GN00982635

TRUMPER

TRUMPER
THE DEFINITIVE BIOGRAPHY

Peter Sharpham

HODDER AND STOUGHTON
SYDNEY   AUCKLAND   LONDON   TORONTO

"Whoever would not be spendthrift of language about Trumper, let him not write on him at all."

Sir Neville Cardus

This work is dedicated to my mother, Nancy Harkness

First published in 1985 by
Hodder & Stoughton (Australia) Pty Limited
2 Apollo Place, Lane Cove, NSW 2066
© Peter Sharpham, 1985
This book is copyright. Apart from any fair dealing for the purposes of private study, research, criticism or review as permitted under the Copyright Act, no part may be reproduced without written permission. Inquiries should be addressed to the publisher.
National Library of Australia Cataloguing-in-Publication entry
Sharpham, Peter.
    Trumper.
    ISBN 0 340 37447 0
    1. Trumper, Victor, 1877–1915. 2. Cricket players – Australia – Biography.
    I. Title.
796.35′8′0924
Typeset in 11/13pt Media Roman at Griffin Press Limited, Netley, South Australia.
Printed by Southwood Press Pty Limited, Sydney.

Contents

CONTENTS

Acknowledgements

This book is the direct result of the skills and energy of the following, without whose co-operation this definitive biography would not have been possible: Victor Trumper's daughter-in-law, Lorraine Trumper (wife of Victor Trumper junior); Victor Trumper's nephew, Charles Trumper (son of Charles Ernest Love Trumper); Victor Trumper's grandson, Victor Trumper III; Clifford Winning, the Honorary Librarian of the New South Wales Cricket Association; Stephen Gibbs, Librarian and Cricket Statistician of Bullaburra, for his compilation of the index and his invaluable help in procuring and searching through old and rare bibliography; Helen Whiteley of Leura, for her assistance with historical research and preparation of the manuscript; Ian Moir of Killara, for his editorial expertise; Val Phillipps of Mount Victoria, for her excellent photographic reproductions from Victor Trumper's various tour albums; Les Petocz and John Bayliss of Lithgow Public Library; the author's brother Dr John Sharpham, Dean of Academic Affairs at the Western Australian Institute of Technology; Dr Don Watts, the Director of the Western Australian Institute of Technology; Dr Robert Koehler, Graduate Director of Physical Education at Illinois State University; Dr John Lill, Secretary of the Melbourne Cricket Club; Rex Harcourt of the Melbourne Cricket Club Library; Dr Maxwell Howell of the University of Queensland; Arthur Tolhurst, Genealogist of Blaxland; Martin Sharp of the Australian National University; Noel and Liz Giles of Port Macquarie, and Stephen Dearnley.

Staffs of the following have also given great assistance: The Mitchell Library in Sydney; The State Library of New South Wales; The State Library of Victoria; The Battye Library of Perth in Western Australia; The Archives Office of New South Wales; The New South Wales Registrar General's Office; The Supreme Court of Australia in Sydney; The New South Wales Land Titles Office; The Society of Australian Genealogists; Rembrandt Photographics of Lithgow, and the Physical Education Department of Lithgow High School.

Sincere thanks are expressed to the following publishers for permission to quote from the various works: Angus & Robertson Publishers for *Googlies*, H. V. Hordern; Collier Macmillan Ltd for *The Game's the Thing*, M. A. Noble (Cassell Ltd); William Collins Ltd for *Autobiography*, Sir Neville Cardus; J. M. Dent & Sons Ltd for *10 for 66 and All That*, A. A. Mailey; George Allen & Unwin Ltd for *A History of Cricket, Vol 1*, H. S. Altham, *Cricket Highways and Byways*, F. S. Ashley-Cooper, and *Was It All Cricket?*, Daniel Reese; Gillingham Ltd for *Not Test Cricket*, J. Elliott Monfries; Heinemann Ltd for *My Cricketing Days*, C. G. Macartney; Kaye & Ward Ltd for *Mr Cricket*, W. H. Ferguson (Nicholas Kaye Ltd); Methuen & Co Ltd for *Life Worth Living*, C. B. Fry (Eyre & Spottiswoode Ltd) and *The Complete Cricketer*, A. E. Knight; Pelham Books for *Cricket: The Great Ones*, John Arlott, and J. Whitaker & Sons Ltd for *The Book of Cricket*, P. F. Warner. Thanks are also expressed to John Arlott for the use of his poem "On A Great Batsman" from Leslie Frewin's *The Boundary Book* published by Macdonald Ltd and to Alan Moyes for permission to quote from A. G. Moyes's *Australian Batsmen* published by Angus & Robertson Publishers.

I wish to record my debt to the reporters responsible for the various newspaper quotes from Trumper's time, especially those from *The Sydney Morning Herald* and John Corbett Davis's articles from the Sydney based *Referee*. It was indeed a privilege to read these splendid descriptions of Victor Trumper's peerless batsmanship. From these contemporary sources the reader may perceive those qualities of greatness which made the man and the cricketer.

Peter Sharpham
November 1984

Foreword

As both librarian and cricket historian I have read hundreds upon hundreds of cricket books over the years. I must say that I am tremendously impressed with this opus which I consider has outstanding potential. The depth of research work carried out by the author borders on mind-boggling and the list of references in the Acknowledgements and the Bibliography support this opinion.

The quotes and references, academically pin-pointed as they should be, because validity and authenticity are the essential ingredients of a work of this nature, have been selected from approved reliable sources and have sufficient variety to suggest that the author has not been dependent on the one "word-bank"—far from it. The anecdotes in the final chapter summarize the author's convictions regarding Trumper's greatness most convincingly. The inclusion of some well-chosen verses gives a pleasant literary balance to the book.

The chronological development of Trumper's cricket career has, in my view, been traced faultlessly and quite objectively. This is particularly pleasing because of the willingness to acknowledge and to report, without any excuses, that even Trumper had human frailties, and, very occasionally, a margin for error wide enough to allow a "duck" or two to intrude into his statistics.

I regard the career analysis of the champion in the Appendix as unique. It will be received by historians all over the world with great gusto.

I found the accounts of the tours of South Africa, New Zealand and northern Queensland fascinating—never before having seen them documented in such surprising detail—again filling a void in our cricket history.

In 1930–31 Archie Jackson undertook a similar tour of northern Queensland with a New South Wales team led by Alan Kippax. The Balmain lad also had amazing success playing 16 innings, 2 not outs, 171 highest score, 1209 runs at an average of 86.35—Shades of Victor Trumper!

9

I've always harboured a kind of "folk-hero" worship about the one and only Trumper who died when I was only six years old. The wonderful Trumper stories my old dad used to tell I'm certain helped to establish the devotion, even reverence, that I have for cricket right up to this very day.

Clifford M. Winning
Librarian of the New South Wales Cricket Association

The Source of Genius

"Trumper with the bat does all things perfectly. There is the simplicity and depth of a full melody."*

So wrote the English international cricketer, Albert Knight, of Victor Thomas Trumper, Australia's Crown Prince of Cricket at the height of the game's fabled Golden Age. During his short but eventful lifetime he was described by cricket's sternest critics as "the wizard of the willow", "the incomparable", "a genius beyond compare", "the dazzling cavalier,". . .

In an article for the *Strand Magazine* of September 1912, Jack Hobbs, the great Surrey run-scoring machine, when commenting on the soundness of Australian pitches, wrote:

> The same prevalence of ideal batting conditions has given us Victor Trumper, the "Champagne of Cricket".
>
> He is the most perfect batsman in his scoring methods I have ever seen. He makes every orthodox stroke quite after the best models, and in addition he has several strokes of his own which it is quite hopeless for other batsmen to attempt.
>
> The way in which he hits a good length ball round to the leg boundary where there are no fieldsmen is enough to break the heart of any bowler, and this is only one of his characteristic shots. He is a past-master of every method of scoring four off a ball most batsmen would be content to play with care, and has more strokes of this type at his command than any other cricketer.

Former England captain, Charles Fry, said in a radio broadcast on Sydney radio station 2FC during the 1930s: "Trumper captured the hearts of English cricket lovers. No matter how many runs Bradman makes, Vic Trumper's name comes up time and again, and his great deeds are discussed. He took a hold on the hearts and minds of people in England as no other batsman has done. It was not only the runs he made but how he made them. He did everything so easily and with such infinite grace. We were not in the least annoyed when he flogged our bowling, he did it so nicely. He will always live in English cricket as something unique, as perhaps the greatest of all!"

---

* A. E. Knight, *The Complete Cricketer*. Methuen, London, 1906.

Charles Thomas Trumper.

The story of the Trumper family in Australia began one winter's day when Charles Trumper, a London hatter, and his wife Jane, stepped ashore from the *Resource* on 24 June 1837. Jane, who was to die from heart trouble at her Oxford Street, Sydney, home at the age of 67 in 1879, bore five children. Her two sons Charles and Thomas became compositors or printers in Bathurst Street, Sydney, in the early 1860s but soon moved to New Zealand to continue their profession in Auckland. They returned to Sydney during 1875 and Thomas housed his wife, Mary Louisa Nagle, and their children, Charles Thomas (16), Thomas (13), John (11), Emily (6) and Jane (4) in Little Piper Street, Woollahra. Charles Thomas Trumper was to become a very successful shoe and slipper manufacturer—at the time of his death in Chatswood in 1920 he left an estate of £2254, a considerable sum for that period.

Victor Thomas Trumper, destined to become one of the game's immortals, was, according to the *NSW Public Service Gazette*, born on 2 November 1877 but no trace can be found in New South Wales records of any birth certificate for a child named Victor Thomas being born to either a Trumper or a Coghlan between the years 1875 and 1879.

Charles Thomas Trumper married Louisa Coghlan on 15 May 1883. Charles was 24 and Louisa 27. She lived with her widowed mother, Margaret Coghlan at 432 Riley Street, Surry Hills. The wedding ceremony took place in the residence of John Penman, the officiating minister for the Primitive Methodist Church, at Harris Street, Ultimo. Charles, like his father, was a strict Anglican.

Louisa gave birth to the Trumper's first daughter just ten months after the marriage. On 22 February 1884, Alice Mary was born at 432 Riley Street. The second child of the marriage, Una Margaret, was born in the Surry Hills home on 16 June 1885. Her birth certificate quite clearly shows that the "previous issue", any other children of the marriage, was "1 female living."

The inescapable conclusion is that Victor was not a product of the union of Charles and Louisa as it is doubtful if they knew each other seven years prior to their marriage, although it is possible. Was Victor an orphan who was adopted by Charles Trumper? As adoption records for the era are non-existent we do not know this. Another possibility is that he was the son of a relative of Charles or Louisa; he came to visit and eventually became a permanent and integral member of the family. One fact is certain, Victor was loved by both Charles and Louisa, and adored and worshipped by his younger brothers and sisters.

Victor's siblings, after Alice and Una, were born as follows:

Louisa Hilda, 1887
Clarice Emily, 1889
May Louisa, 1891
Sydney Charles, 1895
Charles Ernest Love, 1897

It is generally believed that Victor Trumper was born in Darlinghurst, however as there is no genealogical evidence to support this notion, his exact birthplace remains a mystery.

The Trumpers moved from Riley Street to 30 Little Arthur Street, Surry Hills in 1886 and lived in the latter street for two years. During this time the young Victor learned to play the piano and, like most young boys of his era, devoted much of his free time to cricket. Charles Trumper recalled this period in Victor's life in an interview with John Corbett Davis in *The Referee* of 8 February 1913:

> Ever since Victor was nine or ten years old he showed a passionate devotion to cricket. I always prophesied that Victor would make his reputation as a cricketer. After all it was not a wonderful prophecy, as those who remember Vic in his boyhood will admit. At an early age he displayed no little skill in the art of wielding the bat, and it was evident from the beginning that he was the making of a great cricketer. He would practise assiduously in our backyard for hours every day, and when I saw to what extent he was taken up with the game I decided to encourage him in every possible way I could. Early every morning I would accompany him to that magnificent playground, Moore Park, where I would assist him in his practice. We would remain there from 6 a.m. to 8 a.m. and only knock off then on account that I had to prepare to go to my business, and Victor to his school. It was surprising to note the rapid headway he made as a result of his constant practising. Every day I would note some degree of improvement in his skill with the bat and in his style of play, which, needless to say, was a source of much gratification to me.

In 1888 the young family moved to 487 Crown Street, but stayed at that address for only one year before occupying 10 Nichols Street in Surry Hills during 1889 and 1890. The latter year was to prove a traumatic one for the Trumpers as tragedy struck three times. Victor's paternal grandfather Thomas died at the Nichols Street residence from the wasting effects of tuberculosis on 8 July 1890. He had been ill for three months and was a widower as his wife Mary had died years before. He was only 47 years old.

Just fifteen days after Thomas died, young Louisa Hilda Trumper also became a victim of the dreaded disease. She was barely 3 years of age.

Shattered by two deaths in such a short space of time, Victor's parents decided to move house yet again, this time settling at 119 Cooper Street in Surry Hills. In early December of that same fateful year the baby of the family, tiny Clarice Emily, only 17 months old, became the third victim of the insidious lung affliction. Thus in the space of six months young Victor saw three beloved members of his family perish. The effect on an affectionate and sensitive 13-year-old boy must have been devastating.

By this time Victor was attending Crown Street Superior Public School. Monty Noble recalled his arrival: "My first recollection of Trumper was at school. He came just as I was leaving. A short, spare, narrow-shouldered boy, he did not inspire one with the idea of athleticism in any direction."* Yet it was not long before the same small boy, at the age of fifteen, began to play regularly for his school.

On Friday 5 May 1893 Trumper had second top score against Rockdale Public School with 25 runs as his team won on the first innings by 40 runs. Facing Paddington Public School at Victoria Barracks on Friday afternoon 27 October 1893, he top-scored with 35 runs and took 7 wickets for 23 to lead his side to a 70-run victory.

Later in the season in early March 1894 the budding champion opened the batting against Woollahra Superior Public School in the match to determine the champion school team for the summer. He carried his bat right through his team's score of 128 for an impressive 86 not out, even though six bowlers tried to capture his wicket. Then bowling unchanged, he snared 7 wickets for just 14 runs to orchestrate the dismissal of Woollahra for 42 as Crown Street won the afternoon's sport by 86 runs.†

On Saturdays Victor was playing for the Carlton Cricket Club and attending practice under the watchful eyes of Charles and

---

* M. A. Noble, *The Game's the Thing*. Cassell, London, 1926.
† Trumper's school matches are documented in the *Sydney Morning Herald*.

A youthful Victor Trumper, seated third from the left, with the Crown Street Superior Public School Cricket Team.

Alexander Bannerman. Charles Bannerman, who was to later umpire many first-class matches in which Trumper would reveal his superb artistry to the world, was the first cricketer to score a century in an Anglo-Australian Test Match. This was in Melbourne in 1877, when he was forced to retire hurt after receiving a blow on the finger from the bowling of Ulyett. The year 1877 is celebrated as Victor Trumper's birth year and Australia won this, the very first Test Match, by 45 runs. Alexander, a resolute batsman, played in twenty-eight Tests for Australia.

Dr L. O. S. Poidevin described Trumper's early years of cricket with the Carltons:

On the field he was always a personality. It was so from the beginning. His whole career was one long series of thrills, either in promise or in fulfilment. I saw him play first in knickerbockers on a mud and matting pitch on the sands of Tempe, a good distance, as far as I can remember, from the station, whence we all (22) carried our implements. It was the rendezvous of the second elevens of the Sydneys (for which team I played) and, I think, the Carltons (for which team he played). I do not remember the results of that game, but I well remember with what interest his play was watched on that

16

occasion, for had not Charlie Bannerman already proclaimed him "the coming champion?" Even at this early stage of his career he surprised one and all by the graceful turn of the wrists and the free sweep of the bat, backed up by those innate qualities of daring confidence and cheeky enterprise so characteristic of his halcyon days. (*Sydney Morning Herald*, 29 June 1915.)

Most of Australia's great cricketers began the cultivation of their craft on these lively, but true, coir matting pitches. Aggressive leg-side technique learned on the mats they moulded and perfected as they progressed to turf pitches.

Charles Trumper recalled Victor's first encounters in week-end cricket against older players:

Do I recollect the first match in which Victor took part? I should rather think I do. He was only a small boy, wearing knickerbockers. It was on a Saturday afternoon, and he was passing through Moore Park, where a match between the second elevens of Carlton and Warwick was about to be commenced. The Carlton second team was short of a man, and as soon as Victor was sighted he was asked to take the missing man's place. This he readily consented to do, and performed so excellently as to open the eyes of all present. If memory serves me right he scored 24 runs off his own bat and took no fewer than eight wickets. A precocious cricketer, eh? Oh, no! We did not think so. In connection with this match I would like to mention a little incident which at the time struck me as being somewhat humorous. Charlie Patrick was present and at the conclusion of play he mischievously took up a bat and dared the youthful bowlers to bowl at him. The latter were not slow to accept the invitation. The first ball served to Patrick was sent soaring away skywards, but the second, which was bowled by Victor, scattered the stumps in all directions, to the amusement of all, and the surprise of the batsman. (*The Referee*, 8 February 1913.)

Charles Trumper reminisced further:

Just by way of showing the reputation which Victor, boy that he was, had already gained in those days, I will mention another little incident. He had promised to take part in a match one day in order to fill the place of an absentee. But when the teams arrived at the ground where the match was to come off, and the opposing side saw that Victor intended taking part, they refused point-blank to play. I looked upon this as rather extraordinary, in view of the fact that my son was, at the time, only 14 years of age, whilst the two teams under notice were composed of full-grown men!

Something unique in connection with Victor's cricket career is the fact that he has never played in junior cricket. I remember when he was 14 years old he went on a visit to his uncle down at Bulli. While there his uncle took him, in company with a local team, to Mount Keira, for the purpose of playing the Mount Keira eleven. In this match Victor once more covered himself with glory, taking nearly all the opposition wickets for about 19 runs.

In January 1893 Victor, who had just turned fifteen, began playing regularly for the Carlton First Eleven, beginning the year with a match against the Warwicks on the southern wicket of the Domain. The former international Edward Evans took 5 for 30 as the Carltons were dismissed for 116 and in reply the Warwicks made 7 for 97, the afternoon match being drawn. Trumper scored 12 and Charlie Bannerman, who still occasionally appeared in club cricket, added 14. S. H. Bowden, who captured two wickets and top-scored for the Warwicks with 22, recalled the encounter while writing for the *Town and Country Journal* in January 1913:

> Some 20 years ago, on the Sydney Domain Cricket Ground, in a match between elevens from the Carlton and Warwick Clubs, the trundling of the veteran Ted Evans and the writer was negotiated for quite an hour by a slim youngster, who met every delivery with the full face of an impeccably straight bat, which dealt with anything off the wicket, if not in a powerful, yet in an irreproachably artistic manner. Said Evans, "That youngster, given opportunity, will develop into a world batsman." Charles Bannerman, in his day one of Australia's most brilliant batsmen, evidently thought so too, for he at once took this lad, who was Victor Trumper, under his cricketing aegis, and by precept, and, better still, example, instilled into him the fundamental principles of the grand old national game.
>
> Time after time we have been at the nets at the Association Cricket Ground, noting Charlie, the champion that had been, instructing Victor, the champion of the future. For a time all went well, but young Trumper, having mastered the defensive tactics of the game, began to do a little original work in the way of most daring strokes. In vain Bannerman called out, "Leave it alone, Vic; that wasn't a ball to go at." Victor "went" at all such deliveries, and, more than that, made off them scoring strokes with consummate ease. After a while, very wisely, the experienced coach left the young batsman to his own devices. Sam Jones, Harry Moses, and several other top-notchers of that day, with foresight based on insight, also saw Trumper and "named a star." But it is worth while remembering that the subsequent conjuror with the willow laid for himself the foundation of solid defence before, confident in his strength, he

began to execute those strokes which for many years have been the delight and despair of fellow cricketers. In his most brilliant period no one knew better than Victor Trumper the risks his magical strokes evolved [sic].

J. C. Davis, "Not Out" of *The Referee,* made a point of attending club practice sessions in those early days to spot any potential young talent. He wrote of his first glimpse of the young Trumper in June 1915:

When I first saw Victor Trumper he was a tiny lad in knickers. He was short, but neat and trim in appearance, and apart from school hours, appeared to live with the game. Afternoon after afternoon he was to be seen at the Association Cricket Ground. There was only one oval, no bicycle track, and all practice was carried out on the oval where Test Matches are now played, as they were then. Down at the southern end the clubs of that period—Carlton, Albert, Belvidere, Warwick, and Sydney—had their practice nets. And there everyone soon knew the phenomenal boy who batted and bowled and fielded, without a word, without an atom of self-consciousness, as though he were born an international player. And such a player!

For Carlton in the 1893–94 Sydney cricket season Victor was honing his talents against the other clubs. This was the inaugural year for the new Sydney Electorate Competition for the Hordern Shield, carried off by East Sydney. The clubs competing in the First Grade competition were East Sydney, University, Glebe, Redfern, Paddington, Cumberland, Canterbury and Manly. During this season the old clubs still played each other but all of them, with the notable exception of I Zingari, were doomed with extinction.

In October against I Zingari, "Trumper who was playing very stylish cricket, had his middle stump knocked back by Radford after scoring 28."* At Redfern Park in February 1894 he had the second highest score of 25 for the Carltons versus Surrey United, and at the Sydney Cricket Ground during the same month he captured 3 Redfern wickets for just 16 runs in an invitation match.

At the beginning of the following season (1894–95) the *Sydney Morning Herald* looked back on the old competition with some nostalgia:

Saturday marked the opening of the season. The first of October

---

* *Sydney Morning Herald,* 23 October 1893.

always was eagerly looked forward to by large numbers of enthusiasts, probably not so much now, or apparently not so much, as in the old days of the Albert, Warwick, University, Belvidere, and Carlton Clubs when the double-decked tramcars used to be over-crowded by young and old players on their way to the Sydney Cricket Ground, then the best practice wicket obtainable, anxious to have their first strike of the season. How electorate cricket has changed all that!

Four new teams joined the competition that year; South Sydney, Waverley, Leichhardt and North Sydney. Living at 119 Cooper Street, Surry Hills, young Trumper was eligible to play for the new South Sydney Club. Sydney Gregory also lived within the same electoral boundaries. This stylish batsman, suave and dark, with a pointed, waxed moustache, was to have considerable influence on Trumper's emerging batsmanship. A. G. Moyes, in *Australian Batsmen* stated: "There has possibly never been among Australian batsmen a better model for the young than Sydney Gregory, who was one of the most gifted players for his inches that the game has ever seen." By this time Charles Bannerman had dropped out of Sydney cricket to concentrate on his umpiring duties, but he still followed Trumper's career with considerable interest.

In early November 1894, Trumper opened with Gregory on the renovated Waverley Oval. He made 14, while his partner went on to make 152 not out. South Sydney won by 212 runs.

In April 1895, Trumper rattled up 77 not out for South Sydney against Manly on Manly Oval. However the display that was to launch him to eventual international stardom took place just before Christmas 1894 when he was selected to play for the Eighteen New South Wales Juniors against A. E. Stoddart's touring English Eleven. Such matches against odds were not uncommon for representative or touring teams and were a tremendous incentive for the youth of the colony.

As the day of the big match approached Victor caught influenza and was confined by the family doctor to his bed. Despite his mother's pleading he left his sick-bed to participate in the important game. Batting at number three for the Colts, Trumper, who had just turned 17 years old, soon reached 22 runs with some impeccable strokes, when he was almost caught behind the wicket. Shrugging off this near-miss, the slim, blue-eyed and fair-haired teenager square-cut Lockwood to the

Trumper photographed in Brisbane, March 1895.

off boundary. In the next over from Briggs he pulled the esteemed Lancashire left-hander's good length delivery through the air over the heads of the astonished crowd, which included the State Premier, George Houstoun Reid. The ball lodged on the top of an awning in the outside enclosure for five runs.*

At the time, batsmen were only credited with five runs for what today would earn them six, and they then had to change ends as the stroke was an odd number. This scoring law was to be changed during the first decade of the twentieth century to the one with which we are familiar today.†

After fifty minutes at the crease Trumper brought up his half-century against the cream of English bowling, which included the under-arm lob expert, Walter Humphreys. At the luncheon adjournment he was 56, including seven fours and the one five. After lunch Poidevin joined him and Trumper brought up the hundred for his team with a square-cut, forward of point, to the pickets from a Peel delivery. He was then bowled by that bowler for 67 runs made in 85 minutes. The *Evening News* reported to its readers, "The retiring batsman played a most creditable innings, during which he did not give the semblance of a chance." M. A. Noble in the same innings hit up a splendid 152 not out for the Colts and the encounter was drawn. After returning home, accompanied by his father and sisters, Trumper went back to bed for several days.

J. C. Davis reported this match in *The Referee*:

> The batting of young Trumper, the Crown Street schoolboy, against the Englishmen on Saturday, was very refreshing. He is the most promising Colt I have seen since Syd Gregory's time, and appears to be now quite up to the Intercolonial standard.

---

* This superb stroke was documented by the *Evening News*.
† See "Boundaries" by G. B. Buckley, *Cricket Quarterly*, Autumn, 1967.

The Coming of Age

The New South Wales selectors agreed with Davis's opinion as Trumper was selected to represent his State in Adelaide shortly after the New Year vacation in 1895. He scored 11 and 0, yet impressed astute judges of the game with his obvious potential. Elliott Monfries, in his autobiography *Not Test Cricket*, described how George Giffen delighted in enticing young players to move out to his slower flighted delivery, only to be caught and bowled:

> This reminds me of Victor Trumper's first Interstate game in Adelaide. After Vic had made about a dozen runs, Giffen attempted what I have just tried to describe, when Vic, remembering what he had been told to watch out for, hesitated for a split second and then did what was palpably discernable from the fence. He moved the body back slightly, forced the bottom of his bat forward and deliberately cocked the ball over Giffen's head and gave what would have been the dolliest catch imaginable had the wily George remained where he usually did after delivering his ordinary type of ball. This time everybody but Giffen did the smiling. At that early stage of the great Trumper's career was demonstrated the quick thinking of this marvellous cricketer, who, though making fewer than twenty runs in that match, gave a very attractive display, which strangely failed to secure his selection in the next Interstate game. South Australians wondered why, and later performances abundantly justified their wonderment.

Trumper was named as thirteenth man in the Victorian match played in Sydney in late January, and later during the same season travelled to Brisbane with the New South Wales Eleven to play Queensland, scoring 6 and 5 not out as his State won by six wickets. He was also named as thirteenth man in the return fixture against South Australia, played in Sydney.

During the following 1895–96 season Trumper was not selected for the Sheffield Shield engagements, and made only 107 runs in 12 innings for South Sydney, his highest score being 22 not out versus Central Cumberland in December. In April 1896 he took 3 Paddington wickets for 17. Trumper was a bowler endowed with some pace and considerable talent, not only for his school, the Carltons, South Sydney and Paddington, but later for his country in England and South Africa. M. A. Noble described Trumper's bowling in his *The Game's the Thing*: "He bowled a very fast ball and introduced variety by serving up a slow one with exactly the same action."

In the spring of 1896 Trumper joined Paddington Cricket Club when his father and mother moved house to Selwyn Street in Paddington. This change of address ensured Trumper's eligibility to play for the club under the current rules of the Association. During the summer of 1896–97 he twice captured three wickets in an innings; 3 for 9 and 3 for 32, both against Waverley. His batting aggregate was 149, with one score of 48. However, his form in representative engagements was excellent. For the Next Fifteen against a Metropolitan Eleven, on a Sydney Cricket Ground pitch badly affected by rain, he flayed the bowling of Noble, C. T. B. Turner and A. Coningham, all Australian Test bowlers. During his 113 not out he forced the ball to the pickets and continually pulled and cut good length balls from in front of his wicket.

At the turn of the century the pitches were not covered for important matches as they are today. Preparation included watering, cutting and rolling, but once the game began the only treatment allowed was the option of the pitch being rolled and swept before each innings and the customary ten minutes' rolling before the start of each day's play.

On Boxing Day 1896, for a Sydney Representative Eleven on the Albion Sports Ground at West Maitland, against the Hunter River District team, Trumper dominated proceedings, scoring 60 not out. The *Newcastle Morning Herald* reported:

> The finish of the game was quite exciting for the few hundred-odd spectators who were crammed into the small enclosure: The excitement at the pavilion was unbounded as ball after ball was delivered and the runs crept slowly to 160. Trumper made the winning hit of the innings by cleverly placing Waddy to mid-on for a brace. The innings of the not out man was a sterling one.

The following season (1897–98) witnessed the young cricketer indulge in an orgy of run-getting for Paddington which still evokes admiration. Against North Sydney he began the onslaught by making 82 and taking 4 for 57. At this time Hampden Park (later to be renamed Trumper Park) was a virtual swamp, thus the belief that Monty Noble persuaded Trumper to join Paddington because of the excellent turf pitch is misleading.

By the middle of April 1898 Trumper had demonstrated his penchant for centuries by scoring six of them from eight innings, finishing the season with an astonishing batting average of exactly 204. He became the first man to reach 1000 runs in Sydney grade cricket, amassing 1020 runs. His scores are set out below:

Venue	Opponents	Match Commenced	Trumper's Score
Sydney Cricket Ground	North Sydney	9/10/97	82
Parramatta Park	Central Cumberland	23/10/97	123
Sydney Cricket Ground	South Sydney	20/11/97	125
Sydney Cricket Ground	Waverley	4/12/97	84
Wentworth Park	Glebe	12/2/98	120 not out
Sydney Cricket Ground No. 2	Burwood	5/3/98	191 not out
Sydney Cricket Ground	Redfern	19/3/98	133
Sydney Cricket Ground	Leichhardt	2/4/98	162 not out

His score in the innings against Waverley has in the past been incorrectly published as 85. However, on the Monday morning after the game, both the *Sydney Morning Herald* and the *Daily Telegraph* gave Trumper's score as 84. When this score of 84 is added to the 1 sundry plus the totals of the other Paddington batsmen, the result agrees with the correct first innings total of 201. This 201 is further verified, as is the score of 84, by the bowlers' statistics and the scorebook records of the New South Wales Cricket Association.

It was during this summer that Trumper faced A. E. Stoddart's English team while playing for New South Wales. His 43 made for the Next Fifteen against the State side a few days before the England match had ensured his selection. The *Sydney Morning Herald* commented on his inclusion:

Great satisfaction was expressed amongst those in the pavilion, as soon as the names were made known, at the inclusion of Trumper, who during the afternoon had shown brilliant batting. Trumper stood head and shoulders over anyone else in the fifteen, and showed better cricket than some of the eleven in compiling his 43. None of the bowling presented any difficulties to him, and all his strokes were hard, clean and perfectly timed. It was a masterly innings, and in conjunction with his other performances during the present season has placed him in the New South Wales eleven to meet the Englishmen.

Trumper managed only 5 against the tourists in the first innings. In the second Richardson bowled him with an express delivery which smashed the leg stump, sending half of it sailing past wicketkeeper W. Storer, who was standing well back from the wicket. A personal highlight in this match was Trumper's first wicket in first-class cricket—the promising N. F. Druce caught by Monty Noble for 109.

In the field he made amends for his scores of 5 and 0. At long-off he brought off an amazing catch, which J. T. Hearne described in his diary: "Noble bowled well for NSW. Similar action to S. M. J. Woods, but not so fast. Trumper made a great catch in long field dismissing Tom Hayward (poor old Tom, dead out of luck, daren't give half a chance—Melbourne to wit). Next to Jimmy Douglas, the best catch I have ever seen." (*Cricketer International*, September 1982.)

Monty Noble in *The Game's the Thing* wrote:

> If he had little success with the bat, however, he made amends on the field by bringing about Hayward's dismissal with, perhaps, the most sensational and spectacular catch ever seen in the outfield. Hayward hit a ball which I bowled, long and low over mid-off's head. Calculating where it would lodge, Victor dashed in at top-speed, made a baseball dive at the ball, caught it, turned a somersault, and finished on his back with the ball in one hand held high in the air. It was a catch such as one sees but few of in a lifetime.

In the return engagement, played in early February 1898, Trumper was batting confidently on 23 in the second innings, when he was completely deceived by Hearne. "Trumper did not know what to make of it, and that the break on the ball caused wonderment among the Englishmen is proved by the fact that no fewer than five examined and felt for some time the spot where the ball had pitched." (*Sydney Morning Herald*, 7 February 1898.) In the Test Matches Australia recaptured The Ashes which England had held since 1893.

Trumper had still to play for Australia or score a century for his State, his best form occurring against South Australia. On the Adelaide Oval in the first innings he reached 48, being splendidly caught and bowled by George Giffen. At Sydney, in the return match, Trumper took the bowling honours with his 4 for 32. He also scored a polished 68 runs, made in even time.

Monty Noble described Trumper's development from boyhood through to adulthood:

> Although the magnitude of his ultimate triumph could not then be foreseen, those of us who were intimately associated with him were

not greatly astonished that cricketing success should eventually be his portion, for it was with pride and admiration that we watched his early efforts during the period when Nature was moulding him mentally and physically—his brain, his eyes and his muscles—to such perfection of harmonious purpose that he might properly fulfil the destiny allotted to him.*

The following 1898–99 Australian cricket season, preceding the 1899 tour of England, was to be one of incredible triumphs for Trumper. He began slowly, producing only 86 runs in three innings for Paddington, and those anxious for him to tour England were perturbed. One exception was the columnist for the *Sydney Morning Herald* who stated, "Trumper's phenomenal scores of last season caused many to look forward to another succession of big innings this season, but so far they have been disappointed. It is not that he is out of form, but rather that he has not yet 'got going'. One of these fine days bowlers will have a bad time. If that occasion is when the big matches are on, few will regret his non-success now." An incredibly accurate prophecy as it was to soon prove.

In just three innings for Paddington, Trumper boosted his aggregate to 562:

Venue	Opponents	Match Commenced	Trumper's Score
Sydney Cricket Ground	East Sydney	5/12/98	113
Redfern Oval	Redfern	14/1/99	103
Waverley Oval	Waverley	4/2/99	260 not out

During the encounter with Waverley Trumper gathered 90 runs in the final hour of play, in quickly fading light. His 260 not out was chanceless and included one five and 35 fours. J. C. Davis, "Not Out" of *The Referee*, wrote:

Trumper does not belong to the ordinary class of batsmen, he is a genius ... The spectators congregated thickly in the vicinity of the pavilion at the close of play, and gave Trumper a grand reception, such as he richly invited. His innings of 260 was a beautiful one, worthy of any batsman in the world—worthy of Ranji or MacLaren.

J. McLauchlin, a vice-president of the Melbourne Cricket Club, was present at Waverley Oval to see Trumper in full flight for the four-hour duration of his batting. Although this occurred

---

* *The Game's the Thing.*

weeks before the selection matches for the English tour, it is reasonable to assume that when McLauchlin returned to Melbourne he shared what he had seen with the members of the Melbourne Cricket Club and Hugh Trumble, an Australian selector.

In the matches, played against the other States and New Zealand, Trumper really blossomed. Coming in to bat at number seven on Saturday morning, 10 December 1898, against Tasmania, with New South Wales 5 wickets down for 313, he just managed to clamp down on a fast yorker from Eady. After this he began scoring at will, reaching his half-century in fifty minutes. Shortly before lunch he attained his first century in first-class cricket, and became the first batsman to score one hundred before lunch in a cricket match in Australia. The 5000 spectators fortunate to be present in Sydney applauded him enthusiastically. At lunch he was 103 not out. After resumption he raced to 150, and one hour later 200 runs appeared next to his name. At tea he was 247 not out. By this time he was fast running out of partners. However, Kelly, Howell and McKibbin managed to stay long enough for him to reach 292 not out, and the innings closed at 839. It was the most number of runs scored in a day's play by a batsman in a first-class fixture at that time, the previous best being 289 by Archie MacLaren while making 424 against Somerset in 1895.

F. S. Ashley-Cooper noted in his *Curiosities of First-class Cricket*, published in 1901, that Trumper had become the hundredth batsman to reach 200 runs, the first being William Ward with 278 at Lord's in 1820.

Trumper's 292 not out was also the highest total ever recorded for a maiden century until Pervez Akhtar exceeded it with 337 not out at Lahore in 1964–65.

Trumper's record-breaking innings was made as follows: 39 fours, 4 threes, 27 twos and 70 singles.

The *Sydney Morning Herald* described proceedings:

Everyone was delighted; even the Tasmanians, who had the work to do, said that it was a pleasure to field to the young Paddington batsman. His exhibition can easily be described. It was the nearest to an absolutely perfect display that has ever been seen in Sydney. Not unlike Massie in the swing of his supple wrist and shoulder play, Trumper lacked his power but was safer, making not a single mis-hit and never lifting the ball. With the sureness and staying powers of

Murdoch, he was more attractive, with more strokes; in fact he never looked like getting out.

The *Daily Telegraph* commented:

Trumper as a scientific batsman possesses one qualification that the spectators greatly approve of, namely, the vigour with which he attacks the bowling. He comes down solidly onto every ball, and his strokes, if not fielded, nearly all go to the boundary. His batting is of the safe order, everything mostly being placed onto the ground. He obtained his runs all round the wicket, his most telling stroke being the leg glance, which he executes very neatly. He also drives powerfully past the bowler, and to the off, and has a hard placing stroke into the slips.

One week later, batting at number six versus South Australia in Adelaide, Trumper reached his 50 in just over an hour, and batting with great freedom against Ernest Jones' express deliveries, hit a succession of fours to boost his score to 68 in the first innings. Then, without warning, the young champion's nose began to bleed profusely and play was suspended for fully five minutes while he recovered. This fact was reported by the Adelaide press and curiously appears next to his name in the official scorebook of the New South Wales Cricket Association as "nose bled." Immediately play resumed he was caught without adding to his score.

In late February 1899 the first New Zealand eleven to tour Australia began a three-day match against New South Wales in Sydney. On the morning of this encounter Trumper needed in excess of 200 runs to win the prestigious Pattisons Trophy, awarded that season to the New South Wales batsman with the highest aggregate in "intercolonial" cricket. After he finished his breakfast and was preparing to leave his home in Selwyn Street, Paddington, he said to his mother, "I'm going to get that trophy for you today!"*

New Zealand, batting first, were all out for 140. New South Wales replied with 588 and then the visitors capitulated to some fine bowling from McKibbin for only 64. Easily the highlight of the game was Trumper's 253 runs, which included 31 fours. He scored at every opportunity and runs flowed from his bat

* Pattisons Trophy was a unique award for the season 1898–99. It was in the form of an ornate shield of splendid dimensions, expertly crafted in silver and gold. The trophy remains in the possession of the family and the author was recently privileged to inspect it.

effortlessly. The execution of strokes by the young prodigy was technically perfect as he forced the ball to the far reaches of the Sydney Cricket Ground. The *Daily Telegraph* stated:

> Noble had some luck, and scored a number of accidental runs. But there was nothing accidental where Trumper was concerned. He cut, drove, pulled and glanced to great effect, and, moreover, he placed his strokes cleverly to the gaps in the field.

Cobcroft, the New Zealand captain said, when interviewed by *The Referee*, "I might say that the greatest innings of the whole tour played against us was Trumper's. His style was that of a thorough artist, and his strokes so perfect that he never once seemed at sea."

Following the New Zealand fixture a series of three trial matches was held to determine the final composition of the Australian team to leave for England at the end of the summer. These trials, played between the Australian Eleven—eleven tour certainties—and the Rest of Australia took place in Sydney, Melbourne and Adelaide. The final team would then leave for England from South Australia and the unsuccessful players would return to their respective States.

The Eleven were Darling, Hill, Jones, Trumble, McLeod, Worrall, Gregory, Iredale, Kelly, Noble and Howell. Trumper was listed as number eleven for the Rest of Australia in the *Sydney Morning Herald*. Press speculation was rife as to which two players would be added to make up the final thirteen players to tour England. Johns, the Victorian wicket-keeper, was considered a certainty, because the need for more than one custodian on such an arduous visit was obvious. This meant that the final berth would in all probability be given to a slow bowler. The most frequently mentioned candidates were Tom McKibbin and George Giffen.

Just before the first trial match in Sydney, the members of the Paddington Cricket Club held a farewell dinner in honour of M. A. Noble and J. J. Kelly, prior to their eventual departure for England with the Australian Eleven. The spacious banqueting room at Paddington Town Hall was gaily decorated and musical items were performed during the evening. Toasts were proposed and drunk to the two tourists and each was presented with handsome travelling and cricket bags. Colonel J. C. Neild, MLA, the club patron, then made the much awaited presentation of the prestigious Pattisons Trophy to Victor Trumper for the highest batting aggregate of 674 runs in the six intercolonial matches played that season. In his speech the politician described Victor as "the best colt in Australia."

After the dinner Trumper hurried home to show his proud parents Pattisons Trophy. His promise to his mother was fulfilled.

This is an appropriate moment to recall that Victor Trumper was throughout his life a strict teetotaller, convinced that alcohol had a long-term debilitating effect on the athlete, strongly believing that the secret of furthering a career in cricket was to pursue a sound, healthy lifestyle. He never smoked and usually retired early to bed at night. He was both shy and modest, and was more nervous when walking from the field to the plaudits of a large crowd than when facing the world's most devastating fast bowlers. Philip Trevor in *Cricket and Cricketers*, wrote, "He was not gauche but he was shy. He loved cricket, and he enjoyed himself hugely, though without vainglory, when he was batting. But he did not love what had been called the attendant glories of the cricket field." Frank Iredale in *Thirty-three Years of Cricket* wrote:

> Through many years of connection with him, which I am proud to say was never clouded by any misunderstanding, I felt how greatly our country was honoured by his presence as a sportsman in the highest sense. To be near him always as it were, seemed to me to be an honour. His was one of those natures which called to you, and in whose presence you felt it was good to live.
>
> His loving nature made many friends, and his cheery optimism was good to see. In all my cricket years, and association with cricketers, I never knew a man who practised self-effacement so much as he. He loved the game, and he respected those that played it. In victory and defeat he was just the same—his demeanour never changed.

In the first trial match in Sydney for the Rest of Australia Trumper scored 6 and 46. In the second played in Melbourne on 13 March Trumper compiled 46 and was then bowled by McLeod. On his return to the crease he was on 26 when he opened his shoulders to Noble. That player described what transpired: "As it came along the thought ran through my mind, 'Miss it, miss it.' It was not an easy catch and could very easily have been dropped without creating suspicion; but I did not miss

31

it. My disappointment at his dismissal was, I believe, greater than his."

Noble had for weeks been advocating his friend's inclusion in the Eleven so the temptation to drop the difficult chance must have been strong, but his competitive instincts prevailed.

After the Melbourne match the Australian selectors, Joe Darling, Sydney Gregory and Hugh Trumble, met and included Johns as second wicketkeeper and twelfth selection. Ignoring popular speculation they decided against the inclusion of a slow bowler and instead chose the Victorian all-rounder, Frank Laver as the thirteenth selection. Influenced perhaps by his record score against Tasmania and his big innings in the New Zealand confrontation, they caused some surprise by naming Victor Trumper as the fourteenth selection or reserve player to make the trip in the unlikely event of one of the thirteen becoming indisposed and not being able to make the long voyage to England.

The *Adelaide Observer*'s man on the spot in Melbourne wrote:

> For the fourteenth place Trumper of Sydney has been chosen, but this is conditionally upon a fourteenth man being taken. The final decision has not been arrived at on this point, but Trumper has been asked and has consented to go to Adelaide to play in the final match, with the understanding that he will be ready to proceed to England if desired. At the same time the general feeling at the meeting was that a fourteenth man was not necessary, and this will in all likelihood be the ultimate conclusion.

The *Sydney Morning Herald* on 16 March was urging his inclusion:

> Trumper is named as fourteenth man, but in such a way as to signify some different financial arrangement to the rest of the team. If it be decided to take that many—and, considering everything for and against, the weight of argument is in favour of the higher number—it will no doubt be generally admitted that Trumper is entitled to a full share of the profits.

Those present in Adelaide for the final trial match witnessed a mature display by Trumper, who compiled 75 in the first innings with considerable flair in just over two hours. The *Adelaide Advertiser* commented:

> Trumper's innings of 75 cannot be too highly praised. It was incomparably the best display of his team and was almost chance-less. His cutting was superb, and his on play almost as good. When

he reached the pavilion he was accorded an ovation which was richly deserved.

The *Adelaide Observer* stated:

> As an exhibition of scientific batting Trumper's display would be hard to beat, and it is not difficult to understand the strong desire in some quarters to include the young Welshman [sic] in the Australian Eleven.

After the match the three selectors again met and confirmed to press and public that Trumper would be sailing to England on the *Ormuz*. This last minute inclusion was warmly received throughout the country although some disappointment was expressed regarding Trumper's financial status, the *Sydney Morning Herald* stating:

TRUMPER'S SHARE

> It was hinted a few days ago in the *Herald* that Trumper would probably go to England on different terms to the rest of the team. It now transpires on good authority that he proceeds there as an amateur, that his expenses will be paid, and that he will receive a bonus of £200 so far as the English tour is concerned. Should the team visit America, South Africa, New Zealand, or Tasmania, he will share alike in the matches played in those countries. Should he be a success in England the agreement provides that his claims to a larger bonus or an equal share in the profits of the tour will be considered.

At 4 p.m. on Thursday 23 March 1899, the Tenth Australian Cricket Team sailed from Larg's Bay in South Australia on the *Ormuz*. On board was a young man who would become a cricketing legend.

Those making their first sea voyage were soon baptised as the steamer negotiated the Great Australian Bight. Just after dinner a storm enveloped the ship and the seas became extremely rough, carrying away the taffrail. Three sailors were dashed against the dining room, one losing an ear and another breaking his leg. Three women seated behind an awning were swept bodily along the deck.

Trumper, who was resting on his bunk, was completely drenched by a large wave which broke over the steamer and burst through the port-hole above his head. He wisely sought drier quarters as Frank Laver and Monty Noble sealed the opening.

Practice in the games deck nets was a daily routine and at night the travellers listened to classics in the music room, joined in group singing on deck, or danced in one of the saloons. Fancy dress was popular and during one such occasion Victor Trumper and Jim Kelly, with blackened faces and towel turbans, caused some merriment by daubing passing revellers with brooms dipped in soot.

Passing through the Red Sea after the customary stop in Colombo, a short stay was made at Port Said, where the Australians rode on the donkeys. The *Ormuz* next berthed in Naples, where some of the tourists travelled to England via the Continent. Trumper and the rest of the team stayed on board and continued by sea.

Some days later a green and gold flag fluttering outside the Inns of Court Hotel in High Holborn proclaimed that the Australian cricketers had arrived for the coming summer.

Trumper (far left), Laver, Darling and Kelly ride the Port Said donkeys, 1899 Tour.

The 1899 Tour of England

On Monday 1 May, the Australian cricketers commenced a week of practice sessions in the nets at Lord's. Only a few officials and the press were allowed to watch, as the MCC committee decided not to admit the public because of the unfinished state of the new buildings under construction. *The Times* reporter watching commented, "Without going into minute details it may be said that Trumper and Noble bat in very taking style."

As the practice pitches and the bowling approaches were quite soft, most of the players found muscle soreness a problem in the cold and damp conditions. Bill Howell did not practise on the Tuesday afternoon as he was suffering from a leg strain which he sustained the previous day. This was to prevent his involvement in the first two tour matches and was to occasionally trouble him during that fine English summer.

That week the Australians were lavishly entertained at dinner by the Surrey Club at The Oval. On the following Saturday Monty Noble and Frank Laver took part in a club game at Esher in Surrey and both hit centuries, Noble 134 and Laver 101. The same night the entire touring party were grandly feted by the London County Cricket Club at a banquet. Dr Grace, who rarely wasted words, welcomed the Australians in a brief address, declaring that they were a "rare good lot." Monty Noble held a high regard for William Gilbert Grace and recounted an amusing incident which reveals the true character of the great cricketer:

> Whatever present-day cricketers may be to the next generation, W. G. Grace will always stand out as the Grand Old Man of the game, and, no doubt, as time goes on and more romance, and probably a good deal of fiction as well, will be associated with his name. The first time I played against him was at the Crystal Palace in the first match of the Australian 1899 tour. Just before I went in to bat, Hugh Trumble came to me and said: "Now, look here, Monty, when you go in, take care 'W.G.' doesn't talk you out." Grace, Hughie explained, had a reputation for getting young players bustled if he could only get them to talk while at the wicket. I promised to heed the advice, and in I went.
>
> Sure enough, after the first over, "W.G." came up and said: "Good

day, young fellow." "Good day," I replied and walked away. At the end of the next over he again tried, but I ignored him. For several overs this went on without my taking any notice of him. I had a very uncomfortable feeling about my apparent rudeness, and wondered just what he was thinking of me. After a while, however, I convinced myself that I was well enough set not to be talked out of the game, so, next time he approached me, I replied, and from then on we conversed freely. When I look back on the incident now I feel certain that, instead of trying to bustle, "W.G.'s" object was really to encourage me, and that the warning given me was simply a sample of Trumble's leg-pulling, for he was one of the most inveterate practical jokers I ever met.*

Trumper's name did not appear on the scorecards for this first tour match against the South of England. The home side led by Dr Grace forced a draw against the visitors: South of England 246 and 222, Australia 375 (Gregory 124 and Noble 116 not out) and 1 for 7. This forceful batting display coupled with the destructive deliveries of Hugh Trumble and Ernest Jones was a portent for English cricket.

In the second match, at Leyton, Trumper, batting well down the order, was bowled by Young for 0. In the second innnings he scored 3, again bowled by "Sailor" Young. The budding cricketer experienced first-hand a pitch which played "queerly" as the result of a heavy spring dew. Monty Noble described an incident in this match, which Essex won by 126 runs:

One does not meet many deaf cricketers, but I recollect a most amusing experience at Leyton when we were playing Essex—the team we were never able to vanquish—in 1899. A. P. Lucas, who had then passed his cricketing prime, but was still a fine batsman, had been playing well and making strokes many young players might envy. He was deaf in one ear. Fielding mid-on for us was Charlie McLeod, who was also deaf on one side. Between overs Charlie made several attempts to open up conversation with Lucas, but the batsman took no notice. This annoyed Charlie very much and he mentioned the fact to Hugh Trumble—of all people. Hugh looked very serious and replied: "Yes, Charlie, he has the reputation of being a bit particular about those to whom he speaks." Soon afterwards Lucas asked what sort of a fellow McLeod was. "I've been trying to talk to him for half an hour," he said, "but he won't take any notice." "No," said Hughie, "Charlie is a bit stuck-up, you know." And so the practical joker had the two glaring at each other during

---

* The Game's the Thing 1926.

the remainder of the innings. I remember Lucas made fifty*, by the by; and what a capital knock it was. Trumble took good care to let everyone else know of his little joke, and most of them watched developments with ill-concealed amusement. It was not until the day's play was over that he let McLeod and Lucas into the secret. Fortunately both of them possessed a sense of humour and they soon became good friends.†

The next engagement, against Surrey at Kennington Oval, was won by the tourists; Australia 249, Surrey 114 and 64. Trumper, at number seven, made 13 before Hayward bowled him off his pads on the soft, rain-affected pitch. Bill Howell, the Penrith bee farmer, in his debut in England, had the wonderful bowling figures of 10 for 28 and 5 for 29. Charles Fry said that Howell could make the ball buzz like a bee, and any cricketer who has faced a particularly good pace bowler cutting his fingers across the seam, will recognise the sound he describes. Later in the tour he was presented with a purse full of gold sovereigns and a gold watch for his new wife from Australian admirers.

Victor Trumper, in the next fixture against an English eleven at Eastbourne on 18 May, was run out for 5. In the second innings he was unconquered on 64 at stumps. On the morning of the third and final day showers fell, soaking the pitch. When play eventually resumed Trumper was caught without adding to his overnight score. His was the highest innings of the game, Australia winning by 172 runs with Hugh Trumble bagging 4 for 35 and 7 for 37. In the fifth tour match, versus Yorkshire at Sheffield, the weather was showery and the pitch heavy. With the home team at 3 wickets down for 83, the heavens opened up and the game was eventually washed out.

On 25 May the match with Lancashire began, and although the weather was fine, the wicket and surrounds were soft from the recent rains. Joe Darling, on winning the toss, decided to bat but the Australians were soon in trouble on the sticky wicket until rescued by a plucky innings from Victor Trumper. His elegant 82 on the treacherous surface was to prove a match-winner as Lancashire had no batsman who could master the conditions, and the visitors won handsomely by an innings and 84 runs. The *Sydney Morning Herald* commented:

---

* Lucas's actual score was 46 not out in the first innings.
† *The Game's the Thing.*

Trumper in England, 1899.

The first innings of the Australians against Lancashire will no doubt stand as one of the best recoveries recorded during the present season. The first five wickets fell for 65, and the second five added 202, a performance that indicates again the strength of the batting side of the Australians. Trumper has now played two fine innings in succession, 64 and the present 82, and he was well supported by Trumble, Kelly and Howell.

Immediately after this match the tourists accepted the invitation of Lord Marcus Beresford to spend an afternoon at the Manchester Racecourse as honorary members of the Club. An anonymous tip to back Portobello proved a wise investment as the horse was successful. After the race the Australians left for London with bulging pockets.

In the seventh match against Oxford University, Trumper scored a breezy 25. Here B. J. T. Bosanquet opened the bowling with considerable venom. He was to later completely change his style to concentrate on "googly" or "Bosie" deliveries, much to Australia's cost. In the match, which was drawn, it was arranged to draw the stumps early on the last day to allow the visitors to travel to Epsom Downs in time to watch the Derby. They witnessed an exciting race in which the well-named colt, Flying Fox, owned by the Duke of Westminster, stormed home at 2 to 1 on favourite to win the mile and a half classic.

The interest throughout England leading up to the First Test at Nottingham was very high. The Post Office at Trent Bridge sent off 80,000 words by telegraph on the first two days of the big game. It was a historic occasion in many ways as it was to be W. G. Grace's last Test Match for England at the age of fifty, and the first of many battles for The Ashes for the twenty-one year old Victor Trumper. As well, Wilfred Rhodes, the Yorkshire left arm finger spinner was making his debut for England, as was Frank Laver for Australia. It was also the first occasion that five Test Matches in the series were played on English soil, and the first in which a Test was played at Trent Bridge. The line-up for both countries was awesome. The following are justly revered names:

ENGLAND	*AUSTRALIA*
W. G. Grace (Gloucestershire) (captain)	J. Darling (South Australia) (captain)
C. B. Fry (Oxford University and Sussex)	S. E. Gregory (New South Wales)
	C. Hill (South Australia)

W. Gunn (Nottinghamshire)
T. W. Hayward (Surrey)
J. T. Hearne (Middlesex)
G. H. Hirst (Yorkshire)
F. S. Jackson (Cambridge
University and Yorkshire)
K. S. Ranjitsinhji (Cambridge
University and Sussex)
W. Rhodes (Yorkshire)
W. Storer (Derbyshire)
J. T. Tyldesley (Lancashire)

W. P. Howell (New South Wales)
F. A. Iredale (New South Wales)
E. Jones (South Australia)
J. J. Kelly (New South Wales)
F. Laver (Victoria)
M. A. Noble (New South Wales)
H. Trumble (Victoria)
V. T. Trumper (New South Wales)

A crowd of just over 14,000 avid spectators attended the Trent Bridge ground on the first day, Thursday 1 June, as Darling won the toss and Australia batted on a fast, true pitch with the sun streaming down. Despite the early inclement weather, the summer of 1899 was one of the driest ever experienced by an Australian eleven in England. P. C. Standing described it as "a beautifully fine summer."*, and it was certainly a wonderful vintage year just across the Channel in Bordeaux.

Just after 12 o'clock Iredale and Darling walked to the wicket to face Hearne's right arm off-cutters and Rhodes's left arm orthodox spinners from around the wicket with little or no run-up. Both bowlers kept a tight length and at lunch Australia were 1 for 80, Iredale having been caught at mid-on for 6 by Hayward from the bowling of Hearne. In the mid-afternoon Hill and Gregory pushed the score along to 151, Joe Darling having played a typical captain's innings for 47.

With the score at 3 wickets for 166 Gregory was bowled by Hirst for 48. Hirst troubled all the batsmen with his fast left arm deliveries. Later in his career he slowed his pace somewhat to concentrate on very effective in-swingers, coming from around the wicket. Victor Trumper was next man in and he was bowled by Hearne, without scoring, from a sharply breaking ball, which, according to one member of the Notts. County Eleven who was watching from the pavilion, "might have bowled any man in the world." At stumps at 6.30 p.m. Australia were 8 for 238. The Test resumed on Friday morning at noon and Hearne and Rhodes soon cleaned up the Australian tail with the total at 252.

The very first ball of the England innings was a scorching

---

* P. C. Standing, *Anglo-Australian Cricket 1862–1926*. Faber & Gwyer, London, 1926.

no-ball from Jones which almost shaved Dr Grace's beard. When a similar incident occurred in 1896 at Sheffield Park against Lord Sheffield's Eleven, W.G. admonished the fast bowler. The ebullient Jones on that day had reputedly quipped, "Sorry, Doctor, she slipped," as the ball flew over the wicket-keeper's head and sped toward the boundary. The champion then methodically proceeded to go after the bowling and on the fiery pitch made a hearty 49 runs.

In the Nottingham Test, however, the England captain went on to score 28 falling to Noble, caught at the wicket by Kelly. Jones was bowling with great speed that day, one of his first balls to Fry clean-bowled that batsman but it was also a no-ball. The Sussex player went on to make 50 before Jones skittled his stumps. Ranjitsinhji then put together 42 only to hear a Jones thunderbolt rattle his wicket and England were soon dismissed for 193, giving Australia a first innings lead of 59. At stumps on this second day the visitors were 1 for 93.

On the Saturday, under cloudless skies and in front of a substantial crowd, Noble and Hill resumed the innings. Noble and then Iredale were soon out and at 3 for 151 Victor Trumper came to the crease. He quickly made 11 runs before Jackson bowled him with a fast ball as he attempted a leg-glance. Hill was then smartly caught low down at point by Grace for 80, put together in sparkling fashion. At lunch with the score at 8 for 230 Joe Darling declared the innings closed, leaving his bowlers just over three and a half hours in which to dismiss England. The home country thus needed 290 runs for victory, an extremely difficult task, considering the wide Trent Bridge boundaries.

After scoring a single, W. G. Grace was bowled by a Howell "break-back", similar to the ball which dismissed Trumper in the Australian first innings. Soon Jones and Howell had England reeling at 4 for 19. Ranjitsinhji then endeavoured to save his team. Darling placed two short legs in an attempt to restrict the Indian prince's favourite leg-side strokes, but he merely reverted to a series of conjured drives to all corners of the field off Jones, Noble and Trumble, who bowled with victory seemingly in sight.

Ranji considered that Monty Noble was the most effective medium-pace bowler that he ever faced, but now none of the Australians could claim his wicket and at stumps he was 93 not out, out of a total of 7 for 155, and the match was saved. Ranjitsinhji received a standing ovation on returning to the

41

pavilion. The evening newspaper placards proclaimed, "Ranji saves England." Although this historic Test Match ended in a draw, it was generally agreed by the press that the Australians had much the better of play.

Afterwards W. G. Grace voluntarily decided to stand down from the England team to make way for Archie MacLaren, who succeeded him as captain. Because of his huge size he found it difficult to get his hands down to a fast ground ball in the field. Even though they loved him, the Trent Bridge crowd, a discerning selection committee in their own right, barracked the great man in a good-natured manner while the Australians were batting. He told Stanley Jackson after the Test, "It's no use, Jacker, I shan't play again," and although his co-selectors thought that an England team without W.G. at the helm was unthinkable, they had no choice but to accede to his momentous decision. His service to England over the years was unique.

In the following match against the MCC at Lord's Victor Trumper was batting with flair when he was bowled by W. G. Grace for 29. On the afternoon of the second day Trumper and the rest of the Australians were presented to the Prince of Wales and the Duke of York.

Later in the tour, the imposing figure of W.G. suddenly loomed into view inside the Australians' dressing room demanding that Trumper hand over a bat with his autograph on it. This was done immediately. The great man then placing one of his own hallowed blades into the youth's hands, delivered the following oration in his high voice, "From today's champion to the champion of tomorrow." He then turned and strode majestically from the room.*

At 10 o'clock on the morning of the Second Test Match at Lord's 8000 people were already seated at the ground. The crowd later swelled to 30,000. England batting first were all out for 206, Jackson scoring 73 and Jones taking 7 for 88. The Fleet Street reporters were impressed with the sharpness of the Australians in the field even though they went into the match without Frank Iredale, who had the measles.

On the second day of the match with Australia's score at 4 for 189, Victor Trumper came to the crease. He got to work

---

* W. G. Grace's bat is still in the possession of the Trumper Family and has been viewed by the author.

immediately by stroking a single and then a superlative leg-glance for four off Jackson. At this stage Clem Hill was nearing his century.

Trumper was soon batting in dazzling fashion, meeting the ball sweetly in the middle of his bat. With awesome precision he drove hard and often into the long field, and his cutting and glancing drew admiring applause from the Lord's crowd. At the other end Hill had moved to 135 when he was very well caught by C. B. Fry, almost on the pavilion rails. Kelly then joined Trumper, who continued to bat fluently. With the score at 278 MacLaren called for a new ball to replace the badly damaged old one. In Rhodes's next over with it, Trumper drove his first delivery past cover-point to the pickets. Mid-off and extra cover were kept extremely busy continuously retrieving hard, penetrating drives from the young batsman. At the break for lunch he had made 48.

On resumption Trumper off-drove Jessop for four and then forced the very next ball to the fence with a perfect on-drive. Kelly was then caught at the wicket with the score at 306. Trumble was next man in and Rhodes replaced Jessop. Trumper welcomed him with a cover-drive for four and then pulled the next for three. He then hit a two and a four off Mead to bring his score to 74. During Rhodes's next over Trumper square-cut the Yorkshireman for two successive fours. Jackson was then employed and received similar treatment. Finally, in desperation, Hayward was tried and Trumper immediately on-drove him for three to bring up his hundred, made in barely 143 minutes. He was immediately approached from behind the stumps by Lilley, who had replaced Storer as the England wicket-keeper. Lilley described the conversation between himself and Trumper at Lord's in 1899 in his book, *Twenty-four Years of Cricket*.

Lilley said, "Well played, Victor." The reply was characteristic, "Thank's very much, Dick, but I have had a bit of luck." The members in the pavilion at Lord's rose to a man to acclaim the young maestro. When the applause finally ceased Trumper continued to go after the bowling, pulling Jessop around to the leg-side boundary and in the fast bowler's next over he claimed two successive fours with a cover-drive and a leg-glance. He finally ran out of partners as the Australian innings closed at 421. The lead of 215 set England a daunting task and the match was really a lost cause for the home team from this juncture.

Trumper was loudly cheered for his score comprising 20 boundaries and which occupied 195 minutes. Dick Lilley was impressed by the innings, "Victor Trumper gave a superb display without the semblance of a chance, and he is undoubtedly the greatest Australian batsman I have ever seen. There is no stroke of which he is not a complete master."

The press were equally lavish with their praise for the innings of 135 not out:

> ... the innings of Trumper was the innings of the match. When Trumper got his runs last month at Eastbourne almost everyone was impressed by his style; and yesterday he won everbody's admiration by his timing of the ball and by his driving and cutting. He played like a master on a great occasion, and by winning his spurs in a match of this importance he has justified the committee who brought him over here. (*The Times*, 17 June 1899.)

H. S. Altham, in *A History of Cricket*, remarked, "It was Trumper's third innings in an international game, and before he had batted for half an hour it was obvious that a new star of unsurpassed brilliance and charm had joined the cluster of the Southern Cross."

The correspondent for the *Sydney Morning Herald* wrote from London:

> Trumper carried his bat out for 135, tying Hill for top score. It is impossible to give Trumper too much praise for his magnificent score made without a blemish. His was by far the most attractive batting in the match, and his success was very popular with the other members of his team. His splendid conduct in every way has endeared him to his comrades off the field as well as his excellent play on it.

England sent in to bat a second time reached 240, highlighted by MacLaren's famous innings of 88 not out, supported by Hayward's 77. Australia then required 28 runs and soon won by ten wickets.

ENGLAND

First Innings		Second Innings	
A. C. MacLaren, b Jones	4	not out	88
C. B. Fry, c Trumble, b Jones	13	b Jones	4
K. S. Ranjitsinhji, c and b Jones	8	c Noble, b Howell	0
C. L. Townsend, st Kelly, b Howell	5	b Jones	8
F. S. Jackson, b Jones	73	c and b Trumble	37

First Innings		Second Innings	
T. Hayward, b Noble	1	c Trumble, b Laver	77
J. T. Tyldesley, c Darling, b Jones	14	c Gregory, b Laver	4
G. L. Jessop, c Trumper, b Trumble	51	c Trumper, b Laver	4
A. A. Lilley, not out	19	b Jones	12
W. Mead, b Jones	7	lbw, b Noble	0
W. Rhodes, b Jones	2	c and b Noble	2
Sundries	9	Sundries	4
Total	206	Total	240

	O.	M.	R.	W.	O.	M.	R.	W.
Jones	36.1	11	88	7	36	15	76	3
Howell	14	4	43	1	31	12	67	1
Noble	15	7	39	1	19.4	8	37	2
Trumble	15	9	27	1	15	6	20	1
Laver					16	4	36	3

AUSTRALIA

First Innings		Second Innings	
J. Worrall, c Hayward, b Rhodes	18	not out	11
J. Darling, c Ranjitsinhji, b Rhodes	9	not out	17
C. Hill, c Fry, b Townsend	135		
S. E. Gregory, c Lilley, b Jessop	15		
M. A. Noble, c Lilley, b Rhodes	54		
V. T. Trumper, not out	135		
J. J. Kelly, c Lilley, b Mead	9		
H. Trumble, c Lilley, b Jessop	24		
F. Laver, b Townsend	0		
E. Jones, c Mead, b Townsend	17		
W. P. Howell, b Jessop	0		
Sundries	5		
Total	421	Total	0 for 28

	O.	M.	R.	W.	O.	M.	R.	W.
Jessop	37.1	10	105	3	6	0	19	0
Mead	53	24	91	1	–	–	–	–
Rhodes	39	14	108	3	5	1	9	0
Jackson	18	6	31	0				
Townsend	15	1	50	3				
Ranjitsinhji	2	0	6	0				
Hayward	6	0	25	0				

Major Wardill, Hill, Trumper and the team companion in England, 1899.

Despite the fact that the length of the over in England was five balls (changed to six in 1900), the over rate for both teams was remarkable. 379 overs were bowled in the three-day Lord's Test.

In the fixtures leading up to the Third Test Match at Headingly in late June, Trumper's batting proceeded as follows: 55 *v.* Oxford University Past and Present at Portsmouth, 12 *v.* Leicestershire at Leicester, 11 *v.* Derbyshire at Derby.

At the start of play on the first morning of the Leeds Test the wicket was quite soft but the weather was fine and warm. Darling won the toss and chose to bat in front of 12,000 spectators. Soon after lunch the tourists were all out for 172. Trumper was bowled by Young for 12. At stumps England were 4 down for 119. That evening both teams, who had accepted an invitation to attend the Empire Theatre, gathered in the foyer. A pleasant evening was anticipated but instead they were upset by witnessing a grand mal epileptic seizure which attacked that plucky little all-rounder, Johnny Briggs, who had been recalled to the England ranks. Dick Lilley described the distressing occurrence:

"An unfortunate incident happened on the first evening of the match in the sudden seizure of Briggs which cast a gloom over all the players during the time we were in Leeds. The teams had accepted an invitation to be present at the Empire . . . Briggs was occupying the same box as myself, when during the performance the illness suddenly developed which for long kept Lancashire's wonderful little all-round cricketer from the field."[*]

The match was eventually drawn when rain completely disrupted play on the third day; Australia 172 and 224, England 220 and 19 without loss. In his second innings Trumper scored an invaluable 32 before cutting a ball from Jackson into the waiting hands of Ranjitsinhji. In this match, during which J. T. Hearne secured a hat trick (M. A. Noble, S. E. Gregory, and C. Hill), Dr Laver (Frank's brother accompanying the tourists) presented each member of the touring team with a watch made from Australian gold to commemorate the ten-wicket victory at Lord's. Afterwards Clem Hill was forced to enter a London hospital for the removal of a small growth in his nose and Jack Worrall was treated by a specialist for a knee injury. Frank Iredale, who had missed the Lord's and Leeds Tests because of an attack of the measles, rested at Bradford for two weeks but was permitted to play in the following match at Trent Bridge.

The Australians opposed Nottinghamshire on 3 July on a very soft pitch. Notts. were dismissed for 188, Trumble taking 5 for 82. At stumps on the second day the visitors were 3 for 106 with Trumper 31 not out. He got going immediately and played fluent cricket. On the third and last day Australia declared at lunch with the score 7 for 234. Trumper made 85 before Attewell caught and bowled him. He was in for 195 minutes and according to one journalist, gave "a chanceless and excellent display." His was the highest score of the game.

Notts. batting in their second innings hit up 132 for the loss of 6 wickets and declared leaving their opponents 87 runs for victory. With about an hour left the Australians hit out vigorously but were soon in trouble when four batsmen, including Trumper, were sent back to the pavilion without scoring. At the close of play with the game drawn, the tourists had made 38 runs and lost 6 wickets. On this last day there were two declarations and 15 wickets fell.

---

[*] A. A. Lilley, *Twenty-four Years of Cricket*. Mills & Boon, London, 1912.

In the fixture immediately preceding the Fourth Test Joe Darling won the toss at Bristol and decided to bat. By this time W. G. Grace had resigned from Gloucestershire because of the dispute concerning his involvement with the new London County Club as well as his wish, as County captain, to select his own teams.

Trumper, batting at first drop at Bristol, played with great freedom and panache. He was bowled by Roberts for 104, made up of 7 fours, 6 threes and 17 twos. *The Times* reported:

> The great feature of the day's cricket was a very bright and skilful innings of 104 by Trumper who, going in first wicket down, was fifth man out at 212.

Australia won at Bristol by six wickets, and once again, Trumper top-scored for the match.

Laver, Trumper, Trumble and the team companion at Clifton Bridge in Bristol, 1899.

The Fourth Test at Old Trafford was full of incident. On the first day 40,000 people packed the ground and police were forced to close the gates with hundreds more waiting to enter. MacLaren won the toss and England, batting first, were all out for an exhilarating 372 just before stumps. Hayward scored a fine 130 for his country. At stumps Australia were 1 for 1 with Kelly and Howell the night-watchmen.

Just before 3 o'clock on the second day Australia were all out for 196 (Trumper 14), the chief destroyers being Bradley and Young. Forced to follow on, the visitors were 2 for 142 at the close of play with Noble, 59 and Trumper, 18 the not out batsmen. During the afternoon a number of spectators crashed through the roof of a refreshment booth, injuring a waiter.

Overnight heavy rain fell in Manchester making the pitch more slow than difficult. On this final day the partnership of Noble and Trumper was to save the game for Australia as they brought the score to 3 for 205. Trumper was bowled for 63 about half an hour before lunch. Noble went soon after lunch for 89, made in five hours and twenty minutes. As the visitors dug in the crowd whistled the "Dead March" from Handel's *Saul*. Finally at 7 for 346 the innings was declared closed leaving England the impossible task of making 171 runs to win on the wearing pitch. At the end the home team were 3 for 94 and the match was drawn. The correspondent for the *Sydney Morning Herald* wrote:

> Noble and Trumper played wonderfully well, though the change in the pace of the ground caused Noble to be less completely master of the bowling than he had been during his splendid display on the day before. Trumper, on the other hand, was seen at his very best. While quite prudent and watchful he hit out in a way that no one else on the side ventured to imitate, and really played a most finished and attractive game.

Frank Iredale recalled an experience shared with Victor while fielding in this Test:

> In big cricket when I had the pleasure of playing with him, I loved to talk to him of the different phases of the game as it appeared to us both. I remember in a Test Match at Manchester in 1899. We were both fielding in the long field, and during the period when a new batsman was coming in, we had our yarn, and notwithstanding the fact that he loved his trip and the experience he was going through, I felt somehow or other that his mind and thoughts were of his home; he loved his home and the ties that surrounded it, and

though he came with us on many occasions to theatres and elsewhere, one felt that whatever may have been in the place where we were, it was certainly not the real man.*

Besides his wonderful conquest of Lord's, Trumper's greatest triumph was in the match with Sussex played on the picturesque Hove ground adjoining Brighton, in late July. Darling lost the toss and Sussex batted all day, at the end of which they were 6 wickets down for 389. Clem Hill, who had missed seven matches in a row after his operation, became exhausted in the field in the hot afternoon sun, and had to rest. He was replaced by Frank Iredale, who had completely recovered from his earlier illness. Sussex were dismissed for 414 shortly before 2 o'clock on the afternoon of the second day, Charles Fry putting together an erudite 181, the highest score against the 1899 Australians.

At 3 o'clock, with the score at 1 for 62, Victor Trumper entered the fray. His partnership with Jack Worrall lasted until shortly after 5 o'clock when Worrall was caught in the slips for a fine 128. During this period Trumper reached his hundred in 130 minutes, the partnership producing 178 runs. The *Sydney Morning Herald* described the rest of the day's play:

> No other successes fell to the Sussex bowlers that evening, Trumper, when he had Gregory for a partner, batting in most brilliant form. It is possible that he might once have been taken at long-on had Marlow gone for the catch, but this was almost the only blemish in his play, despite the fact that he never stopped driving, pulling and glancing the ball on the leg side. When stumps were drawn he had made 175, Gregory 48, and the total stood at 388, the Australians, despite the fact that they had to face a total of 414, being able to claim much the better of the game.

Commenting on Trumper's 175 not out *The Times* stated:

> Trumper, who played most brilliant cricket, had the satisfaction of making the highest score yet hit for the Australian eleven, and also completed his 1,000 runs during the tour.

The *Sydney Morning Herald* report of the third day is graphic:

> The match was resumed to-day. The weather was fine and the wicket excellent. Trumper and Gregory continued their innings. The former played with great dash, and being well supported by his

---

* Frank Iredale, *Thirty-three Years of Cricket*. Beatty, Richardson & Co., Sydney, 1920.

partner runs came apace. Eventually Gregory went forward to one from Killick and missing it he was stumped by Butt for 73. When Gregory was 64 he gave a chance to Brann at point but it was declined. His score included eight fours. Trumper had long since passed the second century, and his score now stood at 261. Hill came next and the score still mounted up. After adding 28 to the total Hill was caught at the wickets off Brann. Four for 547. Darling joined Trumper, and soon assumed an aggressive mood. Various changes in the bowling were resorted to, but without effect. Trumper hit all round, and punished the bowling with vigour. He treated all bowlers alike, being particularly strong on the pull and the off-drive. Six hundred appeared on the board, and soon afterwards Trumper reached his third century. Darling also continued to play with spirit. When the total reached 624 the Australians declared their innings closed with four wickets down, Trumper being 300 not out, and Darling 56 not out. Trumper batted in slashing style all through his long innings, which lasted six hours and a quarter, and never gave a chance until he reached his third century, at which stage he was badly missed at mid-off. His big score included 36 fours, six threes, and 29 twos.

Trumper became a little tentative when approaching Murdoch's previous record of 286 not out and this was reflected by the fact that his last hundred took 165 minutes. The second hundred had taken 80 minutes and the first, as mentioned, 130 minutes. Thus Trumper achieved the unique record of becoming the first Australian to reach 300 runs in an innings in England. *The Times* commented admiringly:

That most true of all grounds—the Hove, Brighton—remained kind to batsmen on the third day, when Trumper, one of the most skilful members of the Australian Eleven, established a record by scoring 300 runs not out. This is the highest individual innings ever played for or against the Australians in England, and, curiously enough, it was at Brighton that the previous best was recorded, when Mr W. L. Murdoch made 286 against Sussex in 1882 which is generally acknowledged to be the year when the Australians had the most brilliant side ever sent to this country. It was the year that England lost on the Oval by seven runs. Trumper, although one of the last to be selected for this year's team, is one of the most accomplished of their batsmen. He comes down very straight on the ball, and perhaps among a variety of strokes, his best is that by which he gets away a ball pitched on his middle and leg stumps. It is something of a Ranjitsinhji stroke but it gets the ball well away in front of square leg.

51

With respect to this stroke, described by *The Times*, Monty Noble wrote: "Victor's best, most effective and most beautiful stroke, was one made off a fast ball well up on the middle stump. The bat would meet the ball at half-volley, and, with a flick of the wrist at the moment of contact, it would be forced along the ground at great pace forward of short-leg into the country. No assistance was given here by the pace of the ball from the bowler as there is in making the leg glance; it was pure wrist-work and wonderful timing."*

Joe Darling, while batting with Trumper in the Sussex match, felt that this exquisite exhibition of batsmanship made his own innings pale into insignificance and he told those Australians in the dressing room after the declaration that none of the Eleven could bat on the same level as the young champion. Weeks after this game Darling was rummaging in one of his cricket bags when he discovered the bat with which Trumper had made his record score. On it was written a dedication to the Australian captain with compliments from his most junior player: "To Joe Darling with V. Trumper's compliments." This bat is in the museum of the Melbourne Cricket Club.

The Sussex fixture, which ended in a draw, was an outstanding feast of cricket, 1181 runs being scored in three remarkable days with exactly six wickets falling each day. The tourists then met and decided to extend Trumper full financial status, thus foregoing a portion of their own share of the gate profits.

It is interesting to note that Trumper did not bowl in either innings of the Sussex match, even though Hill and Kelly were used. He was only called upon three times by Joe Darling in 1899, and against Somerset he took his only wicket. The Australian captain maintained that he did not use Trumper more often because his health was delicate and he was nursed to ensure that his batting did not suffer.

After the Hove match Victor was exhausted and although he played in the next encounter versus the MCC at Lord's, which Australia won by nine wickets, he was bowled by Trott for 4 in his only innings of the game. He was rested for the next match at Southampton when the tourists met Hampshire.

Trumper was in the field when Albert Trott, the expatriate Victorian, made history by driving Monty Noble over the Lord's

---

* *The Game's the Thing.*

Trumper demonstrates his strength on the leg stump, 1899 Tour.

pavilion into a garden of a neighbouring house. Noble had the last word, however, when he had the Australian caught by Darling for 41. Here is a description of that remarkable stroke:

In the match MCC v. Australians at Lord's, A. E. Trott, unable to restrain himself, set about the fulfilment of his heart's desire—to land a ball over the pavilion. First he lifted a delivery from Trumble over the members' seats to the north of the pavilion, and then drove another which pitched among the seats at the top gallery of the pavilion. He was determined to go "one better," and did, for Noble having taken the place of Trumble, Trott opened his shoulders, and sent the ball with terrific force through the air. The ball struck one of the posts of the chimney appearing above the top-most outline of the pavilion, and rebounding, disappeared behind. It was a tremendous hit and, to adopt theatrical parlance, "fairly brought down the house." (The London correspondent for the *Sydney Morning Herald*.)

It is probable that the young Trumper was impressed by Trott's exuberant hitting. Later in his career he would astound the world with his own lofted drives. During the Lord's match the members of the Paddington Cricket Club sent a cable to Victor congratulating him on his record score at Sussex.

During the progress of the Southampton match, Trumper, Laver and Johns visited the Cowes Regatta. They walked for lunch to the Marine Hotel, pausing on the way to inspect the numerous sideshows. Over lunch they met an acquaintance of Laver, a Mr Harcourt, who entertained them on his yacht *Heloise*. Next he took them to see the finish of the Australian Cup at the Royal Squadron Yacht Club. Here Victor Trumper was re-introduced to the Prince of Wales (the future King Edward VII), and also some European dignitaries. Strolling on the lawn behind the Club House the three Australian cricketers were surrounded by an excited group of elegant and titled beauties eager for an introduction to the handsome young men. Here the guests encountered the horse-drawn carriage of Queen Victoria. As Victor and his team-mates bowed their heads the elderly monarch returned the greeting.

The final Test Match at The Oval was notable for the high scoring, especially by England. At the close of play on the first day the home team were 4 for 435. Chasing a final total of 576, Australia were all out for 352 on the third day and, forced to follow on, had made 254 runs for the loss of five wickets when the match ended in a draw. Fine centuries were compiled by

54

Hayward and Jackson for England, and Gregory improved Australia's precarious position with his fighting 117. Trumper in this match made only 6 and 7, and caught MacLaren in the long field off Trumble when the England captain was 49.

After much team discussion it was decided not to visit South Africa, due to the gathering war clouds. Instead the tourists travelled back to Australia in two main groups. The first consisted of Darling, Trumper, Worrall, Iredale, Gregory, Howell, Kelly and Jones, who embarked on the *Oruba* on Friday 15 September, soon after the final match. Trumper and Howell were both keen to return, the former to rejoin his family at 31 Liverpool Street, Paddington, and the latter to be reunited with his new bride.

Major and Mrs Wardell and the remaining cricketers sailed a fortnight later on the *Ormuz*. However, plans were made for Johns to return early on the *Oroya* because of the sudden illness of his father.

Hill, Trumble, Kelly, Trumper and Guide on Nelson's "Victory", 1899 Tour. The plaque in front of Kelly's foot is where Nelson fell.

55

In the remaining matches after the final Test Trumper's best performances were his 62 at Lord's versus Middlesex and a brisk 51 made at Taunton against Somerset. Fielding mostly in the out-field, usually at long-on, he took fifteen catches during the tour. He was third in the Australian batting aggregates with 1556 runs, and fifth in the averages with 34.58, an outstanding effort considering that he was the last man selected in the team.

Victor Trumper had indelibly made his mark on world cricket in a manner and style that no one before him even remotely approached. Frank Iredale mirrored the wonder expressed in England and Australia at his innovative batsmanship:

When he came forth into the cricket firmament, and played his game, no one knew what to think. Old canons of the game were broken, and new ideas were submitted by this mere stripling of a lad.

Old players gasped with astonishment at the extraordinary strokes he made, and the seeming indifference to either the bowling or the field. In later years we knew that this meant a master had come forth and was making history. We saw new things, new strokes, and a brilliancy of execution which we had never seen before, and one wondered whether it would last. Slow, perhaps, to develop, yet never altering his ideas or his desires, he went on in his own way until the time came when he blossomed forth as the greatest batsman in the world.*

---

* *Thirty-three Years of Cricket.*

The New Century

In South Africa, late in 1899, the Boers invaded Natal and the impending attack on Ladysmith was only weeks away. As the British retired to Mafeking, patriotic fervour in Australia and New Zealand in support of the Empire was rapidly gathering pace. Not all reports from the front line were humourless. Dick Lilley tells the story:

> A company of the Coldstream Guards was ordered in Lord Methuen's first battle to storm one of the kopjes held by the Boers. The advance had just been sounded when a shell came from the enemy, and without bursting buried itself in the earth close to the men. The one nearest to where it dropped looked across at his neighbour, and said, "If I had only got my bat here, I'd have hit that beauty for six."*

In the early hours of Saturday 28 October, the *Oruba* sailed through Sydney Heads. On board were Victor Trumper, Sydney Gregory, Bill Howell and Frank Iredale. At 7.30 a.m. the executive officers and several delegates of the New South Wales Cricket Association boarded the steamer from a launch to welcome home the winners of The Ashes.

The four heroes were then conveyed to Circular Quay where family and friends were waiting to greet them after their seven-month absence. One observer, having cast his eye over the returned cricketers commented, "Trumper has developed into a sturdy looking chap with a pair of substantial shoulders."

Bill Howell left with his wife by the morning train for Penrith to inspect his farm and his bees. Later that day a more formal and substantial welcome was given at the Australia Hotel attended by officials and dignitaries, past and present cricketers, family members and friends. Association president, George Houstoun Reid (the future fourth Prime Minister of Australia), in a speech frequently punctuated by cheers, said, "Australians appear to be getting in their cricket as near perfection as possible, but with regard to the tenth team it can be said that they

---

* *Twenty-four Years of Cricket.*

have excelled in harmony. Their record, I believe, is the best. Although we admire the doings of our old representatives, we are naturally gratified when we find colts coming to the fore. In the tour just closed the colts of the team have met with greater success than has perhaps been recorded on any previous occasion. I won't mention names but we have taken a special pride with the advent of certain colts, both because of their sterling ability and their invincible modesty of demeanour."*

Two weeks later Monty Noble and Jim Kelly arrived in Sydney on the *Ormuz*, which Kelly had boarded in Melbourne after his stay with his family. Later that day Noble travelled to the Sydney Cricket Ground to watch some of the play in the Metropolitan Eleven versus Country match which had commenced the previous Thursday. His friend Victor Trumper, playing for the Metropolitan Eleven, had earlier scored 116 runs in a powerful exhibition. This match against the Country Thirteen was drawn.

The following Wednesday night was spent by both Paddington players as guests at a smoke concert run by the old boys of Crown Street Superior Public School at Quong Tart's Elite Hall. Mr E. Banks, the Headmaster was chairman, and the 300 people present were entertained with musical items directed by Mr Spaull. When the toast of the evening to "Messrs Trumper and Noble!" was submitted, there was prolonged cheering.

At Paddington Town Hall on the following evening Trumper, Noble and Kelly were guests of honour at a sumptuous banquet. G. H. Reid, president of the New South Wales Cricket Association, John Cash Neild, MLA, the Paddington Club patron, other politicians and officials, and Phillip Sheridan, the secretary to the Sydney Cricket Ground Trust, were present. During the evening many popular songs were sung with piano accompaniment. G. H. Reid, who proposed the toast of the evening said, "All Australians, whether they represent the colonies on the cricket field or serve their country in the Transvaal, will give a good account of themselves. Our guests have done honour to the colony in England, and I sincerely hope that they will live long on the cricket fields of Australia." After toasting the heroes of the occasion Mr Reid called for three hearty cheers which were given with enthusiasm.

In South Africa the siege of Kimberley and the assault on

---

* *Sydney Morning Herald*, 29 October 1899.

Ladysmith had begun in earnest. A large Boer force under Colonel Cronje had surrounded Kimberley and was bombarding it with heavy artillery. These events were followed daily by an intensely interested Australian public. The sale of newspapers containing cable reports of the fighting was brisk.

Heavy rain on Friday 17 November 1899 caused a delayed start to the intercolonial match with Queensland on the Sydney Cricket Ground. When the surface was fit for cricket on the following day, Jim Kelly won the toss and chose to bat. Frank Iredale and Sydney Gregory were victims of the current influenza epidemic and could not play, and Bill Howell was still recovering on his farm from the leg injury sustained in England.

Victor Trumper came in at first drop when Monty Noble was out leg before wicket for 15. During the next 45 minutes before lunch Trumper and Donnan added 52 runs to bring the score to 1 for 84. On resuming Trumper made his half-century:

> Donnan was 98 when Trumper was 96. The latter, however, was the first to bring the individual century on the board. It was beautiful cricket at both ends, each stroke hard and well timed, and the running between the wickets by these two was one of the features of the day's play. (*Sydney Morning Herald*, 20 November 1899.)

Trumper on reaching his hundred opened up, and hitting in all directions soon grossed 145. At this point his partner was caught for 113. Unruffled Trumper continued to bat with great gusto and soon raced to his double century. After 185 minutes at the wickets he was caught at long-off for 208. It was a whirlwind innings:

> He went after the bowling on all sides, every bowler was alike to him. He punished all and hit very hard indeed. Many of his hits, dropping on the cycling track, went bounding up the terraces, and one pitched at the southern end of the stand near the scoring board. His style is if anything more attractive than before he went to England, simply because it is more vigorous, but where he used to keep the ball well on the ground, he now lifts it and consequently takes risks. He is now a most pronounced hitter. (*Sydney Morning Herald*, 20 November 1899.)

New South Wales won the Queensland match by an innings and 315 runs. Trumper in the Queensland second innings had figures of 2 for 12 from 7 overs. The customary toasts and speeches were made in the pavilion, and the cricketers prepared to journey northwards to Brisbane for the return engagement.

This took place before 4000 as the visitors won the toss and batted first on a hostile and rain-affected pitch. Kelly, Duff and Noble soon capitulated and Trumper at number five decided to decimate the bowling. This positive attitude won the game for the southern team, as Queensland couldn't handle the treacherous wicket, scoring 156 and 129. Trumper's State made 371, of which his 77 was the match winner. One Brisbane reporter wrote, "Trumper gave a splendid exposition and received an ovation on retiring."

The New South Wales team on their journey back to Sydney played a one-day game against a New England fifteen at Armidale. The excessive dust and heat prevented many from attending and the city men had difficulty when bowling and batting as their spiked boots kept catching in the matting on the pitch. Nevertheless Victor Trumper had the imposing bowling figures of 9 wickets for 27 runs with Monty Noble taking 5 for 32. Trumper also made second best score for his side with 42, Noble hitting 43:

> Trumper followed and showed the spectators some of his brilliancy, the force of his drives being the most notable feature of his display.
> . . . Several ladies kindly regaled the cricketers and several of those present with afternoon tea, which was appreciated very much, the visitors called for three cheers for the ladies which were heartily given. (*Armidale Chronicle*, 2 December 1899.)

During a similar game in the country E. G. Noble, Monty's brother, was batting and an easy two was hit into the outfield. The batsman having crossed for the second run stood with bat inside the crease but with his feet outside. The return smacked into the 'keeper's gloves and he knocked all three stumps out of the ground appealing to the square-leg umpire. Without hesitation a finger was raised skywards. "What am I out for?", cried the indignant batsman. "You're out because you didn't have both feet inside the crease, and don't come up here with any of your Sydney tricks!"

Arriving back home with very little sleep from the overnight train trip Trumper backed up again with the bat, this time for Paddington against Glebe at Wentworth Park. He led the bowlers and fieldsmen a merry dance in scoring 119 before lofting a drive into the long field. The following week he took 4 for 30 from 13 overs, as Paddington marched to a win by an innings and 158 runs. Despite this resounding victory Paddington was not to win the premiership this year, Central Cumberland proving successful from North Sydney and South Sydney.

Trumper's next century took place one week later in Adelaide in the Sheffield Shield fixture. Batting at first drop with his side chasing the home team's 155, he reached 38 before stumps were drawn. The *Sydney Morning Herald*'s man in Adelaide wrote: "Trumper played the bowling with consummate ease, and made his runs in little over half an hour, during which short time he played such brilliant yet safe cricket that the spectators lustily cheered him, and many golden opinions were expressed about his play at the close." It is food for thought that such a short innings should be so lauded. The *Adelaide Advertiser* reported:

> Trumper's innings was simply delightful, and he seemed to play all the bowling with the most perfect ease. His back play, especially, is charming, and it is doubtful if he has his equal as a batsman in Australia.

Play continued on the Monday and Trumper batted as if Jones and Giffen were novices, which of course they were not. He raced to his half-century and in less than fifty minutes added 50 to his overnight total. At lunch he had scored 107 and Donnan, who went in before Trumper on the previous day, was on 66.

After lunch Trumper continued to be severe on Jones and Giffen, bringing up his 120 off the latter with a majestic sweep to the leg chains. Soon reaching 100 runs for the day he surged on to 150. When he had reached 165, much to everyone's amazement, he misjudged the ball while attempting to leg-glance a Giffen off-break and was out leg before wicket. He occupied the crease for 190 minutes and hit 16 fours. The *Adelaide Advertiser* described his batting:

> With perfect hitting all round the wicket Trumper went on giving a delightful display. All bowling alike seemed easy to him, and he had the South Australian trundling tied in a very bad knot indeed. So bad was it that Clem Hill was presently called up to take a hand, while Reedman was put on. Nothing, however, seemed to avail, and soon the South Australian first innings score was passed with the loss of only one wicket. The force that Trumper put into his strokes was shown when straight driving Hill he broke one of the stumps in his companion's wicket. And yet he does not give one the impression that he is hitting hard. It is the beautiful timing of the strokes that makes them travel so.

He was about three hours and a quarter making his score, and his innings can only be described as superb. He gave no chances, and hardly made a faulty stroke. There can be no doubt that at present he is far the best batsman in Australia.

New South Wales were all out for 807 with Noble 200 and Gregory 176, but Trumper's exposition was regarded as the innings of the match. The home team scored 260 in their second attempt, Pye bagging 4 for 71 and Trumper 2 for 1, as New South Wales won by an innings and 392 runs.

News of the events filtering back from South Africa were by now a daily feature in the newspapers, and public interest increased because of the involvement of Australian troops in the fighting. Australians living in Cape Town raised funds to provide extra items of comfort for their soldiers in the field, and back home donations to patriotic funds flooded in from all over the Island Continent. In New South Wales, for example, the Patriotic Fund was swelling rapidly and had soon exceeded expectations, with contributions ranging from monies gathered by the employees of the Department of Public Works, to silver thrown on the stage of Her Majesty's Theatre after the singing of "The Absent Minded Beggar" by Miss Dorothy Vane.

Despite the war, celebrations for New Year's Eve went ahead as usual and, in Sydney, George Street was packed with thousands of gaily dressed revellers, each one present to herald in the twentieth century. Brightly lit trams and young people blowing trumpets joined in the festivities until well after midnight.

By the end of January 1900 the Patriotic Fund had reached substantial proportions. A benefit match to support the New South Wales Bushmen's Contingent and the Patriotic Fund, which was held at the Sydney Cricket Ground in early February 1900, was well supported by the public. Trumper made 41 and 49 and took 2 wickets for 21 for the Australian Eleven, which defeated the Rest of Australia by 151 runs.

New South Wales won the Sheffield Shield that season and, in all the intercolonial matches, were only vanquished once in six matches, by South Australia in Sydney. Trumper's batting in the intercolonial encounters was impressive; 208, 77, 165, 57, 45, 7, 31, 41, giving him an aggregate of 631 runs and an average of 78.88.

For Paddington he made 354 runs, an average of 59, and collected 13 wickets for 261 runs.

During early August 1900, the Paddington Baseball Club played Leichhardt at Hampden Park before a crowd containing the USS *Culgoa*'s baseball squad. This was one of two selection trials conducted that day by the New South Wales Baseball Association.

After a Probables versus Possibles fixture in which Trumper was the only Probable player to make it home twice, the scene was set for the inaugural intercolonial series with Victoria to decide the holders of the J. C. Williamson Trophy. Victoria, led by Frank Laver, won the first game in an exciting finish by 11 runs to 9. According to the press reports Trumper, fielding at short stop, played well. The second and third games, also on the Sydney Cricket Ground, were both won by the home State by 9 runs to 6, and 8 runs to 5 respectively. Monty Noble, Jim Kelly and Victor Trumper all shone in their particular departments of the game. In his later life Trumper was to advise young, aspiring cricketers to take up baseball in the winter months to improve their fielding skills.

The 1900–01 Sydney season proved as outstanding for the Paddington Club as it was for its leading light, Victor Trumper, the First Grade team winning six engagements and drawing two, and easily carrying off the Hordern Shield. Trumper's all-round performances were outstanding; he scored 557 runs from ten innings and captured 28 wickets at an average of only 11.07 runs per wicket. In fact his medium-paced deliveries were so incisive that twenty of his victims were clean-bowled. Among those who fell to his vigorous deliveries were Frank Iredale, Reg Duff, Bill Howell, Leslie Poidevin and Charles Gregory.

His best batting performance was at Hampden Park in early March, when he blazed 213 runs against Glebe without losing his wicket. In December his bowling on the North Sydney Oval was devastating, as his statistics indicate:

O.	M.	R.	W.
26.4	7	90	9

That season the opening bowling combination of Trumper and Noble proved so successful that between them they collected 69 out of the 72 wickets which fell to Paddington during the innings in which they bowled, and in three matches they took all the opposition wickets between them. On three separate occasions in the field Monty Noble did not use Trumper and himself as he wanted to give his other bowlers the chance to bend their backs for a change. Trumper's impressive all-round figures are reproduced:

Opponents	Venue	Match Commenced	Batting	Bowling
Central Cumberland	Hampden Park	15/10/1900	94	3/22
Redfern	Redfern Oval	29/10/1900	75	6/50
Sydney	Hampden Park	17/11/1900	3	0/21
North Sydney	North Sydney Oval	1/12/1900	49	9/90
Waverley	Waverley Oval	12/1/1901	2 & 30	5/49
Leichhardt–Balmain	Birchgrove Reserve	18/2/1901	35	0/21
Glebe	Hampden Park	2/3/1901	213 not out	1/33
Burwood	Sydney Cricket Ground	16/3/1901	26 & 30	4/24

New South Wales cricket supporters received a rude shock when in December their State side was humbled by South Australia in Adelaide. Trumper's contribution of 32 and 53 was not sufficient to prevent capitulation by an innings and 35 runs. Easily the highlight of the struggle was Clem Hill's 365 not out. He ran out of partners while chasing Archie MacLaren's world record score for first-class cricket of 424 made in the Lancashire versus Somerset encounter of 1895 at Taunton.*

The South African War still evoked public interest and it was amid satisfaction that Lord Roberts announced in Johannesburg that Lieutenant J. H. Bisdee, of the Tasmanian section of the Imperial Bushman's Contingent, had been recommended for the Victoria Cross for valour in the face of the enemy. The Citizen's Life Assurance Company promised a life annuity of £1 per week for the first Australian to be thus decorated.

In late December pride and excitement were increasing as the day of Federation approached. Australia's successes in the international clashes with England in cricket during the decade up to 1901 and the veneration of home-grown heroes such as Trumper, Darling, Hill, Trumble and Noble grew alongside the swelling national desire to break away from the apron strings of the mother country.

---

* Initially surpassed by W. H. Ponsford, Victoria v. Tasmania in Melbourne, 1922–23 season with 429.

A national referendum, heavily supported by the diggers on the Western Australian goldfields to the cries of "One people, one flag, one destiny!", had acted as a catalyst for the legislative manoeuvres between Westminster and Melbourne.

The New Year rolled in and with it the birth of a new nation. The London *Standard* reported to English readers that the celebrations in Australia on and after Federation Day resembled a chapter from the Arabian Nights. This was by no means journalistic exaggeration, as myriads of pleasure craft and yachts dotted Sydney Harbour like confetti from Circular Quay to the Heads. Brass bands on large mail steamers moored at Farm Cove, with flags flying in the easterly sea breeze, entertained thousands under the golden January sun.

The following Friday the New South Wales Government held a mammoth Federation sports carnival on the Sydney Cricket Ground at which several thousand spectators witnessed Australia's champion athletes striving to win such contests as cycling races, track and field competitions and gymnastic displays. There was considerable interest in the results of "The Australian Cricket Ball Throwing Championship." The record established the previous summer was a mighty throw on the full of 124 yards 10 inches by Victor Trumper. The contest for the champion's medal this year was very much a one-act affair as the results clearly indicate:

Medal for First Place:	Victor Trumper (Paddington CC)
	120 yards 1 foot 6 inches
Medal for Second Place:	Jack Marsh (Sydney CC)
	92 yards
Third Place:	E. B. Dwyer
	91 yards 1 foot 6 inches

Another event comprising cricket skill involved throwing a ball at a wicket for accuracy, and the placegetters were A. J. Hopkins (North Sydney CC), H. Goddard (Stanmore CC) and S. E. Gregory (Waverley CC).

On the next day 5 January 1901, the twenty-first meeting between New South Wales and South Australia began before 16,000 onlookers in Sydney. The match was unique as the home team batting second set a world record total of 918 runs, which eclipsed the previous best, a score of 887 by Yorkshire. Century innings were recorded by Iredale, Noble, Gregory, who top-scored with 168, Duff and Poidevin. Trumper's contribution was a polished 70, including 11 fours made in 88 minutes. One connoisseur wrote:

> His cricket was much steadier than what he showed last season or before he went to England. Though from a spectator's point of view the exhibition was not so attractive as when he last appeared in a first-class match in Sydney, it was, however, safer, and more likely to win for his side.

South Australia were completely routed as the victors exacted inspired revenge for their previous defeat in Adelaide. The visitors were without Joe Darling, who was farming in Tasmania, and they could manage only 157 and 156. Jack Marsh, the controversial Aboriginal fast bowler, had the fine match figures of 5 for 34 and 5 for 59, while Trumper, who opened with Marsh in the second innings, took 2 for 23 and 1 for 39 as the home State were triumphant by an innings and 605 runs.

Just two weeks later the Empire was rocked by the death of Queen Victoria who passed away at Osborne Manor on the Isle of Wight from the effects of a cerebral haemorrhage. In Australia the new nation mourned for weeks, and shops and businesses closed for several days. Flags were consistently flown at half-mast and masses of floral wreaths surrounded the late Queen's statue in Sydney. Many shop-front window displays were converted into memorial tributes lined with black materials. Grace Brothers' store in Broadway featured a marble bust of Queen Victoria, tastefully placed on a black-draped pedestal surrounded by a wreath of violets, accompanied by the words "In Memoriam" and "An Empire Mourns". Interstate and Electorate cricket was suspended for nearly two weeks during the period of mourning.

In the last Sheffield Shield match of the season in February 1901, Trumper was again among the runs, hitting his first ever century against Victoria. *The Referee* described his performance:

> V.T.'s strokes were very sound all round the wicket, some of the late cuts being gems. . . . Trumper exhibited superb cricket from start to finish. When he plays a big innings the cricket is always beautiful, and never fails to give delight to everyone—if the field and their sympathisers be excepted. He did not give the ghost of a chance to get rid of him, other than that which was accepted. He hit 31 fours and was as fresh as paint at the finish. Trumper's lasting powers are

really wonderful, for in this big innings one might have thought that the heat would affect him. As I have already said, his strokes were all round the wicket. They included cutting of all kinds, square and fine, and driving on both sides of the wicket. He used a Glenville bat, which prior to his getting the 100, had a piece about 4 in. by 1 in. knocked out of the face centre within a couple of inches of the bottom. Later on he had to take another strip out, and many of his runs were got with as badly a battered bit of willow as any man used in a big innings. ("Not Out", John C. Davis)

When he opened with Iredale he was a little more sedate than usual, but later he continually forced the hostile and accurate deliveries of Trumble, Saunders, Laver and McLeod all over the ground. The *Sydney Morning Herald* described the play after lunch on the third day:

On resuming Trumper added a couple and then his great innings came to an end. He was caught by Ross at the wickets off Saunders. Trumper's contribution was 230, and it was indeed a magnificent effort. He was in four hours 50 minutes without giving the faintest chance or even making a miss-hit of any kind. It was just such another of those long occupations of the crease which he showed the Australian public before he joined the eleven for England. Safe, every ball along the turf, every loose ball severely punished, and he was never in difficulties.

Despite Trumper's effort, plus a contribution of 3 wickets for 71 with the ball during the Victorian second innings, the visitors won a thrilling finish by one wicket and the Sheffield Shield was to reside in the trophy room of the Melbourne Cricket Club. Trumper's seven innings in the Shield encounters yielded him 458 runs, the highest for the State, his average being 65.43. He also took 6 wickets at a cost of 232 runs.

The following spring, preparations for the 1901–02 tour by the England Eleven were well under way, and in Sydney the Electorate competition began on 28 September on wickets made heavy by soaking rain. Paddington met Redfern in the first round and on the first afternoon's play on a swamp-like pitch Trumper greeted the new season with 158 runs. The following Saturday his lively bowling caused Redfern to be dismissed for 116. Trumper's statistics were:

O.	M.	R.	W.
22	7	37	6

Although mostly occupied in State fixtures and the Test clashes with England that season, he still managed to amass three innings of 158, 108, and 112 for Paddington in only six attempts, giving him 479 runs with an average of 79.83. He also took 11 wickets at a cost of 218 runs.

A most unusual occurrence took place while Trumper was carving out his 112 against Waverley on the Sydney Cricket Ground in February 1902. Both the Paddington second and third teams were involved in two tied results in their matches with Burwood and Petersham. The Paddington second team hit up 161 runs and Burwood replied with the same total. In the third grade match both Paddington and Petersham scored 236. The latter side on batting for the second time were all out again for 236.

The eyes of the new nation were diverted from cricket scores for two minutes on Tuesday 5 November 1901 when nearly 100,000 racegoers cheered home the 6 to 4 favourite, the aptly named Revenue, in the Melbourne Cup on the Flemington Racecourse. The five-year-old bay gelding won the two mile classic by half a length, ridden by the eighteen-year-old local jockey F. Dunn.

Trumper's first tilt at English bowling that year took place in late November in Sydney. Opening with Monty Noble on the first day he top-scored for New South Wales, stroking 67 charming runs in 79 minutes. He made nine boundary hits and the *Sydney Morning Herald* reporter at the match wrote, "Trumper's cricket was delightful to watch, all his strokes being perfectly timed, and containing a great deal of force." The home combination won by 53 runs, Archie MacLaren for England making 145 and 73 and Dick Lilley 80, the wicket-keeper being caught and bowled by Trumper, who took two wickets in the match.

Prior to the First Test Match in Sydney, the tourists defeated a Glen Innes District Eighteen by an innings and 89 runs, Blythe capturing 17 wickets for 101 runs in a game punctuated by thunderstorms. Even without Rhodes and Hirst, prevented from touring by Yorkshire, in the English party, the mother country humbled Australia on the Sydney turf by an innings and 124 runs, Barnes and Braund bowled in great style to a hesitant Australian batting combination. Trumper made 2 and 34 and his curious lack of form in most of the international fixtures was attributed by *Wisden* to his working at night in an office. He was, in fact, a junior clerk in the Probate and Intestate Estates Office in Macquarie Street, on an annual salary of £90.

On leaving Crown Street Superior Public School during 1895, Trumper was accepted as a junior clerk with the NSW Public Service at £40 per annum in the New South Wales Government Stores Department. He did not open a sporting goods store until 1904, so the oft-quoted story of him pulling a bat from the rack before scoring 185 not out with it in 1903 is obviously apocryphal.

The Trumpers at this time lived at 31 Liverpool Street, Paddington and did not move to 112 Paddington Street, Paddington until 1902. The story that Victor lived his childhood days at the latter address is misleading. The full household movements of the Trumper family are in the Appendix.

Victor's best effort against MacLaren's men was at Adelaide in January 1902 during the Third Test. He compiled 65 and 25, opening the batting on both occasions. *The Referee* described his dismissal in the first innings:

> At 138 Hill hit a ball to Gunn at mid-on, and Trumper started an impossible run. He was sent back, but could not get home in time, being run out. Trumper played a grand innings for 65, towards the end being especially brilliant and charming.

Trumper hit 8 fours. A remarkable dust storm after lunch on the fourth day brought down the flagpole in front of the Governor's box as the tempest enveloped the ground. Victor Trumper and the others on the field lay prone on the grass and then beat a hasty retreat back to the pavilion. The velocity of the wind did not diminish and stumps were drawn at 5.25 p.m. with visibility almost down to zero.

Australia won this Test by four wickets, having won the Melbourne match in which Hugh Trumble took the hat-trick (A. O. Jones, J. Gunn, and S. F. Barnes). The Adelaide struggle is chiefly remembered for Clem Hill's 98 and 97. He had scored 99 in the Australian second innings in Melbourne. The unfortunate breakdown of Sydney Barnes in Adelaide ensured that he did not play for the remainder of the tour. He had captured nineteen Australian wickets in the first two Tests.

The host country, winning the last two Tests, retained The Ashes. Despite a mediocre season in the international arena, the selectors had no hesitation in naming Trumper in the Australian

Eleven to leave for England in March. On the journey south the Eleven played a Bendigo Eighteen and during the local batsmen's stay at the wickets Trumper took the bowling figures for the match with five wickets, Bendigo hitting 180 runs to the Eleven's 440.

While visiting Ballarat for a game with the town's Eighteen cricketers, Trumble, Howell and Armstrong were returning to the surface after inspecting the underground shafts of the Last Chance United gold mine, when their cage was suspended in space for half an hour following a malfunction. Fortunately they were freed without any ill effects.

The Englishmen, having won against South Australia by six wickets, were formally farewelled at the Adelaide Oval. Two days later the two Elevens, who would again play on the verdant English fields, made their farewells before sailing on the *Omrah*. The *Sydney Morning Herald*, reviewing the prospects for the coming tour, commented:

> Trumper has had a peculiar experience since his return from England. He changed his style from safety to one full of risks, and for a time did well, but during this season his desire to score off impossible strokes, accompanied by some bad luck, was a bar to the accumulation of runs to the extent that was anticipated from so brilliant an exponent of batting.

The description of the *Herald*'s Adelaide correspondent conveys to the reader the colourful scene that greeted the eye on that clear March morning of departure so long ago:

> There was an extraordinary bustle at the Adelaide railway station this morning when Mr MacLaren's team and the members of the Australian Eleven left the city to board the mailboat. A number of local cricketers and enthusiasts were on the station, and many proceeded to the vessel with the players. Mr and Mrs MacLaren and Messrs Jessop, Hill and Jones were the only voyagers by the special which left the city at 10.30, the others coming down by a later train. It was a lovely day at the anchorage. The waters were lightly rippled by a cool south-westerly wind. The South Australian Cricket Association had been striving for the past week to secure a special launch for the cricketers and their friends, but the tug company could not comply with the request. Consequently there was a crush at the pier to get on the vessels plying to and from the *Omrah*. Some alarm was excited at first by a report that the mailboat had been quarantined, but subsequently it was found that the yellow flag,

70

after flying for about three hours, had been hauled down and the coast was clear. The vessel presented a very busy appearance, over 600 passengers being on board. The good feeling which had existed between the Australians and their opponents throughout the tour was indicated by the hearty manner in which the two fraternised. After hearty farewells the *Omrah* left her anchorage on the homeward trip.

One Wet and Glorious Summer

The Australian team making the journey on the *Omrah* was an extremely formidable combination comprising J. Darling (captain), E. Jones, C. Hill, (South Australia); V. T. Trumper, M. A. Noble, R. A. Duff, S. E. Gregory, A. J. Hopkins, J. J. Kelly, W. P. Howell, H. Carter, (New South Wales); H. Trumble, W. W. Armstrong, and J. V. Saunders, (Victoria).

During the long sea voyage the two teams mixed freely. Concerts, usually organized by Monty Noble, often featured the Paddington player performing with his distinguished baritone voice along with Len Braund's repeated renditions of that popular music hall lament, "The Blind Boy". It was obvious to the English cricketers that the Australians were very determined to retain The Ashes as they kept in good physical condition. Dick Lilley wrote:

> It was this determination to win that could not but appeal to every one. It was so obvious, this one dominating idea that they were out to play cricket, and were expected to give the very best they had. It is, of course, the proper spirit in which to make the journey, and it is difficult to estimate how much of their success was due to it; and the splendid physical form in which we always found them showed that they were carefully carrying out their resolution, and that cricket, and cricket only, occupied their time and thoughts.*

The Australians practised in the nets at Lord's accompanied by incessant winds and showers. Hugh Trumble while fielding a ball driven by Clem Hill, dislocated the thumb of his right hand and tore the webbing. This was to prevent his appearance in a match for over five weeks.

The first engagement of the 1902 Tour of England was with a very strong London County combination led by the ageless W. G. Grace. This began after lunch on a sodden Crystal Palace ground on 5 May, and the tourists were bundled out for a meagre 117, the South African left-arm medium pacer C. B. Llewellyn claiming 5 wickets for 52 runs. The fifty-three-year-old Doctor Grace, resplendent in his London County cap of bottle green with red and yellow stripes, took 2 for 25 with his deceptive

---

* *Twenty-four Years of Cricket.*

round-arm, slow-flighted deliveries for which he had become so renowned over the years. One charming anecdote from his Crystal Palace years begs to be retold here.

A promising young batsman invited by W.G. to turn out for his team, was asked benevolently where he would prefer to bat in the order. The reply was a slightly boastful, "It really doesn't matter, Doctor, I've never made a duck in my life." His gargantuan skipper with large brown eyes narrowing into slits thundered back, "Never made a blob, eh? Then it's number eleven for you. Not enough experience!"

Batting at fourth drop in this match, Trumper was run out for nine while Syd Gregory top-scored with 34. At the close of play London County were 2 for 34. The next day was overcast and cold, play being interrupted for twenty minutes by rain. Len

Trumper, watched by admirers, rides a goat cart, 1902 Tour.

Braund blasted 104 runs in 125 minutes for the home team, pushing the score to 235. Australia, batting next were 7 for 203 at stumps, with Joe Darling hitting 92 runs and Victor Trumper, who opened with Duff, making 64, which included 8 fours and a five (not over the boundary).

Only ten more runs were added to the overnight total on the third day before heavy rain and hail set in and the match was washed out. The London media were not impressed with the display and commented that the Australians were feeling the exceptional cold intensely. The London *Evening News* printed the following:

> Does your circulation fail, Kangaroo?
> Got a frost-bite in your tail, Kangaroo?
> Do you find it hard to play
> When it's hailing half the day,
> And it's even cold for May, Kangaroo?
>
> Are your Noble, Duff and Hill, Kangaroo
> And poor Trumper feeling ill, Kangaroo?
> Had the voyage made them stale,
> Since Llewellyn did not fail,
> When he started "finding bail", Kangaroo.
>
> 'Tis no doubt a sudden change, Kangaroo,
> But you'd sooner find your range, Kangaroo,
> If in coming o'er the seas,
> In the chambers where they freeze,
> You were hardened by degrees, Kangaroo!*

M. A. Noble wrote: "It is doubtful if ever an Australian eleven began a tour of England under such unfavourable auspices as the team of 1902. From the time practice was started, and during the following six weeks, everything seemed to go against us. Wretched weather and sickness among the players each did its utmost to knock the heart out of the team. The rain fell almost without cessation, and the biting easterly wind of the Mother Country almost froze one's marrow, so that all our games were played under the most depressing conditions. Fires in the dressing-rooms were much in evidence, and most of the days usually set apart for cricket were spent by members in playing cards, poker being the favourite game, with nap a good second."†

* Samuel J. Looker, London *Evening News*.
† *The Game's the Thing.*

The second match of the tour was won by the Kangaroos by an innings and four runs. Darling 128, Hopkins 80 and Kelly 66 were the most fruitful contributors to a total of 474. Trumper hit seven fours in his score of 47 and took 3 wickets for 59 runs from 21 overs, in the first innings, as Notts. succumbed with innings totals of 287 and 183 (Armstrong 8 for 47).

During this miserably cold and dank summer Trumper's penchant for centuries was astonishing. F. S. Ashley-Cooper wrote:

> Trumper's batting was "sui generis", and, although he could play an orthodox game as successfully as anyone, it was his ability to make big scores when customary methods were unavailing that placed him above his fellows. His timing has never been excelled, and in the art of placing the ball he was unsurpassed. He always seemed to divine far quicker than most men the best way in which a ball should be played, and then brain, wrist and bat acted in perfect unison. At times he would apparently change his mind at the last moment—he was always very quick on his feet—but, even then, the resulting hit was, more often than not, pre-eminently a master stroke. So many were his devices, in fact, and so pronounced his versatility, that, when at his best, even the greatest bowlers seemed to be at his mercy. At times it was useless to atempt to place the field for him, for his repertoire of strokes was remarkable and, as stated, his ability to place the ball was exceeded by none. His wonderful pulling was so successful because it was due to a combination of great confidence in himself and a marvellous eye.
>
> In his prime he would often get a yorker to the square-leg boundary, and it was by no means unusual to see him cut a ball off the middle stump for four. Some of his biggest hits, which sent the ball over the ring, were made without any apparent effort—the result of perfect timing and judgement.
>
> For him the season was one long triumphal progress, and those who were fortunate to witness his amazing brilliance will never be able to forget the unrivalled skill and resources he displayed. On sticky wickets he hit with freedom and scored well, often whilst his companions were puddling about the crease, unable to make headway and seemingly content if they could keep up their wickets.*

Trumper's first century innings occurred in the third match of the tour at Kennington Oval in the Surrey fixture. It was

---

* F. S. Ashley-Cooper, *Cricket Highways and Byways*. George Allen & Unwin, London, 1927.

compiled in 150 minutes. *The Times* report gives a clear description of the playing conditions:

> Delayed by weather in the morning the players went on until late in the afternoon, when a promise of sunshine gave way to a drizzle and a bad light, and the wind was always keen. Mr Trumper's batting was extremely good to watch, and the wonder was that the play all round could have been so good under the miserable conditions. Mr Trumper came down very hard on the ball, and was strong on the leg side, and dealt relentlessly with any short bowling.

Trumper's 101, consisting of 9 fours, 9 threes and 9 twos, was made on a very difficult pitch on which the ball kicked randomly. He was finally caught in the slips from a Hayward delivery. The Prince of Wales visited the ground during the day but missed out on seeing Trumper's exhibition. Australia declared at 5 for 296, Surrey in reply scoring 96 and 122, Bill Howell proving almost unplayable taking 5 for 23 and 6 for 33 and one wonders what the Surrey scores might have been with Hugh Trumble bowling from the other end.

At the function held at The Oval on the second night of the Surrey match the Club president, Lord Alverstone, while proposing the toast to the Australians proclaimed, "There is little doubt that our colonial friends no longer come to learn but to teach us cricket. We are proud of our tutors and wish them good luck."

In the next match at Leyton a draw resulted as play was continually interrupted by scudding showers. Trumper, who had only made nine before he hit a ball from Young onto his wicket, took the bowling figures for the game: 5 wickets for 33, three of which were clean-bowled. His statistics, although excellent, only partially reveal the accuracy and vigour which had the Essex batsmen continually playing at balls of perfect length which moved both ways off the seam:

O.	M.	R.	W.
13	4	33	5

In the evening the tourists were invited by Sir Henry Irving to watch Gounod's *Faust* at the Lyceum Theatre. After the opera the party were taken back to their hotel with the steaming horses trotting through the driving wind and rain. It was on such a night during the 1905 Tour that Victor Trumper and Monty Noble were leaving the London Coliseum when they noticed a small boy sheltering in a murky doorway selling sheet music. Trumper

76

went over and speaking quietly to the lad in his own gentle way, bought all his merchandise and sent him home.

The above incident, which was recounted by Monty Noble, could not have occurred before December 1904, as this was the month during which the Coliseum, situated in St Martin's Lane, first opened for business. This most fantastic of all music halls was owned and managed by an Australian, Oswald Stoll, who built an enormous revolving stage, numerous food stalls, an information bureau and a tramline which led straight from the street to the Royal Box.

Frank Iredale, who was later to become very well acquainted with Trumper when Victor joined the Gordon Club in 1909, wrote: "He was splendidly loyal, and a firm believer in what was right. He was a hard man to know, because he made you so indebted to himself for many kindnesses extended. All the children loved him because he was easily approachable and so adaptable. He thought of others so constantly that one could almost believe he lived for the rest of the world."*

Trumper's next century was made on the Christ Church Ground at Oxford in late May, the first day being a complete washout. On the second, the pitch was surprisingly firm but the Oxford batsmen put up little resistance against Jones, Noble and Armstrong, scoring only 77 runs. Trumper and Duff opened for Australia and after 12 overs 78 runs were posted, Trumper's share being 46. In just forty minutes he reached his half-century and in another fifty minutes he raced to his century, having completely demoralised the bowling with his wizardry. Trumper and Duff made 108 for the first wicket in just fifty-five minutes, while Trumper's second wicket stand of 105 with Hill took only fifty-nine minutes. Trumper could not be contained and his pulling to the square leg boundary was breathtaking. His 121 made in 114 minutes, caused *The Times* to comment:

> His batting was delightful to watch. He drove well, pulled with certainty, and scored skilfully on the leg side, his chief hits being 15 fours.

Joe Darling closed the innings at six wickets for 314 and in their second innings Oxford could manage only 183, Saunders taking 7 for 67. Thus Australia won by an innings and 54 runs.

---

* *Thirty-three Years of Cricket.*

Two days later W. G. Grace, who had played for the Maryle-bone Cricket Club and Ground against the First Australian Eleven in that famous encounter twenty-four years earlier, won the toss and elected to bat on a fine and sultry Monday morning. At the close of play the MCC were all out for 240 (Ranjitsinhji 67, Grace 29), and Australia were 1 wicket down for 74, Trumper being 46 not out. The following morning he hit his third century innings of the 1902 Tour adding 59 runs in seventy minutes. The *Sportsman* in its report commented:

> For the third time in the tour Trumper managed to place three figures against his name, reaching the century after a stay of a couple of hours, his proportion being one hundred and one out of 174. Five minutes later, with his contribution raised to one hundred and five and the total to 182, he was bowled middle stump by a good length ball from Hearne. Nothing in the shape of a chance marred his fine, free innings, which included as its principal strokes eleven 4's, a 3, and five 2's.

The visitors were all out for 271, W. G. Grace taking 5 for 29, a wonderful performance for a man who had been born in 1848.

The visitors took the field for the MCC second innings and during an early over from Ernest Jones a sensation occurred. As he released one of his rocket-like deliveries a sparrow flew in front of the ball and was knocked to the grass. As it fluttered in seeming agony towards the fence a spectator hurried onto the field to end its misery while the sympathetic crowd chanted, "Kill it! Kill it!" At this approach the bird suddenly flew up and out of Lord's amid scenes of relief and laughter from both players and spectators. Such was the uproar that the match did not resume for fully three minutes.

The MCC in their second attempt were soon five wickets down for 119 when W.G. came in and put together a tidy 23. Darling then brought Trumper on to bowl and his success was almost immediate as William Gilbert Grace had the symmetry of his wicket impaired by a fast full-toss, which, striking the batting pads, cannoned on to the stumps dislodging the leg bail. The MCC second innings was closed at 8 for 280, leaving the Australians 250 for victory.

Trumper and Duff opened and with the total at 91 (made in 55 minutes) Duff was caught by Trott in the slips. Trumper was 48 and rain fell halting play for thirty minutes. On resuming 33 runs were added before Hill was bowled by Hearne. Trumper went on his way until he was bowled by Trott for 86. His display lasted 105 minutes and included 13 fours. Darling joined Gregory and hit out with great vigour but with the score at 3 for 217 time ran out with Australia needing only 33 runs to win this most memorable match, and without the interruptions caused by rain they would have probably done so. The English press agreed that Trumper was easily the man of the match scoring a total of 191 runs and taking 3 wickets for 30.

In the first of the 1902 Test Matches, at Edgbaston in Birmingham, England, batting first on Thursday 29 May were 9 for 351 at stumps (Tyldesley 138, Jones 3 for 76, Trumper 2 for 35). Heavy rain fell overnight and during most of Friday morning and play did not resume until five minutes to three. The wicket was very soft but Lockwood and Rhodes added 25 runs before MacLaren, eager for his bowlers to test the tourists on the slow, wet pitch, closed the innings at 9 for 376. He was not disappointed as after 85 minutes batting the Australians were all out for a paltry 36, which included 3 wides. Trumper who opened, was seventh man out for 18, as Rhodes with 7 for 17 and Hirst with 3 for 15 both bowled magnificently. Although the light was poor and the pitch like putty, it was not technically a sticky wicket as the sun did not appear during the day.

Forced to follow on, Australia were 0 for 8 when bad light halted play around six o'clock. Trumper had made all eight runs while Duff held up his end, thus the former batsman was credited with 26 runs from 41 made from the bat that day by Australia. On Saturday morning a crowd of 14,000, eager for an England victory, clamoured for admission and a dozen people were trampled as hundreds broke into the ground. They were thwarted, however, as the torrential overnight rain had completely soaked the playing surface and the cricket did not begin until late in the afternoon. When Trumper and Duff finally resumed the innings at 5.15, Trumper added 7 more runs to his overnight score before Braund caught him in the slips from Rhodes. Duff was caught by Fry for 14 but shortly afterwards the umpires called a halt at 6.25 and the Test Match was drawn.

The dismal performance of the Australian batsmen at Edgbaston produced the following verse:

Our Cornstalk cousins like us well,
Our country, our abodes,
And yet the truth they fain must tell:
They cannot face our *Rhodes*.[*]

The next engagement for the Australians at Leeds in the beginning of June resulted with a win for Yorkshire by five wickets, the condition of the wicket at Headingly must have had to be seen to be believed. The surface was thoroughly soaked and the heat of the sun transformed the pitch into a steaming swamp. Trumper was to top-score for the match with 38: Australia 131 and 23 (Trumper 7, Gregory 10 not out), Yorkshire 107 and 5 for 50, while George Hirst had match figures of 9 for 44 for the White Rose team and Jackson (9 for 42) without performing the hat-trick took 4 wickets with five balls. On the first day 33,705 fiercely patriotic spectators swarmed onto the playing area and took the stands by storm, the police being powerless to stop them. Before play resumed after lunch, both teams stood in the centre of the ground and, in an attempt to restore order, performed the national anthem with the crowd joining in the singing. Three cheers for Edward VII then rang out and play was eventually allowed to continue with people continuously spilling over the boundaries. Crowd disorder in cricket is not, it seems, a phenomenon restricted to the late twentieth century.

Yet again in the tenth tour match, at Old Trafford, play was interrupted by the weather, and Lancashire did not even bat. With Australia 7 wickets down for 356 at the end of the first day, wintry conditions returned and the match was abandoned. Trumper was once again dominant under overcast skies hitting 70 runs out of 109 for his team in seventy minutes. He executed 12 fours and had the crowd constantly applauding the audacity of his strokes. Ironically in Australia, New South Wales farmers who had suffered the effects of years of relentless drought were tentatively hailing the end of the "dry" as scattered thunderstorms fell throughout the State.

English cricket fans did not have long to wait for Trumper's next century as in the following meeting with Cambridge University at the Fenner's ground he produced a superlative all-round performance. By this stage of the tour Trumper's name

---

[*] P. C. Standing, *Cricket of Today and Yesterday*. T. C. & E. C. Jack, London, 1902.

had become a household word in English families. Neville Cardus described how, as a schoolboy he worshipped this ideal of the perfect batsman; fair with grey-blue eyes, quite tall and with slender build, not too muscular, and above all, graceful and courtly in his every movement at the wicket—the Crown Prince of Cricket.

On the night before each Test Match the youthful Cardus prayed by his bedside for an England victory as well as a century innings from his Australian idol.

With Noble recuperating from influenza at Brighton, and Darling, Saunders and Howell feeling the effects of the same virus, Dr Roland Pope, the physician to the Australian team, took the field against Cambridge. A Sydneysider, he had previously played three times for the tourists in 1890. Once again rain affected the day's cricket and in the eleven consecutive games since the beginning of the 1902 Tour not one match had escaped this fate. After lunch Cambridge, who won the toss, were all out for 108 on the soft but slow pitch. Victor Trumper bowled very well and his analysis deserves reproduction:

O.	M.	R.	W.
8.3	4	19	5

He took the last five Cambridge wickets in only twenty-seven balls for just 6 runs, four of his victims being clean-bowled and the fifth stumped by Carter standing up to Trumper's slower ball. Hugh Trumble making his first appearance in England in 1902, took 4 for 33.

The start of the Australian innings was delayed by more rain and at stumps the score was 87 for the loss of one wicket, with Trumper, who had opened as usual with Duff, on 27 and Clem Hill with 25. The following day in Cambridge dawned bright and sunny and the wicket soon became sticky and treacherous under the influence of the warm sun. Most of the visiting batsmen could not cope with the conditions, although Syd Gregory hit a polished 72. Trumper, having stroked 11 charming fours was stumped for 128 which took just under two hours to compile and Australia completed a first innings total of 337. In their second attempt the students were routed for 46 runs, Hopkins capturing 7 wickets for 10 runs as the touring party achieved victory by an innings and 183 runs. Trumper's achievement in top-scoring for the match and taking 5 for 19 in the home side's first innings, evoked admiring praise from the English cricket journalists.

F. B. Wilson in his autobiography, *Sporting Pie*, recalled in 1922:

K. R. B. Fry was a wicket-keeper, but not quite a first-class one: a fine bat if an erratic one; and the very worst field who ever played in first-class cricket. Who that saw it can forget the two catches which Trumper presented him with at Fenner's in 1902? Trumper knew that the Australians could make almost what they liked against Cambridge—the wicket was very easy on the first day—and was quite willing to see some of the tail end have a serious knock. Trumper was, perhaps, the most unselfish great cricketer who ever lived. He mistimed a hook, when he had made seven, straight to Fry at mid-on and was walking out, but Fry was paralysed, He held out one hand like a soup-plate but could not close it from sheer fright! A little later Trumper played the same shot and this time—he was at the Pavilion end—he turned round and went for home. The ball hit Fry on the chest—he was too absolutely unnerved after the first effort to move his arms. It would have been an absolute impossibility to throw a man an easier catch from a distance of twenty-two yards. I was at short slip at the time and had to use physical force to turn Trumper round and make him go back to the wicket. "You don't play that trick on me," said Trumper, who really thought I was joking: he was too modest to know that a fellow struggling for his "Blue" would about as soon as attempt a "joke" like that as to pull Padoubny's moustache. "Look at the poor devil," said I. Fry was still standing there with the ball at his feet and there was not a man on the ground—not even the bowler—who was not sorry for him. Trumper got an extra hundred after that in about an hour and a half, and then got out on purpose. Those two catches lost Fry his last chance of a Blue in 1902, for he was still thinking of them, I do believe, when he went in to bat. Fry could catch a hard hit one but never a "dolly."

Monty Noble in *The Game's the Thing*, wrote: "We invariably drove to the cricket grounds in a charabanc, Joe Darling, the captain, being always the first aboard. He was very severe on the laggards and a heavy fine was imposed on those arriving on the field late. Sometimes, I fancy, he had the impression that, provided Vic and a few others were there, nothing else mattered, for, when the time arrived to leave, he would look around and ask, 'Is Vic here?' If the reply was 'Yes' he would tell the driver to go on, without even troubling to inquire if any were missing." Whenever Darling chided Victor for getting out soon after surpassing a hundred in 1902, Trumper's stock reply was, "If the rest of you chaps can't pull your weight, then it's a pretty poor show!"

H. S. Altham, although British to his bootstraps, was a great admirer of Trumper and witnessed many of his finest innings in 1902. He wrote: "From start to finish of the season, on every sort of wicket, against every type of bowling, Trumper entranced the eye, inspired his side, demoralized his enemies, and made run-getting appear the easiest thing in the world. To try to reduce to words the art of this consummate batsman is almost an impertinence, but to those who never saw him at his best I would suggest that they should study the glorious series of photographs of Trumper in action contained in Beldam and Fry's *Great Batsmen*. From these they will catch at least a reflection of the ease, the balance, the perfect naturalness that made him perhaps the most fascinating batsman to watch in the history of the game."[*]

Drenching rain welcomed the players for the Second Test at Lord's on 12 June. The Australians could barely make up the eleven contestants for the game as some were still recovering from the effects of colds and influenza, with Trumble and Howell confined to bed. Only two hours' play took place during the match and this occurred on the afternoon of the first day. Batting first England were 2 wickets down for 0 runs, with Fry and Ranjitsinhji both dismissed by Hopkins without scoring. Archie MacLaren and Stanley Jackson took the score to 2 for 102 when play was halted at around six o'clock. The two not out batsmen played excellent cricket in the bad light. For Australia Hopkins finished with 2 for 18 and Trumper had 0 for 33 from 8 overs, although he had MacLaren dropped in the slips when the England captain was on 34. Play in the remaining two days was completely obviated by the torrential rain.

Excitement in England at this time was not only confined to cricket. Indian princes such as the Maharajah of Jaipur, and premiers and prime ministers from the far-flung corners of the Empire, along with their colourful and numerous retainers were gathering for the Coronation of Edward VII, whose health, however, was cause for increasing concern among Buckingham Palace officials. Anticipation was high, and in Australia celebrations for Coronation Day were well under way. The Governor-General, Lord Hopetoun, donated 300 bottles of French

---

[*] H. S. Altham, *A History of Cricket, Volume 1*. George Allen & Unwin, London, 1926.

champagne to be distributed to hospitals throughout Sydney, and also gave £100 for 300 poor families, so that each could enjoy a substantial meal. Throughout Australia parades by schoolchildren, picnic race meetings complete with brass bands, and sporting displays were planned for the great day. This festive mood was heightened by the final surrender of the Boer commandos to Lord Kitchener and his officers in the Transvaal, the Orange River Colony and Cape Colony during the middle of June. Gloom, however, was to soon descend on the Empire as Edward VII hovered close to death from severe appendicitis and an urgent operation was performed to save his life. The Coronation had to be postponed while he recovered.

Victor Trumper's next century innings took place on 26 June during the England XI match at Bradford. A few days earlier Sir Percy Walker, the president of the Derbyshire Cricket Club, had entertained the travelling cricketers over lunch at his palatial Osmaston Manor at Ashbourne. For once the sun shone and the guests spent a splendid day relaxing away from the rigours of the tour.

Refreshed by the Ashbourne visit Trumper was in scintillating form at Bradford reaching 113 in two hours in brilliant sunshine on an excellent wicket. He cracked 19 fours and reached his 1000 runs for the tour, making him the first batsman in the land to reach four figures in the wettest English summer since 1860. The *Sportsman* commented:

> The batting honors on the Colonial side were carried off by Duff and Trumper, who came together when matters were going very badly with the Cornstalks on Thursday morning—Darling, Noble, Hill, and Hopkins having all been sent back with 35 on the board—and by splendid cricket completely turned the tables on the attacking party. In an hour and fifty minutes they increased the total to the extent of 191 before Trumper was bowled by Knutton round his legs. The outgoing batsman was responsible for half the score of 226 at the time he left, and the only blemish in his display was a sharp chance to Sowden at point, when he had made 61.

The Australians comfortably won this engagement by seven wickets. Trumper rested during the next match, a two-day fixture at Edinburgh against Scotland. The Australians were grandly fêted by their Scottish hosts. They were entertained at the Australian Club, then the following day were driven to the Forth Bridge and to Lord Hopetoun's estate, after which they

FIVE CRICKETERS OF THE YEAR.

C.J.BURNUP   W.W ARMSTRONG.

V TRUMPER

1902.

J IREMONGER   J.J KELLY

PHOTOGRAPHED BY
E HAWKINS & COMP! 32 PRESTON ST BRIGHTON

The "Five Cricketers of the Year 1902," from the 1903 Wisden.

returned in the evening to dine at the Grange Club in Edinburgh. The Scottish match was won by the tourists by an innings and 105 runs.

The Third Test Match at Sheffield starting on 3 July was to be the only one ever played on that ground. The task of scoring runs in the poor light of this industrial city prompted many a batsman to insist that he could see the gas lamps burning in the pavilion, even at mid-day. Australia won this international by 143 runs, assisted by some fine batting on a soft pitch from Hill and Trumper in the second innings. Trumper, who made only 1 in the first innings, mauled the England bowling from the outset during his second visit to the wickets. The Australians began the second innings with a lead of 49 as Trumper began scoring at will, among his strokes being a fine off-drive for four off Rhodes. He quickly added 19 while Duff at the other end could manage only a single and was soon after caught. Trumper then in daring manner stroked 12 runs from a Rhodes over. One eye-witness wrote, "Hill came and practically looked on while Trumper, exhibiting the greatest dash, punished the bowling severely."

Batting for just fifty minutes for his 62 he hit eight scorching fours before skying a ball from Jackson to Lilley behind the stumps. Charles Fry, who had been recalled for this match after Ranjitsinhji was forced to stand down with a strained leg, described Trumper's style in his autobiography, *Life Worth Living*:

> Victor Trumper used to walk to the wicket and start making beautiful strokes from his first ball onwards. No matter how good the bowling, he made it look easy, and he never permitted any wicket to appear difficult. Trumper was tall and shapely with slightly sloping shoulders and a rather long body. He had a natural grace of movement and played his strokes with a swing from the wrists which was not a flick but rather, as it were, a stroking effect. . . . Trumper gave one the impression of generous abandon.

In his four engagements preceding the Fourth Test at Manchester, Trumper's batting was highlighted by his innings against Gloucestershire on 15 July and Surrey on 22 July. Prior to the Gloucestershire match he rested during the Australian victory at Worcester after which he enjoyed a day with the other tourists on a horse-driven trip through rural Worcestershire and a visit to Malvern College. On returning to Worcester the Australians were shown around the Royal Worcester Porcelain Works.

Trumper's 92 at Bristol against Gloucestershire was both majestic and faultless until he was caught by Jessop off Roberts. He smote fifteen boundaries in only 75 minutes as Australia cruised to victory by an innings and 222 runs.

Against Surrey on Kennington Oval rain frequently halted play but Trumper still managed to force the heavy ball over the sodden turf for 10 fours on his way to a total of 85 made at a run per minute. The Surrey match was drawn.

The Australian Rifle team were also visiting England during July, 1902, and, against formidable opposition at Bisley won the Kolapore Cup, the symbol of world supremacy in the sport.

Rain fell during the night and on the morning of Thursday 24 July the first day of the Fourth Test Match at Old Trafford. As Joe Darling and Archie MacLaren walked onto the sodden outfield to toss, grey clouds obscured the sun. Despite the soft wicket, Joe Darling, on winning the toss, decided to bat. MacLaren was not perturbed at the prospect of bowling out the Australians on such a wicket with the likes of Jackson, Rhodes, Lockwood, Braund and Tate at his disposal. His main tactics were directed at Trumper: "Keep Victor quiet," he told his men, "the pitch will be sticky as the day goes on, then we'll bowl them out as fast as they come in to bat."

Thus the most imperious and subtle of England's captains concentrated all his energies in attempting to subdue Trumper's genius, yet, despite everything seemingly working against the making of runs, Trumper was supreme. He and Duff hit 9 runs from the first two overs from Rhodes and Jackson, punishing the bowling with great freedom, and within one hour's play one hundred runs appeared for Australia on the scoreboard. Despite frequent bowling changes Trumper and Duff raced to a first-wicket partnership of 135 in only seventy-eight minutes before the latter was smartly caught behind by Lilley from Lockwood's bowling for 54. Trumper, who was on 80 when Duff retired, had reached his 50 in fifty-two minutes. Clem Hill joined Victor, who did not slacken the pace or alter his incredible range of strokes. Two of his lofted drives went straight over the sightscreen into the practice ground and play was held up while the ball was recovered. Archie MacLaren said of this wonderful morning's batting, "Victor had half a dozen strokes for the same kind of ball!"

The Australian 150 was soon reached in an hour and a half, and six runs later Rhodes went on in place of Jackson. After ten more runs were added Trumper was 92 and Hill 12. In the next over the good-looking opening batsman reached his hundred by pulling Lockwood off his stumps for two scorching fours just five minutes before lunch. The century, which had taken just under 105 minutes and included 14 fours, 3 threes and 6 twos, was chanceless and those at Old Trafford rose to congratulate the young master batsman. *The Times*'s reporter at Old Trafford stated:

> Mr Trumper played a grand innings, and his sixth century for the team. His innings was marked by splendid hitting on the leg side, and his placing on the off side was remarkable. He is certainly the finest cricketer on all wickets that we have had from Australia.

Neville Cardus gave an eye-witness account of Victor's appearance and flawless technique that day:

> I was only twelve years old when I saw Trumper at Old Trafford on this deathless morning of 24 July 1902. His cricket burns always in my memory with the glow and fiery hazard of the actual occurrence,

the wonderful and consuming ignition. He was the most gallant and handsome batsman of them all; he possessed a certain chivalrous manner, a generous and courtly poise. But his swift and apparent daring, the audacity of his prancing footwork, were governed by a technique of rare accuracy and range. Victor was no mere batsman of impulsive genius; he hit the ball with the middle of his bat's blade—even when he pulled from the middle stump round to square leg. In my memory's anthology of all the delights I have known, in many years devoted to the difficult but entrancing art of changing raw experiences into the connoisseur's enjoyment of life, I gratefully place the cricket of Victor Trumper.*

Thus Trumper not only became the first Australian to record six century innings in England for a touring team but achieved the hallowed distinction of being the first batsman to complete a century before lunch on the first morning of a Test Match. In over one hundred years of Test cricket this has occurred only four times up to 1984.

Trumper was soon out after lunch for 104 when he added one run to his score before succumbing to Rhodes, bowling from the city end. The London based *Sportsman* described the dismissal:

> His [Rhodes] fifth ball saw the termination of Trumper's innings, the great Australian batsman, who at first shaped as if to cut the ball, apparently changing his mind and just directed it into the hands of the wicket-keeper, Lilley, who effected a very neat catch.

Australia went on to score 299 (Trumper 104, Lockwood 6 for 48), and England replied with 262 (Jackson 128). With the wicket in a very soft state Australia could manage only 86 in the second innings (Lockwood 5 for 28, Darling 37, Trumper 4). After lunch on the third and final day, England, needing a total of 124 for victory, were 44 runs without loss when a succession of wickets fell to the accurate onslaught of Trumble and Saunders on the difficult pitch. With the score at 8 wickets for 109 the intense expectation among the spectators became almost unbearable. The final minutes of one of the greatest of all Test Matches is described by the *Sydney Morning Herald* correspondent at the ground:

> The excitement increased apace, each stroke being watched with anxiety. Rhodes occupied the vacancy and the score was raised to 116. Lilley hit Trumble up to square-leg, where Hill effected a

---

* Neville Cardus, *Autobiography*. Collins, London, 1947.

splendid catch. Nine for 116. Tate was last man in, as he came out a shower fell. The Englishmen wanted still 8 runs to win. Tate did what scoring remained, and he obtained a quartette, but was then bowled by Saunders and the innings, amidst an indescribable scene, closed for 120. The Australians thus won by 3 runs.

Writing in 1903 in the *Sydney Morning Herald*, one of the touring party described the finish of this justly famous Test:

> I remember the red-letter day at Manchester when Australia won by three runs. The Australians ran off the field with delight, and as they bolted up the steps of the members' pavilion those noble-hearted, grievously disappointed Englishmen—who an hour before had reckoned England "must" win—thumped the backs of our fellows, and cried out, though their hopes had been rudely flung down and trampled on, "Well played, Australians; well played." We got upstairs to the dressing room, and leaped and yelled to get the surplus froth off our wild joy. It was more than we could contain.

Seemingly not content with his record-breaking performance at Old Trafford, Trumper in the next fixture against Essex at Leyton established yet another record, one that could also never be broken.

Essex batted first and were all out for a handsome 345, the Australians while fielding wore black crepe on the left arm in respect for Bill Howell's mother who had died in the Penrith district a few days earlier. Howell who understandably was very upset, did not participate in the match. His father also was to pass away shortly after the game's conclusion.

With thunderstorms threatening, Trumper and Duff opened before lunch on the second day. Duff was soon caught by Russell from Young's left arm deliveries for 10. Trumper's display was chronicled by the reporter for *Sporting Life*:

> Apart from one man, the Australians gave a most disappointing display of batting, nobody approaching Trumper in a remote degree in brilliancy of execution and mastery over the attack. This famous batsman played an innings of 109—his seventh of three figures for this tour—which in grace and style could hardly be equalled. It was noticeable that he made fewer runs than usual by his famous method of pulling—relying chiefly upon powerful and well-kept-down drives and clean, hard cuts—and hardly once did he mis-time a ball until beaten by a beautiful break-back from Mead. It is very doubtful if the Australians have ever sent over a batsman with such fertility of resources in scoring off so many good balls. Even Massie, with all

his wonderful powers, had not such extraordinary aptitude in making runs by all sorts of strokes—and good ones, too—as this young cricketer from New South Wales. He certainly made the batting of his colleagues look very poor stuff yesterday, and but for his brilliant innings the Australians would have been in a bad way indeed.

Australia were all out for 232 and the home team in their second attempt declared at 3 for 184 just after lunch on the third day. Australia, needing 298 runs for victory, made a valiant attempt to reach the Essex total, but at stumps had registered 253 runs for the loss of six wickets and the contest was drawn.

Victor Trumper in his second innings was out leg before wicket to Reeves for an immaculate 119. This second century in the match earned him the unprecedented feat of becoming the first Australian to score two separate hundreds in a first-class match in England. Trumper also became the second Australian to register two centuries in a first-class match anywhere, this having first been achieved by C. J. Eady in Tasmania during the 1894–5 season.

The *Sportsman*, although noting that the second hundred took longer than the first, was nevertheless impressed with the manner in which it was compiled:

> On Tuesday Trumper rattled up 109 in an hour and thirty-five minutes, and yesterday he was not disposed of till he had subscribed 119 out of 237 for five wickets. His runs were not made at the same pace as on the previous day, seeing that they occupied two hours and thirty-five minutes in putting together, but his contribution was again faultless and a treat to witness, by reason of its grace, ease, and brilliance. He started, however, unusually slowly, and occupied nearly 40 minutes in reaching double figures. He was dismissed leg-before. His great and faultless innings of 119 included seventeen 4s (one a grand drive between the pavilion and stand), two 3s, and seven 2s.

During the Essex match Trumper was approached with the offer of a substantial job at the end of the tour and the chance to play County cricket during the following English summer. This news filtered back to Australia causing some consternation. Copies of the *Sportsman* shipped to Sydney added fuel to the flames of controversy:

> The *Daily Mail* has somewhat prematurely published the news that Victor Trumper may qualify for an English county. The intelligence

is, of course, not novel to a good many of us who are keenly interested in cricket, but until something was definitely arranged it did not seem politic to allude to this most important matter. An anonymous correspondent of the *Liverpool Post* towards the end of May mentioned that an Australian, who was efficient in all departments, might qualify for Lancashire. This was generally assumed to be Warwick Armstrong, but, as a matter of fact, the writer must have heard some premature whisper about Trumper. I have not the least idea which the other county may be to which allusion is made, but there is good reason for believing that the great Australian cricketer will in 1904 appear for Surrey. Of course there may yet be a lapse in negotiations, but if he does appear for any English county it is quite probable that Trumper may emulate the example of Sewell, Llewellyn, and Trott, and play as a professional. He will earn the honest admiration and enthusiastic support of everyone if he does so. I am expressing the opinion of more than one prominent amateur when I say it is believed he is too good a sportsman to be ashamed of owning he is earning a living as a cricketer, and to that honourable calling he will give new lustre. To add here any panegyric on his ability would be superfluous, but it may be mentioned that he is personally a real good fellow, full of generous enthusiasm, keenness, and a healthy manliness which wins for him hosts of friends.

Joe Darling immediately countered the Surrey offer with a position in his Adelaide sporting goods shop coupled with the chance to play for South Australia, but Victor remained unmoved by any of these overtures, his strong ties in Sydney being of primary importance. Alderman Allan Taylor, the ex-Mayor of Annandale agreed to assist him in obtaining a position of importance in Sydney, however on his return he continued working in the Probate Office. Victor said, "I took his word as a gentleman."*

English critics wrote in glowing terms of Trumper's dual centuries at Leyton. The *Sydney Morning Herald* reported how Home Gordon epitomised this praise:

Virgil and Dante invoked the Muse to help their pens, and some such assistance is needed to do justice to the magnificent batting of Victor Trumper. It seemed to some of us on Monday that the Australians after the test match were, excusably, taking matters a little easy. But the subsequent days showed no relaxation in the fascinating

---

* *Town and Country Journal*, 10 December 1902.

punishing powers of Trumper. Essex were a thorn in the flesh of the colonials in 1899, and if their present attack is not of the star type, it is certainly calculated to inspire respect. But apparently all attack is powerless to trouble Trumper, for, as the balls kept fairly below bail-height, he proceeded to make happy havoc of them and succeeded in piling up two centuries as flattering in the quality of their brilliant freedom as they are useful to his average. To convey in phrases the ease with which he played in both innings is impossible, and so admiration can only be expressed in compliments, sincere and deserved.

"The Cornstalk" of the *Athletic News* composed the following:

VICTOR TRUMPER—AN ACROSTIC

Victor be in name and deed, pride of Austral seas,
In a blaze of glory such as few recall.
Clinking strokes that blind us, dazzle and remind us,
Trumper, Victor Trumper is the peer of all;
Onward still where'er he be, England or Australia,
Reeling out his hundreds while the crowds acclaim.

Timing, driving, glancing, hooking that's entrancing,
Rushing up the pathway to the Hall of Fame;
Under all this triumph what do we discern—
Modesty, refreshing as a desert rain,
Pride, well-curbed and glowing,
Earnest and straight-going,
Round his brow the victor's wreath will long remain.

At the same time as Trumper was procuring his two record-breaking innings at Leyton, Nellie Melba was making a farewell appearance to a wildly enthusiastic audience at Covent Garden in Verdi's opera *Rigoletto* before her return to Australia. Meanwhile Major Wardill, the Australian team manager, was being inundated with congratulatory letters and cards from Australians living in England applauding the Test Match victory at Manchester and praising Trumper's batting in the Test and against Essex. Cables arriving from Australia were in much the same vein.

During a team meeting the Australian cricketers decided to abandon the originally proposed tour of America and decided instead to await the reply of an offer sent to South Africa for a stop-over during the return to Australia, during which it was hoped to play a series of Test Matches.

Ten days after the Essex match Victor Trumper and the rest

of the touring party witnessed the glittering and opulent Coronation procession from a special vantage point provided for them overlooking the immense crowds which lined the route between Buckingham Palace and Westminster Abbey. The Hampshire match, in which the South African professional C. B. Llewellyn took part and which Australia won by an innings and 79 runs, occurred immediately before the Coronation, and was rescheduled to two days so that the visitors could travel back to London to join in the celebrations. King Edward VII's gift to the Empire was the stately Osborne Manor, on the Isle of Wight, which had been originally bought by Queen Victoria and Prince Albert. One minor incident marred what was almost a perfect day in London. After the royal procession had passed through Parliament Street, a horse pulling a private carriage took fright and charged into some Indian soldiers. Two officers and some privates were taken to Westminster Hospital for treatment.

In Australia the Coronation was celebrated amidst much rejoicing and thanksgiving. The main event in Hobart was the conferring of the Victoria Cross on Lieutenant Bisdee by the Governor, and in the evening the local fire brigade organised a torchlight procession and pyrotechnic display as bonfires blazed in the surrounding hills.

Ships in the harbour at Fremantle and on the Swan River near Perth were gaily festooned and school children participated in sports carnivals and picnics and were driven through Perth in the trams free of charge. Brisbane and Melbourne not to be outdone, held numerous thanksgiving church services on the Sunday after the Coronation, and riverside picnics and dinners were commonplace on the grand day.

At Pittwater, north of Sydney, each child was presented with a commemorative medal and several large bonfires were lit. That night a flotilla of boats adorned with bunting and lanterns formed a charming picture on the water. In Sydney, portraits of King Edward VII and Queen Alexandra were displayed in numerous windows, and a gymnastic exhibition, a game of association football and Punch and Judy shows entertained over three thousand school children at Kensington. Afterwards the massed school choirs sang "Sons of the Sea", "Rule Britannia" and "God Save the King."

The final Test at The Oval was to see England win in a thrilling finish by one wicket. This was due largely to some wonderful

Armstrong, Kelly and Trumper, with a Scottish lass, 1902 Tour.

hitting by Gilbert Jessop, who made the only century in the game, his contribution being 104 made in just 75 minutes. Trumper, who opened in all his Test Match innings in 1902, scored 42 at The Oval before George Hirst bowled him. His second stay at the wicket was brief as he was run out for 2, but his wonderful batting during the Third and Fourth Tests had secured Australia's grip on The Ashes and added yet another chapter to his shining history. The highly respected *Wisden's Cricketers' Almanack* in 1903 proclaimed him the most illustrious of the five outstanding cricketers for the 1902 season:

In the course of the tour he obtained, despite the wet weather, 2570 runs, thus easily beating Darling's 1941 in the glorious summer of 1899, which up to this year was a record aggregate for any Colonial batsman touring in the country. Pages might be written about Trumper's batting without exhausting the subject. Having regard to the character of the season, with its many wet days and soft wickets, it is safe to say that no one—not even Ranjitsinhji—has been at once so brilliant and so consistent since W. G. Grace was at his best.

Trumper seemed independent of varying conditions, being able to play just as dazzling a game after a night's rain as when the wickets were hard and true. All bowling came alike to him and on many occasions, notably in the Test Matches at Sheffield and Manchester and the first of the two games with the MCC at Lord's, he reduced our best bowlers for the time being to the level of the village green. They were simply incapable of checking his extraordinary hitting. Only a combination of wonderful eye and supreme confidence could have rendered such pulling as his at all possible. The way in which he took good length balls off the middle stump and sent them round to the boundary had to be seen to be believed. Though this exceptional faculty, however, was one of the main sources of his strength on soft wickets, he was far indeed from being dependent on unorthodox strokes. His cutting and off-driving approached perfection and he did everything with such an easy grace of style that his batting was always a delight to the eye. Risking so much, he plays what I should call a young man's game, lightning quickness of eye and hand being essential to his success, and for this reason I should not expect him after twenty years or more of first-class cricket to rival such batsmen as Shrewsbury, A. P. Lucas and W. L. Murdoch, but for the moment he is unapproachable.

He was not in the smallest degree spoilt by his triumphs, bearing himself just as modestly and playing the game as sternly at the end of a long tour as at its beginning. Incidentally I may express my extreme satisfaction that the efforts to secure him for an English county failed. It would have been a paltry and unworthy thing to deprive Australia, by means of a money bribe, of her finest batsman.

Trumper's ninth century for the 1902 Australian Eleven blossomed forth at Cheltenham during the return match with Gloucestershire in the middle of August. Showery weather made the pitch soft and the visitors batted first, but little cricket took place that day because of the rain. On a wicket that became a glue pot he gave a dashing display on the second day as he raced to his hundred after just over ninety minutes batting. He was appropriately caught by Champain from Jessop's bowling for 125 runs which was posted on the scoreboard in exactly two hours and which included 16 scorching boundaries. Not even Jessop could master the sticky wicket and the tourists won easily by an innings and 10 runs. Such was Trumper's absolute mastery with the bat that Warwick Armstrong's 56 not out was the only other score which remotely approached the innings of the Paddington genius.

Following scores of 69 against both Kent and Middlesex Trumper's next hundred was at Harrogate in the Players Eleven encounter on 2 September. At stumps on the first day the Players were all out for 184 on the muddy pitch and Australia were 59 without loss, with Trumper on 41 and Duff 15. The conditions presented no terrors for Trumper as he carved 8 fours and added insult to injury with a towering straight drive for six out of the ground. *The Times* reporter wrote:

> The Australians had barely half an hour's batting. Mr Trumper hit brilliantly; he obtained a six and eight fours, the six and five of the fours being off Llewellyn's bowling. Thus, of Trumper's score of 41 not out, 38 of his runs scored before stumps were boundary strokes.

His final score of 127 was easily the highest in the game, Joe Darling being next best with 67. A feature of Trumper's innings was his last 25 runs being made in only two consecutive overs, three fours being dispatched in the over in which he was stumped. He only batted an hour and three quarters for his 127 and hit 4 sixes and 19 fours. Australia won the Harrogate contest by an innings and 47 runs.

The opponents in the next fixture at Scarborough were C. I. Thornton's Eleven, featuring players of the calibre of Rhodes, Foster, Tyldesley, Jackson and Hirst. This struggle was drawn as Trumper made 62 in less than an hour and hit 10 fours. In his second innings he added 55 runs and executed 8 fours. He was out leg before wicket in both innings and of his 117 runs, 72 came from boundaries. Yet again Trumper top-scored for his country.

His final century of the 1902 Tour took place in the very next match with the South of England, played at Hastings. This game was the third last of the tour and Trumper would have been forgiven for taking things easy, as he had already produced ten innings exceeding one hundred, each a masterpiece in its own right. Prior to the South of England fixture his aggregate stood at 2322 runs, a total which was well clear of any other player. At Hastings Trumper had his off-bail dislodged by a ball from Gill when he was 16 in the first innings, but in his second stay he made some splendid strokes from Hayward, Braund and Vine, one, a mighty pull stroke onto the road beside the ground for six. He was a trout among the minnows on the rain-affected pitch scoring 120 in barely two hours as he dispatched 17 fours and the one six. Once again he registered the highest score in this match, which was ultimately drawn.

The Players team which confronted the Australians at The Oval in the final match of the 1902 Tour of England was virtually a Test side, with included Hirst, Rhodes, Braund, Tyldesley, Hayward and Lilley. Even this game was not spared the cold and wintry conditions which plagued England during that bleak summer, as rain fell spasmodically and the wicket was soft. Royalty was not sacrosanct for even King Edward VII and the Prince of Wales, on a grouse drive in Scotland, were inconvenienced by sleet and snow which fell all day. However there was a good bag.

Trumper too had a good bag at The Oval where he registered 96. *The Times*, described play with the score at 1 for 70:

> The Players bowling had been very good. Haigh twice beat Mr Hill, and Rhodes once got through Mr Trumper's defence. But the hitting after the delay (caused by rain) was wonderful. Hirst and Hayward were severely punished; but Braund ought to have got Mr Trumper out at 74, when Iremonger missed a chance at fine short leg low down. After this Rhodes from the pavilion end caught and bowled Mr Trumper.

To gauge some idea of the esteem in which he was held in England it is pertinent to mention the Cricketers' Benefit Fund Auction sponsored by the *Daily Express* at which one of Dr Grace's bats was sold for £50. One of Ranjitsinhji's went for 13 guineas, Jessop's for £8, and Victor Trumper's bat realised £42.

Despite the dual problem with sickness and weather the Australians had staged a remarkable tour. Not only did they retain The Ashes by two Tests to one, but of the 39 matches contested, they won 23, drew 14 and lost only two. Trumper's contribution was an unprecedented total of 2570 runs (Clem Hill was next with 1614)—an average of 48.49—and 11 centuries and 11 half-centuries. Shrewsbury headed the season's averages but he made only 1250 runs at an average of 50 runs per innings.

Trumper attempts a cut from Lockwood. The Fifth Test Match at The Oval, 1902.

Bobby Abel scored the most runs by an Englishman—2299 at an average of 41.05.

Pelham Warner stated: "During the summer of 1902 Trumper scarcely knew what it was to fail. The state of the wicket made no difference to him—runs flowed from his bat: but of all the wonderful innings he played on that tour, those against the MCC at Lord's and the Players at The Oval will ever remain in my recollection. He just did what he liked with the best bowlers of the day. One straight drive literally 'went through' Braund in the Players match and hit the far screen first bounce with a lovely thud. All bowling came alike to him. The way he hooked good-length balls was amazing and his driving and late cutting were brilliant in the extreme. Exceptionally quick on his feet he did everything with perfect ease."[*]

Years later Hugh Trumble was asked which Australian team he considered was the best ever sent to England. Without hesitation he named the 1902 side as being by far the most superior because they always batted with thirteen men. Asked to clarify this, he explained, "As W. G. Grace was, in his prime, as good as three batsmen for the Mother Country, so was Victor Trumper easily worth three for Australia!"

---

[*] P. F. Warner, *The Book of Cricket*. Sports Handbooks, London, 1911.

In South Africa, 1902

An enthusiastic group of spectators farewelled the Australians at Waterloo Station in London as they boarded the Southampton train which was to convey the party to their waiting mail steamer, the *Dunvegan Castle*, bound for South Africa. As the train pulled out from the station the strains of "Auld Lang Syne" filled the air and spasmodic cheering was heard.

The schedule for the South African visit was to prove exhausting. After seventeen days at sea, Victor Trumper and his companions reached Cape Town on 7 October, and the *Dunvegan Castle* on entering the port crashed into the breakwater at the entrance to the harbour. Shaken, but uninjured, the party clambered into the sleeping carriages on the train in preparation for the long journey of two nights and three days to Johannesburg, the main mining centre of the Transvaal goldfields.

After only a day's rest, during which they attended a reception, the Australians faced an All South African eleven in the First Test Match on the ground leased by the Wanderers Club for their domestic engagements. The impressive complex consisted of four cricket fields, several tennis courts and a fine pavilion on the main ground. The Durban journalist E. W. Ballantine described the playing surface:

> The ground is a bare tract of land, dark red in colour, and in the centre of the Oval a green patch of coconut matting, 8 ft wide is stretched and nailed down, each end about 6 in from the popping crease and outside it. The surface of the ground is hard, and consequently there is a tendency for the bowling to rise considerably. The fielding is generally true, notwithstanding the presence of a few small pebbles that would occasionally give the ball a little bit of hop. On a hot day the ground is naturally trying to the feet, while the dust, which is always more or less prevalent, has the effect of parching the players' throats and causing too much of what would be on another occasion a useful thirst.

The home side chosen for the First Test was formidable, including in its ranks the Hampshire professional C. B. Llewellyn, now an employee in the Wanderers Club office, who had bowled so well against the tourists in England. Also in the team were A. W. Nourse and J. H. Sinclair, two of South Africa's all time great cricketers.

The fine weather brought out a fair crowd as South Africa won the toss and batted. At lunch the score was 179 for the loss of only one wicket. The crowd had by this stage swelled to 6000 and it was Trumper who removed Tancred for 97, to break the second wicket partnership of 172 runs. Trumper then bowled Llewellyn for 90, but the home side again rallied and at stumps were seven for 428.

Australia, set a total of 454, were dismissed for 296; Llewellyn claiming 6 wickets for 92. Trumper opened with 63 and was Llewellyn's first victim, with Reg Duff 82 not out. The middle order batsmen succumbed in the rarified atmosphere 6000 feet above sea level. Asked to follow on, the visitors made 372 for the loss of 7 wickets declared (Clem Hill 142, Victor Trumper 37) leaving South Africa 215 runs for victory. At stumps on the third and final day they were 4 for 101 and the game was drawn.

Moving to Pretoria, the capital of Transvaal, Victor Trumper and his companions engaged a Transvaal fifteen on 15 October, on a field and pitch similar to that at Johannesburg but possessing a grassed outfield.

The Australians' train was late in arriving in Pretoria and the match was over 35 minutes late starting. Transvaal won the toss and at the end of the day's play were 7 for 423. Saunders left the field after lunch, ill with influenza. Heat affected the visitors in the field and the highlight of the day was Sinclair's century which he reached with a massive drive over the press tent for six. On the second day Transvaal added only 39 runs for the loss of 7 wickets.

As agreed, the hosts fielded eleven men when the Australians went to the wickets. Duff and Trumper opened and the latter player began with a single to leg. After ten minutes the openers had put on 30 runs. Duff was bowled by Taberer for 36 with the score 1 for 78. Hill joined Trumper, who drove Niemeyer to the press stand for 4. Soon Hill was bowled off his pads for 3. Trumper then brought up his side's century after only 45 minutes. Armstrong was soon out for 6 and lunch was taken with Trumper 45 not out.

After the break Noble accompanied Trumper, and the score rose steadily as Trumper twice drove Niemeyer for two 2s and then to the onside for 4. He then punished Shepstone by driving

101

him for 4, sweeping the ball for 2, on-driving twice for 4 and finished the over with an off-drive for another 4; 18 being added in the one over. Noble was soon bowled off his pads for 9 while Trumper was on 86 and the score 4 for 169.

The Australian captain then left the pavilion to join Trumper who enthusiastically glanced Thornton for 2, drove him for another 2 and then again to the on boundary. The light soon became very poor and Trumper reached his century, made in 90 minutes, by driving Niemeyer for 2. Soon afterwards it rained heavily and the players ran from the field with the score at 4 for 204. After 45 minutes play resumed but the light was still poor. Trumper hit Thornton for a slashing on-drive to the fence for 4 and lifted a delivery from the same bowler clean out of the ground over the tea rooms as the crowd roared. He then drove Sinclair to the on and off boundaries but soon Darling fell to Taberer for 34. Hopkins was now in and Trumper was dropped at long on. Hopkins was bowled by Sinclair and Trumper brought up his side's 300 by playing Sinclair to leg for 3. Approaching his own second century he drove Cooper to the onside for 3 then drove Niemeyer for two successive sixes out of the ground—an off-drive and an on-drive—and finished off the over with a 2. He raised his 200 with a hard cut past point for 4. A small terrier then fielded a shot to leg by Trumper from Sinclair. During the final wicket partnership with Saunders, Trumper added 40 whilst his partner made no score. Saunders finally made a single and was bowled. The Transvaal fixture was drawn after Australia finished with 392 of which Trumper scored 218 not out, and Hugh Trumble, who only played in the first two tour matches, left South Africa early on the *Australasia*.

The Australians now travelled back to Johannesburg for the Second Test Match and *The Times* reported:

> The second match between the Australians and a team representing All South Africa was begun today in magnificent weather. There was a moderate attendance. The wicket was excellent. The Australians won the toss, and Trumper and Hill opened the innings and began knocking up runs rapidly, but Trumper's wicket fell when he had made 18.

Australia could muster only 175 runs, Llewellyn being the chief destroyer. South Africa replied with 240, Sinclair reaching 101 before being bowled by Howell. His century, made in 120 minutes, included 6 sixes. Victor Trumper had the best bowling figures for Australia in the South African first innings:

O.	M.	R.	W.
12	1	60	3

At stumps on the second day Australia were 5 for 201 and on the final day were dismissed for 309, Warwick Armstrong reaching 159 not out. The home side then collapsed for only 85 under the combined onslaught of Saunders (7 for 34) and Howell (3 for 23) and Australia won by 159 runs.

That evening Victor Trumper and the Australian side were guests at a dinner and the next morning the tourists left by train for Durban, the beautiful seaport of Natal to face the local Fifteen.

The game began in windy and dull weather with a sizeable attendance. E. W. Ballantine described the venue for this match:

> Durban possesses a veritable paradise of a ground. There a 9 ft natural coconut mat was used, and stretched on a pitch of grit. The outfield is of grass on a sandy soil, and the pleasure of fielding on such a ground was freely remarked upon by the visiting players. The Durban oval is a portion of the borough park, and as there is only a two-railed fence round it the public have no difficulty in obtaining admission into the ground free.

Trumper contributed a brisk 52 to his side's score of 268, and at stumps the home team were 27 for the loss of one batsman. Although Natal were to obtain 205 runs, Bill Howell took 11 wickets for 79 runs. Australia batting next declared with six wickets down for 203, and with Natal in deep trouble, losing six batsmen for only 69 runs, heavy rain washed out the match.

Against Western Province the tourists won easily by 282 runs. They made 172 (Trumper a breezy 49) and 274, while the home side could manage only 84 and 80. Bill Howell took 17 wickets altogether for 54 runs.

The final Test Match at Cape Town took place at the spectacular Newlands ground beneath the backdrop of Table Mountain. Reuters described the Australian first innings:

> The visitors won the toss and had first use of an excellent wicket. Trumper and Duff made a splendid start, and, despite the excellent bowling and fielding of the home team, sent up the 100 before being separated. Duff, who was the first to go, played steadily, while Trumper hit in brilliant style. At lunch the score was 115 for one

103

wicket. When the game was resumed there was an attendance of 5000. The Australians did not maintain the advantage they had gained, Trumper was quickly disposed of. His 70 was made without a chance.

The Australians made 252, and South Africa at only 85 were asked by Joe Darling to follow on, this time doing better with 225. With only 59 needed for success, Trumper and Duff reached the required figure with the Paddington genius making 38 not out at the close of the Test. Bill Howell took 9 wickets for 99 runs.

After the customary celebrations the much travelled cricketers prepared to sail for Australia on the *Sophocles*. The tour, besides being a historical first by an Australian team, was a resounding success, not only from the matches won, but as an exercise in diplomacy so soon after the Boer War.

Wisden expressed the following opinion of the value of the trip:

> Following their brilliantly successful tour in England, the Australian team went home by way of the Cape and played six matches in South Africa. Their visit aroused great interest and they were received with enthusiasm by South African players. They did themselves ample credit, winning three matches and leaving the other three unfinished.

Summing up with his impressions, E. W. Ballantine wrote:

> That the visit to South Africa will do much to foster the game there is no disputing. The fielding of the team has been such as to show what the possibilities are of reducing this important part of the game to a fine art, and it is one easier of copying than the examples given in batting, bowling, and wicket-keeping.

The Durban journalist kept his most laudatory comments for just one Australian: "The batting of Victor Trumper has been very much admired, and by his natural demeanour and unassuming attitude he has found many friends in South Africa. His batting has been described as 'poetry and a picture book'."

Golden Days

The dawn hours of Thursday 4 December 1902 saw the *Sophocles* berth in Melbourne. At mid-day the Melbourne Cricket Club welcomed some of the Australian Eleven at Scott's Hotel. Trumper andKelly had earlier left the ship to visit Kelly's relatives before the invitation arrived. One reporter on sighting the cricketers wrote, "The members of the team are all looking tolerably well, but most of them after their hard season's work in England look thin."

Trumper accompanied his Paddington team-mate, Jim Kelly to renew his acquaintance with his friend's parents-in-law, William and Anne Briggs at their home in Oxley Street, Glenferrie. Here Victor met their daughter and his bride-to-be, Sarah Ann Briggs, a tall, blue-eyed, auburn-haired beauty.

Victor Trumper soon sailed for Sydney on the *Sophocles* to be reunited with his own family. On Wednesday 10 December the southern members of the victorious Australian team arrived in Sydney by train to participate in the exhibition match against the New South Wales Thirteen. As the train pulled in to Redfern Station they received a fitting welcome and then left for the Sydney Town Hall to attend a reception. To an overflowing audience the Lord Mayor proposed the first toast and then made a lengthy speech. Here is part of that speech as reported in the *Sydney Morning Herald*:

> "We have with us to-day the members of the best Australian team of cricketers (cheers) ... We all know that they have won as many matches as any other Australian Eleven (cheers) and have lost fewer. (Prolonged cheers.) They have accomplished records in almost every possible department of the game. (Cheers.) Victor Trumper (cheers) will have a celebration in a few days on a very much larger scale. (Cheers.) I understand that the Town Hall will be taxed to its utmost capacity by those who desire to be present to honour him. (Prolonged cheering.) He has achieved records in the highest batting average, the highest individual score,* the greatest

---

* The Lord Mayor should have said "highest aggregate" as M. A. Noble had the highest individual score with 284 versus Sussex.

number of centuries, and the honour of making two centuries in one match." (Loud cheers.)

Joe Darling and Hugh Trumble replied to the various welcoming addresses by the dignitaries present, and were followed by Victor Trumper: "It is very good of you to give us such a welcome, although in one respect it is hardly necessary, as we are only too glad to be back. I think Mr Trumble and myself are very lucky to have been so highly appreciated, but there were others in the team, particuarly new members, who did all that could be expected of them."

Monty Noble while proposing the toast to the NSW Association said, "The members of the team are very proud of the reception given us. Those who were not on the spot could not possibly appreciate the services of Messrs Trumper and Trumble in an adequate degree."

On the second Friday after arriving back in Australia, 12 December 1902, the Eleventh Australian Eleven, possibly the greatest Test combination of all time, began their final match together. New South Wales batting first were all out at six o'clock for 227 on a wicket which began in a soft condition but soon dried out under azure skies and a relentless Sydney sun. When the New South Wales Thirteen were 7 down for 137 Trumper was called into the attack by Joe Darling. The *Sydney Morning Herald* described the action:

> Trumper was called on in place of Noble, and met with an ovation. The challenge had the desired result as Cuffe was almost immediately caught by Trumble off Trumper at short-slip . . . Loveridge, the NSW captain, was dismissed, caught and bowled by Trumper, before he had scored. This was Trumper's second wicket for 1, and he might have had a third at the same cost. Howard who came next, just touched one, and it travelled very adjacent to Trumble.

Trumper went on to take the bowling figures for the Australian Eleven:

O.	M.	R.	W.
12	3	18	3

Noble, Jones, Saunders, Armstrong and Hopkins took the remaining wickets between them. This example serves to demonstrate yet again that Trumper in his prime could bowl with enormous enthusiasm and on his day was at least equal to the best bowlers in Australia.

106

That evening every available space inside the Sydney Town Hall was crammed for the "Public Reception and Presentation" given by the Crown Street School Old Boys' Union in Victor Trumper's honour. When he ascended the stairs leading to the stage the immense audience applauded with deafening approval for several minutes and then gave out three tremendous cheers. Those present on the platform with Trumper were the Lord Mayor of Sydney, Alderman Thomas Hughes, Senator J. C. Neild, the Hon. J. Darling, MLC from South Australia (Joe Darling's father), and Charles Bannerman, Victor's boyhood coach. The members of the Australian Eleven and the New South Wales Thirteen sat with the guest of honour.

The interior of the Sydney Town Hall was bedecked with Australian flags, banners and streamers and signs that welcomed the hero of the evening. All the men wore formal dress and a quartet sang one of Victor's favourites, "Home Sweet Home." Then the Lord Mayor addressed the assembly with the following: "The citizens of Sydney recognize that Mr Trumper is the most brilliant sportsman that we have ever turned out. We hope to have him with us for many years to come!"

Musical items, which constituted most of the evening's entertainment, began with the "Grand Triumphal Chorus" by Capocci played by the City Organist Arthur Mason, himself an Old Boy. Other items included "The Holy City" sung by Monsignor Pauwels and "They Kissed" by The Meistersingers. The climax of the evening was the presentation of a fine collection of sterling silver plate to Victor by D. Levy, MLA, the Vice-President of the Crown Street School Old Boys' Union. When Victor rose to reply he was drowned out by the exuberant cheering and only those close to the stage could hear his, "Thank you to all those who have credited me with the honour of upholding Australian cricket."

The next morning Trumper, before 11,000 cricket fans, batted at third drop for the Australian Eleven and the scene was described by the *Sydney Morning Herald*'s man on the spot:

> Duff on resuming after lunch was accompanied to the wicket by Trumper. The latter met with a magnificent reception. The crowd cheered and cheered again, and the Naval Brigade band struck up "See, the Conquering Hero Comes," and then there was more cheering. Cuffe should have secured his second wicket without cost, for Duff snicked one to the left of Hickson at short-slip. The two

batsmen then warmed Cuffe, 20 coming from two overs. Thirty-one were added to the total in 13 minutes, but at 133 Trumper softly returned one to Howard, and retired with a dozen to his credit.

Trumper opened with Duff in the Eleven's second innings and batted superbly for 78, the highest score for the match. One of his hits was a soaring off-drive from Marsh's bowling onto the lawn in front of the Smokers' Stand for 5. Today this would have landed onto the area in front of the Sheridan Stand, the Smokers' Stand being dismantled in 1909. Trumper's dismissal was described in the *Herald* report:

> Trumper made a terrific straight drive off McBeth's second ball, and the bowler made a magnificent catch. There were very few on the ground who knew where the ball was until it was seen in McBeth's hand. Trumper was in for 1 hour 27 minutes for 78, and hit one five and nine fours. His batting was brilliant in the extreme, and it is impossible to say more.

On the Monday night following the Crown Street presentation the New South Wales Cricket Association held a welcome for the Australian team members and a presentation for Trumper at the Australia Hotel. George Houston Reid, the Association President and a future Prime Minister, chaired the meeting of over 200 cricketers and dignitaries. Next to him sat the venerable Harry Hilliard, a member of the first New South Wales team to play intercolonial cricket against Victoria in Melbourne during late March 1856. Born in Sydney in 1826, Hilliard was a member of the Currency Club and as a youth he sometimes practised cricket in an old graveyard situated in George Street near where St Andrew's Cathedral now stands. The boys rearranged the tombstones to make more room for their game and at the sight of an approaching policeman would all dash behind the church, sometimes leaving a bat on the ground in their haste to avoid detection. Afterwards one of the boys retrieved the implement from the local police station and experienced the practised long arm of the law.

G. H. Reid, who usually sported a monocle, said, "Old men like myself and Mr Hilliard can look back upon a long past of cricket, but the record of the present Australian Eleven is the most brilliant. When one reflects upon our comparatively small population and opportunities, and contrasts them with the teeming millions and enormous wealth of the mother country, I am inclined to feel astonished that the Australian representatives have been able to go to the mother country and put up such an unparalleled record of success. I think the members of the team will take it ill if I do not refer to the success of Mr Trumper and Mr Trumble. Mr Trumble was vice-captain of the team, and we all know there is no stauncher man. He came off both with bat and ball, but conspicuously with the ball. Then there is Mr Trumper, who, so far as I can gather from the best authorities, has marked himself as the most brilliant and successful batsman, not only of Australia, but of the world!"*

Joe Darling responded for the Australian Eleven and then G. H. Reid presented Victor Trumper with a cheque for 100 guineas. This had been collected while the cricketers were sailing home, under the direction of P. K. Bowden, the Association secretary, who had issued collection boxes for public donations throughout Sydney.

Victor also received from the future Prime Minister of Australia a handsome illuminated address made by John Sands, at the bottom of which were the signatures of the executive members of the Association. The full address reads as follows:

We, as representing the State of New South Wales, desire to extend to you upon the occasion of your return to your native land a very cordial welcome. From the scenes of your recent signal triumphs you have come back crowned with the laurel of the cricket field. With honest and deepest pride and gratification we have closely followed step by step the long series of your remarkable achievements, whereby you have rendered memorable the tour of the Eleventh Australian Eleven. Such magnificent performances have not only established and emphasised your own brilliance, but have served materially to enhance the prestige of your associates, and to shed upon the entire community in whose midst you have been born and bred much additional lustre. Whilst thus offering to you our heartfelt admiration of the consummate skill and rare capacity you have evinced in the arena of contest, we take this opportunity to express our appreciation of your manful bearing, genial personality, and all those many qualities of heart and mind which have ever endeared you to all with whom you have been brought into contact. We ask your acceptance of this address and gift as a slight token of our high esteem, and as some recognition of the gallant stand made by you as our representative. It is our earnest desire and constant

---

* *Sydney Morning Herald*, 16 December 1902.

hope that the distinguished status you have gained will be maintained for many years to come. With every good wish for your future welfare.

Victor responded briefly in a voice tinged with emotion, "I am deeply grateful for this presentation."

The following poem written by "Oriel" of the Melbourne-based *Argus* soon after the Tour of England and South Africa gives the reader a real feeling for the excitement and exuberance Trumper's cricket generated in those golden days when the world was yet untainted by the carnage of global warfare.

VICTOR TRUMPER

Some talk of Alexander,
  And some of Hercules
Of Hector and Lysander,
  And such great names as these;
Yea, all those heroes breezy
  Will live beyond all time,
Because their names were easy
  To jingle in a rhyme.

But there is one Australian
  Whose praise few poets sing
Because his name is alien
  To almost everything.
Unjust it is I know it,
  But he must yield his claim—
The most perspiring poet
  Can hardly rhyme his name.

Long life to Victor Trumper
  That record breaker fine;
I drink it in a bumper
  Of clear Australian wine.
And verses would come thronging
  Ev'n as I drink it down,
If only (foolish longing)
  His name was Jones or Brown.

Long life to Victor Trumper!
  That brave, hard-hitting soul,
That pounder, smasher, thumper
  Of all that Rhodes can bowl
Ground, press-box, and pavilion
  Have seen what he can do;

His worshippers are million,
  Although his rhymes are few.

Ask no more rhymes for Trumper;
  There is no English name,
From King to counter-jumper,
  That knows a wider fame.
And in my verse I'd gather
  His records till the morn,
If only Victor's father
  Some other name had borne.

Because of his commitments in South Africa Trumper batted only five times for Paddington that season, his aggregate being 374 and his average 74.80. In four spells of bowling he took a total of 7 wickets for 183 runs, his best figures being in the match against Sydney at Hampden Park on 14 February 1903, won by Sydney on the first innings by 127 runs:

O.	M.	R.	W.
20.1	7	55	4

His batting exhibition that season against Redfern on Redfern Oval is still discussed in Sydney over eighty years after the event. His score of 335 was a record for senior cricket in Sydney and at that time had not even been exceeded in interstate matches, W. L. Murdoch having made 321 against Victoria in 1881–82.

The scoresheet for the match on 31 January 1903 shows that in desperation Redfern used ten bowlers that afternoon for a total of 80 six-ball overs. Six of Trumper's towering fives were lost or souvenired. The most famous hit, a lofted on-drive, cleared the fence by more than 50 feet (17 metres), sailed over the traffic in Chalmers Street, and smashed a window on the second floor of John Hunter's Boot Factory 150 yards away from where Trumper was batting and where the South Sydney Leagues Club now stands to-day. One "fiver" was sent soaring out of the southern end of the ground to the second-floor balcony of a terrace house, and another bounded across Elizabeth Street threatening to enter the bar of the Australian XI Hotel. These incredible shots were clearly described by the world-famous barracker, "Yabba" in the *Truth* of 3 January 1937. With all the fieldsmen on the fence, underarm lob bowling was used in a vain attempt to curtail the onslaught of bat on ball. Trumper's reply was to hit two successive deliveries bouncing among the date palms in the park next to the ground towards Redfern Street. Local shop owners, who had by this stage, boarded the front windows of their establishments joined the thousands who roared their approval at each stroke. The participants on the bowling green adjacent to Redfern Oval prudently ceased their play to obviate being maimed and watched Trumper from a safer vantage point. The drive that gave the great batsman his 300 was another "fiver" that hurtled over a fence well away from the ground and into a carrying yard. In *The Referee* Jack Davis reported to an astonished Sydney:

> Within the past twelve months Victor Trumper has established all sorts of batting records in first-class cricket. They have come one tumbling over another until his brilliant and wonderful faculty for run-getting has passed into a byword and he is proclaimed on all sides the greatest batsman of the world. The public who sees him hitting the ball in all directions, or fielding with speed and accuracy surpassed by no Australian of the day, does not suspect that he is in need of a long rest from cricket. Nevertheless, it is a fact. He has developed into a staunchly built athlete, and were it not so he could never have stood the physical strain he has undergone in the course of twelve months, for Trumper at the wickets compares with the average cricketer as a racehorse might compare with a cab-horse on the race track. He would have dearly liked to put by his bat for this season after the Victoria match on Thursday, but a few more runs are to come from it before it goes into winter quarters.
>
> Between nine and ten thousand people put in an apperarance at the Redfern Oval to see the Paddington v. Redfern match. It is the largest attendance ever seen on the ground, and the attraction was largely—"Trumper". As a rule the caretaker of the ground has some little work to keep the small boy from climbing over the picket fence and depositing himself in the grass in the shade of the crowd, but in this instance he had nothing to do, for the small boy was unable to root his way through the spectators, deep and densely packed round the ground. The trees in the park were peopled and the streets blocked with tradesmen's carts, whose drivers waited to see the hero of the hour operating . . .
>
> He hit 22 fives and 39 fours. The fieldsmen and bowlers were bewildered; the spectators, well one might almost say were spellbound. Redfern cricketers in other seasons were so impressed with Trumper's prowess that they referred to him as a "bally marvel." Now they class him as a freak. The Redfern Oval is a small ground, but Trumper did not rest content with merely hitting them out of the ground, for he sent them into the adjoining streets, which by the

way, presented a peculiar appearance, with vehicles of all sorts lined up, and drivers standing upright on them to catch a glance of the play. No fewer than 266 were the result of boundary hits, so that V.T. was saved a lot of running any ordinary first-class batsman would have to undergo in putting such score together.

His cricket even astonished those who had often seen him score at a scorching pace against bowlers of high repute. His HITTING was extraordinary, and when he did not hit the ball out of the ground, he placed it where he willed. This may afford some idea of the sort of cricket played by Trumper, the Wizard of the Willow.

Trumper and Gee who opened for Paddington put on 423, a record for the first wicket in Sydney Grade cricket. Trumper's 335 took him only 180 minutes, giving him a run rate of more than 110 runs to the hour, an unbelievable figure considering that every time he hit a five he lost the strike. On the very same day on the Sydney Cricket Ground Jack Marsh took 6 wickets for 19 for Sydney versus Burwood, including the hat trick.

On the following Saturday Redfern capitulated for 53 (M. A. Noble 7 for 27, V. T. Trumper 1 for 25, both bowled unchanged) and 122. Thus Paddington won by an innings and 443 having declared at 618 for 9 wickets. Trumper and Noble did not bowl in the Redfern second innings although Trumper took three catches in the match.

During the Sheffield Shield clash with South Australia in early January 1903, Trumper and Duff broke the record for the first wicket by Australian batsmen in a first-class match, the new total being 298 runs. Trumper's contribution of 178 which took only 133 minutes, included 29 fours. Having caned six of the visiting bowlers to the far reaches of the field, the Wizard of the Willow faced Clem Hill:

Hill, who had worked all sorts of changes in his bowling at length went on himself, and had 14 hit off his first over. One stroke from Trumper caused quite a sensation. He drove it hard back with terrific weight. Hill had just time to duck and the ball struck the fence with great force. The batting was the fireworks of cricket, and it was carried on to the accompaniment of thunder and lightning, for heavy clouds had gathered and slight rain was falling. (*Sydney Morning Herald*, 12 January 1903.)

New South Wales went on to win by 10 wickets.

In the next Shield match against Victoria in Sydney Trumper and Duff were at it again, this time registering a first-wicket partnership of 267, of which Trumper was responsible for 130 runs in 137 minutes. His boundary strokes totalled 72 and the home State won by five wickets.

Thus Trumper in two consecutive innings for New South Wales hit 47 boundaries and made 308 runs in barely 270 minutes. A remarkable feat of aggressive and attacking batsmanship against the cream of world bowlers including Jones, Armstrong, Saunders and Laver. It was only two days after the Victorian encounter that Victor blasted his 335 runs on the Redfern Oval. Johnny Moyes, who was to later play for South Australia against the Sydney genius wrote: "Sometimes he would pivot on the right foot, and flick the ball off the crease line past the square-leg umpire. Such batsmen are inhuman, and when in full cry the only thing to do is to wait for them to make the inevitable mistake. They make a lot of runs before the long wait is over."*

Pelham Warner who led Lord Hawke's Eleven in their contest with the Sheffield Shield champions in late March 1903 wrote, when comparing the opening pair: "Trumper is, to my mind, the superior. Indeed I have never seen a better batsman than Trumper. But comparisons are proverbially odious, and both Trumper and Duff are magnificent; one need say no more."†

Against the touring Englishmen the finest batsman that the England captain had ever seen scored 16 and 37. Yet despite the seemingly moderate scores the display of cricket was memorable. Indeed this was the case whenever Trumper batted, each innings, even his most modest total, a cameo masterpiece. Here's how the *Sydney Morning Herald* man on the spot reported the play during Trumper's second innings:

> Trumper was the first to reach double figures, the runs coming along mostly by the aid of neat taps for two and three to leg. A series of brilliant fielding incidents brought forth applause. At 21, Trott replaced Burnup. Duff now moved along briskly; off one over from Dowson he advanced by 10. Then Trott was punished to the tune of nine, and the last three overs produced 27. The hitting was hard, the fieldsmen found it difficult to stop the ball cleanly, and the batsmen caused some amusement by the way in which they stole runs. Hargreave came on in place of Dowson, whose hand was injured in

---

* A. G. Moyes, *Australian Batsmen*. Angus and Robertson, Sydney, 1954.
† P. F. Warner, *Cricket Across the Seas*. Longmans, London, 1903.

trying to stop a hard straight drive by Trumper. The half-century appeared after 25 minutes' batting.

Victor Trumper had a high opinion of Pelham Warner both as a man and a cricketer and said, "When he walks in to bat every blade of grass bows to him."* Warner's description of the above innings, written in 1903, was vivid:

Trumper and Duff began the New South Wales second innings, and in thirty-five minutes actually made 72 runs. Trumper jumped right away at the start, and had scored 21 of the first 28, but Duff soon caught him up, and at 48 each had made 24. Every kind of imaginable stroke was brought into play, and the power with which they hit the ball was astonishing.

Our bowlers seemed helpless, and it really looked as if the two batsmen would be in at the drawing of stumps. But the goddess who presides over cricket loves to bring down the most skilful players, and after 72 runs had been made off twelve overs, Bosanquet went on with his slows, and with his first delivery clean bowled Trumper with a ball which the great Australian batsman thought was breaking from leg, but which came back, and to which he played forward.

The cricket during this first wicket partnership was magnificent, the very acme of perfect batting.†

---

* *The Game's the Thing.*
† *Cricket Across the Seas.*

The 1903–04 England Tour of Australia

In six months' time Pelham Warner returned to Australian shores with a formidable MCC combination which included all-round cricketers of the calibre of Rhodes, Hirst, Braund, Arnold and Bosanquet and batsmen such as Foster, Hayward, Tyldesley and the England captain himself.

Because of his international and Sheffield Shield commitments Trumper took part in only four matches for Paddington that season, his scores being 13, 54, 134 and 114, and he took 7 wickets for his club at the cost of 156 runs.

In the Sheffield Shield clashes Trumper's consistency (his average was 62) enabled his State to win the coveted trophy for the third year in succession, with his scores of 43, 68, 53 and 53 not out versus Victoria and 26, 61 and 6 not out against South Australia. In the first meeting with Victoria, Trumper in the second innings was batting with his usual dash when he was stumped by Elliott Monfries off Harry Trott for 68. Monfries, who like Dick Lilley of England, had many opportunities of observing Trumper's genius from his vantage point behind the stumps, wrote:

> Trumper's batsmanship was in keeping with his beautiful character. Of medium height, lithe and willowy, he was the poetry of motion, as with indescribable grace and ease he made his strokes to every part of the field. It was useless to set a special field to him, as he had not a weak spot anywhere, and young bowlers coming into the Victorian side, before facing up to this very wonderful batsman, were told to take no notice of what he did with their fancy balls but to "just plug away and trust to God he'll make a mistake."
>
> Most of his forward run-getting shots were made with a rhythmic golf-like swing that started and finished high over his head. When first he batted in front of me and made one of these strokes I remember thinking "By Jove, if you do that again and the ball 'does anything' you'll get yourself out." But when the ball did do anything it seemed to make no difference whatever, as it found itself plumb in the centre of the bat and sailing out into the field.*

---

* Elliott Monfries, *Not Test Cricket*. Gillingham, Adelaide, 1950.

116

Having drawn with South Australia and disposed of Victoria by an innings and 71 runs, Warner's tourists arrived in Sydney. During their first meeting with the Sheffield Shield champions they handed their hosts a lesson in cricket, winning by an innings and 10 runs. Not even Trumper's wizardry could save his side, he top-scored with 46 but only managed 11 in his second innings. Warner had won the toss and sent his hosts in to bat on a monstrous wicket soaked by Thursday night rain then transformed into a glue-pot by the baking sun. England replied to the 108 set them by scoring 319 (Tyldesley 80, Hirst 66). The pitch had by this stage dried out and New South Wales could score only 201. The Englishmen won five out of their six matches with the three major cricketing States by substantial margins exhibiting exceptional skill and teamwork.

The stage was now set for the First Test Match and all Sydney simmered with expectation and excitement. On the Thursday morning before the big game members of both sides sharpened their skills at the Sydney Cricket Ground practice nets and rested in the afternoon. Two coats of light green paint were applied to the surface of the cycle track to minimise glare and the Government Astronomer forecast, "Warm to hot, strong, squally and dusty north-east winds." The proprietors of Wolfe's Schnapps announced that any Australian batsman scoring 50 runs in either innings of the Test would receive a gold sovereign plus sixpence for each run in excess of the half-century. Five additional gold sovereigns would be given for a century innings, and for each catch taken in the field one sovereign would be awarded.

Those students of the game who noted that each nation had won the opening Test alternately since 1888, Australia being triumphant in 1901, predicted an England victory.

Monty Noble won the toss and Warner led his men onto the field before a Friday crowd of 17,000. The opening overs were sensational. At 12.05 Hirst bowled to Duff and as the first ball in the Test Match was short of a length it was cut to Relf fielding near the cycle track. Trumper was soon off the mark with a similar stroke from the fourth ball of the same over. Arnold started his first over from the southern end into a north-easterly breeze. His first delivery lifted sharply from a good length and Trumper went after it attempting the cut. The ball flew from the upper edge of the blade of his bat and Foster at second slip dived to his left completing a superlative catch at about knee height. He ricked his side and was incapacitated for several minutes. Soon Australia were reeling at 3 wickets down for 12 runs, but a recovery occurred and at the close of play the total was a sound 259 runs for the loss of 6 wickets. Monty Noble carried his bat for 281 minutes through to stumps making 132 invaluable runs.

Just on 36,000 spectators were present on the Saturday to see the remaining Australian wickets fall quickly with the final total 285 (M. A. Noble 133). After a brittle start the English batsmen put their heads down and when stumps were drawn they were 4 for 243, Foster 73 and Braund 67 being the not out batsmen.

Monday, the third day of this Test, was to be Reginald Foster's day of glory. At stumps England were all out for 577, the highest innings by that country in Tests against Australia up till that time. Foster played a marathon innings for 287 runs in 419 minutes hitting 38 boundaries. He was aided and abetted by Len Braund who scored 102. Foster's innings broke numerous records, including the highest individual Test innings previously held by Australia's Bill Murdoch with 211 at The Oval in 1884, and the highest total ever by a cricketer making his debut in the international Test arena. This last record was previously held by Charles Bannerman with 165 not out in Melbourne in 1877 and Foster's 287 still remains in 1984 the highest score by a cricketer making his debut in a Test Match. At stumps on the third day Australia managed 17 runs without loss, Kelly and Gregory being the night watchmen.

The Tuesday saw a strong fighting stand by Reg Duff who made 84 and Gregory who hit 43. With Australia 101 runs behind England's 577 Trumper came out to join Hill just after lunch with the scoreboard reading 3 wickets down for 191. A. E. Knight who was the twelfth man for England was watching from the pavilion. Writing two years later he recalled:

A slender figure, wan and drawn of face, cadaverous, but spiritualised with the delicacy of ill health, glides to the wicket. Nor ornament nor colour marked his featureless attire, the personality was all-dominating. He took guard quickly, more quickly took a glance around the field, and received his first ball. "Dreams of summer dawn in night of rain" presented no fresher vision than this boy's play to that black sea which hid the blistered grass of the Sydney hill. Not in his fascinating collection of strokes, nor in their frank and open execution merely, lay the charm; it was a man

118

playing away a power which was himself rather than in him. With luxuriant masterfulness, yet with the unlaboured easy naturalness of a falling tear, or rather of showers from the sunny lips of summer, he diverted the ball in every conceivable direction which his genius willed. Not violently nor recklessly, like his comrade Duff the revolutionary slashing with his pike, not with the care-worn, anxious deliberation of Noble, does he reach the heights, but insensibly and unconsciously, lifts us with him to where winds blow cool and the outlook is infinite. Can the force of consolidated mass, a record of two hundred centuries, convey the power of high elevation? Perhaps so, at least we glorify the former more. Aglow with instinctive inspiration, this young prophet played with the world's greatest bowlers, played as men play when "time and the hour" bring out the man and persuade us he is as the gods.

With bat whipping like a flail, he drove the fastest swervers of Hirst, and jumped in with fearless precision to the tempting slows of Rhodes, hooked the dropping "googlies" of Bosanquet and alternatively late cut or pushed to square leg the pace-making deliveries of Arnold. One by one his colleagues fail and pass before an attack of magnificent precision and persistence. "Our Vic" remains, and when a partner's lazy incompetence rendered his last effort to secure the bowling futile, with his colleague's loss, he left the field still undefeated. He had given to his country at least an outside chance of victory, and the glow of a hope once seemingly impossible. Nothing akin to jugglery or contemptuous langour mars the incomparable grace and simplicity of this perfect batsman. His greatness is of that high kind which appeals to the technical no less than to the more human critic. His simplicity has no faintest simplesse, he convinces the onlooker and the bowler that the stroke he executes is precisely what should be done. There is no subtlety, no show miracle, but the perfect openness and the direct simplicity of a master.*

Trumper, despite his apparent illness and the wild demonstration by the chanting crowd after umpire Crockett adjudged Clem Hill run out, remained calm and resolute throughout his long innings. Time and again he cut the ball through the slips and square of the wicket to the fence just wide of the fieldsmen. When Warner moved a man round to obviate a particular stroke Trumper merely redirected the ball to where the man had been fielding. During the over in which Hill was run out, Trumper three times in succession cut Braund through the slips to the

---

* A. E. Knight, *The Complete Cricketer*. Methuen, London, 1906.

pickets from balls that were pitched on or outside his leg stump. The Englishman finally asked his captain to remove him from the firing line, "I can't bowl to a man who continually back-cuts me for four from six inches outside his leg stump!"

Trumper's century was the signal for wild applause, not only on the Sydney Cricket Ground but also at the corner of Hunter and O'Connell Streets, where a large body of onlookers, in excess of 8000, had gathered to watch the progress of their hero's innings as his runs were monitored on the large *Sydney Morning Herald* scoreboard:

> When Trumper reached his century the great surging crowd roared its approval, drowning the rumble of the lorries and cumbersome vans that now and again rolled along to upset the dignity of some of the cheering enthusiasts. Long after stumps were drawn several thousand people remained to analyse the results of the day's play. (*Sydney Morning Herald*, 16 December 1903.)

In Melbourne and the other capital cities throughout the nation the different phases of play were watched with keen interest by crowds outside the newspaper offices as the cables were posted on the notice boards.

The overnight batsmen, Trumper 119 and Armstrong 14, resumed on the Wednesday morning to the bowling of Rhodes and Bosanquet. Trumper reached 133 in exactly half the time that Noble and Foster took to make the same score. He soon raced on to 153 by driving George Hirst crisply to the Shilling Stand. "Plum" Warner exclaimed, "What an innings he played! Such style, such ease, such dash, such power! Against a magnificent and varied attack he put the ball where he liked, and I remember Hirst saying to me: 'It's not much use trying to place the field when that lad's going.' He played as one inspired, and no wonder the thousands who thronged that lovely ground went wild with delight."[*]

Trumper was left undefeated with 185 runs crafted in only 230 minutes, an unbelievable run rate by today's Test standards. However England were to win by five wickets on the sixth day. During his sublime display Victor despatched 25 balls to the boundary and such was the majesty of his batting that A. A. Lilley commented in his autobiography:

---

[*] *The Book of Cricket.*

I have seen Mr. Trumper play many fine innings, but I consider this particular one of 185 not out not merely his own masterpiece, but the finest I have ever seen played from my position behind the wicket. The English bowlers were all in splendid form, and the fielding was keen and brilliant; but against such a powerful combination as Hirst, Rhodes, B. J. T. Bosanquet, Braund, and Arnold he never gave the slightest chance. From the first ball he received till the close he played with perfect confidence and ease, and never gave one the remotest suggestion that he would ever get out. His foot-work was perfection; it enabled him to make his shots on the off with delightful ease—indeed, those forcing shots on the off-side, so perfectly timed and so hard hit, were one of the features of an innings distinguished by a magnificent variety of strokes.

During my long service behind the wickets I have necessarily had many opportunities of witnessing good performances, both by English and Australian batsmen, but in my opinion they have all been eclipsed by this display of Trumper's, and had he remained to double his score, I should never have tired of watching him.*

The bowling of Wilfred Rhodes in this Test provided a wonderful foil to Trumper's batting; on a pitch which was not sympathetic to a slow, orthodox left arm bowler his statistics read remarkably well:

	O.	M.	R.	W.
1st Innings	17.2	3	41	2
2nd Innings	40.2	10	94	5

Every ball a model of length and change of pace and flight, and Trumper during his historic innings quipped to Rhodes, "Just for once, won't you give me some peace, Wilfred?" The answer delivered in a broad Yorkshire brogue was brief and negative.

The total attendance in Sydney was 95,000, a record for Tests in Australia up till that time. Perhaps the final word on this historic international should come from the victorious captain: "Had Hirst been caught from a difficult catch to short-leg before he had scored, the Australians might well have won. But they deserved almost as much credit as the victors, for I cannot recollect another instance of a side which, going in 292 runs in arrears, eventually sets its opponents nearly 200 runs to win. It was a monument of grit and courage, and a glorious tradition for future generations."†

---

* *Twenty-four Years of Cricket.*
† *The Book of Cricket.*

A. H. Garnsey, of Sydney was moved to write the following verse:

VICTOR TRUMPER

He handles his bat like a whip does he,
As if 'twere a rod such as anciently
    Was wielded by Roman Lictor.   .
He cuts and he pulls 'em for fours and for fives,
He glances and hooks, he pushes and drives,
    And piles up the centuries—Victor!

He runs like a hare, he is brilliant at slip,
Or long-off for a change and his throw comes clip,
    Right into the grip of the stumper;
Has the safest hands for all species of catch,
Can bowl a good ball—oh, where is the match
    Of the trump of Australia—Trumper!

The pluck of a hero, a veteran's head,
And modest withal, though his fame it has spread
    To the limits of Empire. A bumper!
We'll call it and take the goodwill for the deed
(He drinks not, nor smokes, let us follow his lead),
    Here's health to you, Vic—Victor Trumper.

The next international in Melbourne not only reminded all concerned about the inclement vagaries of that fine city's summer weather but also the effect such conditions created on the Merri Creek soil on the Melbourne Cricket Ground pitch.

The previous match in Melbourne, the Sheffield Shield encounter between Victoria and New South Wales, was played on Bulli soil. One journalist noted with accuracy: "There appears to be some doubt as to whether the English grass which is grown here will flourish in the cement-like soil from Bulli. There was only one wicket prepared of that soil, so the contest tomorrow will be decided on the usual soil used here. This is to be regretted, for the reason that, should there be a change in the weather, the Bulli soil is never so bad as other Australian soils, and, further, it recovers more quickly." (*Sydney Morning Herald*, 1 January 1904.)

Warner won the toss on the opening day of the Second Test and electing to bat first on a good wicket was well satisfied with his side's total of 221 for the loss of two wickets when stumps were drawn. England were to bat over three days because frequent rain developed during the second day keeping play to two hours. At the tea break a heavy shower soaked the field and with drizzle still falling the umpires after two inspections of the wicket decided to call a halt with the tourists 7 down for 306.

On a very sticky wicket on the Monday the remainder of the England tail were soon all out and Australia went in chasing 315. Tyldesley had made a grand 97. The Australian opening batsmen started sensationally before 8000 spectators. Hirst and Rhodes began the bowling attack, the former from the pavilion end. In Rhodes's first over Trumper cut the ball over the head of slip for a single. Later in the over the ball flew vertically from the bat's edge and Lilley slipping and sliding managed to get both hands underneath it only to see it spill from his gloves to the sodden turf. Had he held the chance, arguably the greatest fighting innings ever made on a wet wicket would never have been documented.

Trumper and Duff took the score to 14 with some smart backing-up when Duff was stumped by Lilley from a Rhodes leg-break. By this stage the ball was rearing to head height from a good length—the Merri Creek soil was playing true to form. Hill was next to fall, caught by Rhodes from Hirst for 5, and Gregory joined Trumper who reached double figures after 35 minutes. Gregory soon succumbed to Rhodes's guile and Hopkins came to bat. Trumper then crashed an off-drive into the fence from Rhodes and from Hirst's next over slammed another boundary. Australia's 50 was reached after 62 minutes with Trumper on 25.

It now became obvious to the excited crowd that Trumper's aim was to avert the follow-on as quickly as possible and enable the Australian bowlers to confront their opposition on the sticky pitch. They settled down to enjoy the ensuing fireworks. Relf came on to bowl and Trumper greeted his second ball with a classic drive through the covers to the fence.

Hopkins was next to go, caught at square leg for a valuable 18 runs. Trumble's stay was brief, falling to Rhodes when on 2. Armstrong and Trumper then added half a dozen, five of which were made by the Sydney man. The Victorian was then caught by Braund from Rhodes, who now had 5 wickets for 33 runs. Kelly joined his club-mate and the *Argus* recorded the action:

Trumper's unique resource in changing his intention and then getting runs was illustrated against Braund. He first went out to him, then stepped back, and with a late cut got 3, making his score an even 50. Immediately afterwards he gave a hot chance to Hayward out near the fence. It was a hard low drive, and the fieldsman, getting a bit too far under tried to take it with one hand as it swerved away from him. Again Trumper dashed out to Braund, and the ball flew over the fence on the bounce, and scattered the crowd on the pavilion seats.

Australia's 100 was reached in 93 minutes, batting time. Kelly was soon out and Australia were 8 for 105 with 11 runs still required to save the follow-on. Howell came in as Trumper continued to hit out, lifting Rhodes high over the sightscreen for five. With the crowd roaring he hit Braund for two straight drives bringing the total to 116, thus forcing England to bat again. The noise from the crowd was now deafening as Trumper walked down the pitch to speak to Howell to advise him to hit out at everything and get England in to bat on the monstrous surface. After some lucky hits Howell was caught at mid-on and Saunders, the last man in to bat, helped add six more runs before Trumper was finally caught on the fence by Tyldesley from Rhodes with the final score at 122. Of this he had contributed 74 on a pitch described by Warner as a "real beast." He opened the innings and was last man out and the next highest score was Hopkins's 18.

The *Argus* stated:

Rarely has admiration for a fine performance been so finely expressed as when Trumper came out. He had batted an hour and 52 minutes on a very difficult wicket, where some of the finest batsmen in Australia looked but mere beginners. He hit one five and five fours, and the points of merit in his play were his quickness of eye and foot, his fine timing, and remarkable aptitude in scoring from the second intention. It has often happened in the past that Trumper has not been seen to great advantage on a Melbourne wicket, but we were able to get some idea now as to what his batting meant to the Australians when wickets were difficult on the last English tour.

Trumper's supreme genius on sticky pitches was due to the combination of his experience on difficult turf during his two previous English tours and his use of a specially prepared practice strip in the Sydney Cricket Ground nets. During regular practice sessions Victor sharpened his skills on a water-soaked pitch and, with the sun turning the surface into putty, he braved fast and slow bowler alike without flinching. This conditioning enabled him to become the most extraordinary and successful batsman on rain-affected wickets that the world has ever known.

England were to fare even worse and at the close of play were 5 for 74. Next day early morning rain turned the turf into a quagmire and the umpires would not allow the Test Match to resume until 3.25 p.m. The tourists were soon all out for 103 on the atrocious surface, Foster did not bat having retired with a high temperature and a chill during his team's first innings. Tyldesley once again top-scored for England before Trumble caught him high over his head in the slips for 62.

The Australians chasing 297 runs for victory opened with Trumper and Duff and the former almost immediately lifted Rhodes over the fence for a perfectly timed five. In fifty minutes he reached 35 and with his team's total at 2 for 73 he hit Rhodes high and deep to long-off where Relf took a splendid catch. Newspaper placards throughout the country proclaimed: "Trumper Dismissed—Hope Abandoned." One Melbourne reporter wrote:

> Trumper was 52 minutes getting 35. He hit one fiver and four fourers. The crowd had some hopes that Trumper would remain until the next day, by which time the wicket would have had a chance of recovering its usual pace and accuracy. Now he was gone all hope had also departed.

Indeed the last seven Australian wickets fell for the addition of only 38 more runs and England won by 185 runs dramatically improving its prospects of winning back The Ashes. Wilfred Rhodes's 15 wickets for 124 runs still remains today one of the greatest achievements by a bowler during a Test Match.

"Old Boy" wrote an interesting profile on Trumper in the *Argus*:

> Standing slightly under 6 ft and of slender build, one wonders at the power which is behind Trumper's strokes. The clean-shaven young man—"The Kid" the other members of the team call him—who chats quietly on the game with never a reference to himself, has abilities such as few other batsmen have ever approached, and none have excelled. He is quick as a cat on his feet, full of resource, able to think quickly, and what is best, think and act in one, and so the ball he has jumped out to drive is by a complete change of design cut down through the slips at such a pace that fieldsman and bowler are alike astounded. No batsman I have ever seen more completely dominates a game when he gets going as does Victor Trumper. The

gentle, winsome young man who a moment ago sat quietly talking in the pavilion is now at the wickets hitting Rhodes and Hirst and Braund all over the field, while his partner at the other end appears to be "scratching" to keep the ball out of his wicket.

The Melbourne pitch was to strike again when England next played Victoria soon after the Third Test in Adelaide. The home State began respectably by making 299 to England's 248. Torrential rain reduced the pitch to a bog as Victoria batted again and in just 45 minutes Rhodes and Arnold had accomplished the unthinkable, sending the opposition packing for 15 runs of which Harry Trott made nine. Rhodes took 5 for 6 from six overs and one ball and Arnold 4 wickets for 8 from six overs, as the tourists won by 8 wickets.

In Adelaide Warner's men fielded first in the opening day of the Third Test when Monty Noble won the toss. Before a Friday crowd of 10,000 under glorious sunny skies, Trumper and Duff faced Fielder bowling from the river end and Arnold with the Cathedral behind him. Duff was severe on Fielder hooking him twice in the very first over of play and Trumper delicately late-cut Arnold to the fence in his first over with the new ball. The running between the wickets was sharp and clever, four being run from a Trumper leg glance. After half an hour 44 runs were posted on the scoreboard, Trumper was 15 and Duff 28. Rhodes replaced Fielder and was promptly hooked by Duff to the boundary. Trumper took fifty minutes to reach 20, but then drove and pulled Arnold to the fence on the on-boundary from two consecutive deliveries.

Bosanquet came on to bowl and puzzled both batsmen and the wicketkeeper with an occasional wrong 'un. Nevertheless Duff soon reached 63 and Australia's 100 appeared after only sixty-eight minutes. Trumper was scoring freely from the other end with a cover drive and square cut just before the century was reached, both shots rebounding sharply from the pickets. Hirst joined in the attack and with his last delivery before lunch he bowled Duff for 79. The opening partnership had put on 129 runs in 88 minutes, an exhibition which makes modern-day Test partnerships pale into insignificance.

Immediately on resuming, Trumper square-cut and leg-glanced Hirst to the cycle track, bringing up his half-century in ninety-one minutes. Clem Hill supported his colleague with sound backing-up between the wickets and contributed to the total with some cracking hook shots from Braund's leg-breaks. Trumper soon had the Adelaide crowd in raptures with his glancing and cutting, it was cricket for the connoisseur! The Australian 200 was hoisted in a mere 133 minutes amid noisy appreciation. The crowd soon had cause for more celebration, as one reporter explained:

> The people were prepared to cheer Trumper for his hundred, and when at length Rhodes let a simple ball get past him, and the three figures appeared, there was a splendid round of cheering. He was occupied 2 hr 46 m in getting the runs, and had not given a chance, nor had he made a mis-hit. The strokes from both men were delightfully crisp.

Trumper increased his total with some firm singles and a drive past square leg for four. With his next stroke he was fortunate not to be run out:

> He played the ball hard to the left side of Rhodes, and started for a run. The Yorkshireman, however, fielded it brilliantly, and returned to the wicket. Hill did not respond to Trumper's call, and the latter turned. Lilley, who was standing back, rushed to the wicket, but failed to take the ball cleanly, and Trumper got home. It, however, made little difference. Hirst was brought on for an over before tea, and his fourth ball was played on. Trumper was in 3 hours 9 minutes for 113.
>
> Trumper's cricket was somewhat different from what the Sydney public are used to witnessing. Instead of the brilliant fireworks, it was solid, though he was not by any means slow. It was not a time for strokes which contained risk, and he, recognising that fact, played the correct game. His batting was attractive all the time, and he was unfortunate to have been dismissed by playing a ball on to his wicket. (*Sydney Morning Herald*, 16 January 1904.)

Australia went on to a first innings score of 388 and England replied with 245, Trumble and Hopkins taking three wickets apiece. On the Monday, just before lunch, Trumper and Duff began the Australian second innings before 7000 spectators. The weather was dull and oppressive and among those watching were the Governor-General of Australia, Lord Tennyson, the Governor-General designate, Lord Northcote and the State Governor of South Australia, Sir George Le Hunte.

Duff hit the first ball of the innings from Hirst to the leg boundary and with the total at 8 an appeal against Trumper was turned down as he snicked the ball onto his pad. The very next ball he dispatched to the square-leg fence and then he cut Arnold off his wicket away past point to the boundary. Bosanquet relieved Hirst, and Trumper immediately produced an off-drive sending the ball slamming into the pavilion fence. Lunch was then taken with the total at 29, Trumper 21 and Duff 8.

After lunch Duff was caught in the slips for 14 with the score at 48. Trumper went about gathering runs and produced some immaculate square drives and late cuts until Rhodes brought his innings to a close with a ball which straightened up striking the pads. His 59 included seven fours and only took an hour and a quarter. Australia eventually grossed 351 (Syd Gregory 112), setting England 495 runs on a perfect batting strip and with no time limit as all the Tests were played to a conclusion. They could muster only 278 and Australia won by 216 runs.

With the result of the first three Test Matches at two to England and one to Australia, interest in the next international in Sydney was high throughout the country.

Trumper before this Test was engaged in the Sheffield Shield encounter with Victoria in Sydney at the end of January. He made 53 in his side's first innings and, set 119 to win, he and Reg Duff scorched a 50-run partnership in 27 minutes. Virtually all Trumper's runs came from on-drives and pulls to the fence. At the end of the match the two openers had reached 119 without loss taking only 55 minutes to do so as the "Mother State" cruised to an easy win by ten wickets to retain the Sheffield Shield.

Elliott Monfries recalled this match in his book, *Not Test Cricket*:

> What an exhibition by both batsmen of supremacy of batting over bowling; and it was no slogging display. Only one ball beat the bat during their stay at the wickets. Trumper was the batsman, and Laver had brought Jim Giller on to bowl.
>
> Old hands will recollect Jim's short run to the wickets and how very simple his bowling looked. Well, Jim's first ball, as usual, was of perfect length, and for once Vic played forward defensively. The ball at the end of the flight seemed to drop suddenly and swung away sufficiently to beat the bat and nearly took Vic's off stump.
>
> "Um," said Vic to me. "This man takes watching."
>
> "Yes," I thought, "and all the others take walloping." Anyhow, they all got the walloping and Jim had to take his share although he was the only one to be shown some mercy, if I remember aright.

Large falls of rain in Sydney during the week leading up to the Fourth Test ensured that on the Wednesday the pitch was completely under water. The next day the Bulli soil had dried out considerably and a large tarpaulin supported by trestles was placed above the pitch to protect it from further rain and allow the wind to pass underneath.

Pelham Warner won a vital toss and England amassed a solid 249. Australia batted on the pitch made increasingly difficult by scudding showers, and could total only 131 (Duff 47, Trumper 7). England increased their advantage, and batting with maturity on the treacherous surface made 210. Australia then capitulated for 171 runs. Even Trumper could not vanquish Bosanquet who captured six wickets for 51 runs. After eight years of frustrated endeavour England had finally won back The Ashes.·

Although the last Test was somewhat an anticlimax it was watched with keen interest in Melbourne and followed closely throughout the nation. This time Noble won the toss and Australia made 247 (Braund 8 for 81). Trumper batted in cavalier fashion for his 88 runs made in just 110 minutes before a crowd of 20,000 appreciative spectators which included the Governor-General, Lord Tennyson; Melbourne being the seat of Australian government until the siting of Canberra many years later. Trumper made half of his runs in boundaries and one reporter wrote that he "played crisp, dashing cricket". Trumper's 88 was easily the highest score as England succumbed on a sticky wicket for 61 and 101 losing by 218 runs. Hugh Trumble in this his last Test for Australia, bowled superbly taking 7 for 28 and performing the hat trick (B. J. T. Bosanquet, P. F. Warner and A. A. Lilley), the only cricketer to do so twice in Tests at this time.

Warner's men returned home triumphant and on the voyage he began writing his classic account of the tour, *How We Recovered The Ashes*. Back in England Bernard Bosanquet was asked what single factor had contributed most to victory in the series: "I am inclined to think that it was the greater variety we possessed in bowling that carried the day. There was little to choose between the teams as far as batting was concerned. Trumper was far the best bat in either side."* Indeed Trumper's

---

* P. C. Standing, *Anglo-Australian Cricket 1862–1926*. Faber & Gwyer, London, 1926.

record in the series was most impressive. He made 574 runs in ten innings for an average of 63.78, the highest average and aggregate by a batsman from either team. He top-scored for Australia in four of the five Tests. He bowled 12 overs conceding only 23 runs but took no wickets.

However, it wasn't just his batting figures that were so impressive as the extreme genius with which they were made that contributed to his wonderful legend. A. E. Knight, who played for England in three of the Tests wrote:

Trumper does not seem to have to watch the ball from the pitch, and then flick it away by wrist and body turn, as does Ranjitsinhji. He divines what the ball will do and where it will be while it is still in the air, and can consequently put the whole force and swing of his body into his strokes. Such a one is scarcely to be written about, however, with a recipe book in hand, or a bundle of statistics at one's elbow. The really highest manifestations of an art so emotional as well as technical as batting, have little relation to time or to quantity. Perchance the statistical expert will yet have many pages to fill with the first-class records of Victor Trumper. Probably not, for such eye and wrist, such lightning celerity, such risk, is for youth alone. Perchance the cold winds of ill-health have already swept across the stream on whose surface lies the glory and the gleam. Howsoever transient his career, none who have been privileged to see him play a great innings will ever forget that spirit, so self-forgetful, so manly, and so true.†

---

† *The Complete Cricketer.*

The 1905 Tour of England

In early June 1904 John Corbett Davis reported to his readers in *The Referee* that "Victor Trumper is still enjoying a spell of rural life on Mr McEvoy's station near Gundagai. He is, I am informed, looking in the pink of health." Victor terminated his stay in the Southern Tablelands and headed to Melbourne to be wed to Sarah Ann (Annie) Briggs, the sister-in-law of the Paddington and Australian wicket-keeper, Jim Kelly. The wedding took place on 7 June in St Patrick's Cathedral. Sarah Ann was the daughter of Anne Guinan and William Alexander Briggs, a retired engine driver, an occupation held in high regard in Trumper's day. Sarah Ann lived with her parents at Oxley Street in Glenferrie, in suburban Melbourne. While courting Annie, Victor had stayed with friends in Burwood Road, Glenferrie.

The best man was Hubert Cooney and the bridesmaid Alice Maloney. On the marriage certificate Victor's profession was recorded as a clerk (he was earning just over £2 per week as a clerk in the Probate and Intestate Estates Office in Macquarie Street in Sydney). Annie's status was recorded as a "lady". As Victor was an Anglican, dispensation had to be first granted before the marriage was solemnized by Father Joseph Murphy.

The wedding was small and extremely private, no reporters and no crowds; not one of the major newspapers even hinting that the nation's most illustrious cricketer was about to be wed. Even the customary marriage announcement was missing from the Melbourne and Sydney newspapers which normally carried such information. After the honeymoon, the couple, both twenty-six years old, returned to live with Victor's parents and his two brothers and four sisters at 112 Paddington Street in Paddington. It was to be a fruitful and harmonious marriage despite the obvious religious differences, both partners being totally devoted to each other.

During the same month in 1904 as the Trumper wedding Monty Noble began his new profession as a dentist in Sydney, and two months later records show that Victor Trumper and

Sarah Ann Trumper (1877–1963).

Hanson Carter opened for business at their "Cricketing and Sports Depot" at 108 Market Street, now occupied by the imposing Centrepoint Tower building. In 1906 they moved their shop to 124 Market Street, where David Jones is now situated, and they remained in business together until 1909 when Carter left to work in his father's business as an undertaker in Waverley.

The New South Wales Cricket Association opened the new 1904–05 season on 1 October 1904. This was described by the *Sydney Morning Herald*:

> A welcome change from the mid-week cold weather gave cricketers and their supporters a perfect day for the opening of the season. Some of the grounds were well attended, notably Waverley Park, where Paddington met Waverley. People will always follow Paddington because they expect Trumper to play a characteristic innings. On Saturday they were completely gratified, for going in first he monopolised one end until the close of the innings, when he was not out 189, which were got in two and a quarter hours.

During his afternoon's sport Trumper pounded fifteen balls over the Waverley Park fence and sent another twenty-two deliveries rattling into the pickets, thus hitting 37 boundary strokes in just over two hours batting. He and Jim Kelly added 219 runs for the fourth wicket partnership in only seventy minutes, an incredible feast of run-getting. His innings analysis makes fascinating reading and it should be noted that from his last eight scoring shots he lofted the ball five times out of the playing area and at one stage of the display thirteen of his fourteen scoring shots either crashed into or over the fence. J. C. Davis wrote: "Victor Trumper opened the season with one of those bewildering, brilliant displays, which make him stand alone among batsmen of the world. Of the three thousand people that went to Waverley on Saturday to see Paddington and the local club meeting, probably 80 per cent were attracted solely by Trumper. He did not disappoint, he thrilled them."

Two days later Trumper took the bowling honours for his team in this match as Waverley were dismissed for 294. Sydney and Charles Gregory and Hanson Carter batted for the local side that day. Trumper's bowling statistics are reproduced:

O.	M.	R.	W.
17	7	31	4

Trumper and Carter's Sports Store at 108 Market Street, Sydney, 1904.

He took nine wickets for Paddington in six spells of bowling that season. His batting figures were 189 not out, 0, 55, 0, 29 and 215. In the round four match with Sydney University played on the University Oval, Victor was dismissed without scoring. He was bowled while attempting to hit the very first ball out of the ground. The ball of good length just clipped the bails and they fell to the ground next to the stumps. Victor with calm nonchalance stooped and replaced them on top of the stumps and took guard to face the next ball as if nothing had happened, while the University players looked on in bewilderment. He remained in his classic upright batting stance for a few seconds longer and then tucked his bat under his arm and walked from the field laughing at his prank. Sir Hector Clayton, MLC delighted in recounting this amusing incident for years after the event.

Victor's last innings for the Sydney Competition was made at Hampden Park just two weeks prior to leaving for New Zealand and England with the Australian Eleven. More than 3000 turned up in the hope of watching him perform as the match got under way. Monty Noble won the toss and Trumper and Chapman walked out to open the innings:

> It is an ill wind that blows no one any good. This match was set down originally for the Redfern oval, but, owing to the condition of the wicket—and there have been a number of complaints about it during the season—the Association changed the venue to the Hampden oval. The residents of Paddington, therefore, had what turned out to be a record display, and one that could not have been ordered better, for the one man the Paddington, the Sydney, or the Australian public want to see, Trumper, registered 215 in 1 h 50 m, and in company with W. W. Chapman put on 330 in that time. The international player hit 33 fours and six fives. While Trumper was batting, the bowling looked such sorry stuff that fivers were expected from every ball, but after his retirement no one could take any liberties with it; in fact, the bowling appeared to improve out of sight; perhaps, as a matter of fact, it did, for bowlers could not be expected to bowl with much heart when the cover was being knocked off the ball. (*Sydney Morning Herald*, 16 January 1905.)

The century partnership arrived in a mere 38 minutes and the double-century partnership after only 80 minutes. Little wonder that the opening stand of 330 had the ecstatic Paddington crowd on their feet for the entire duration of the partnership, such was the elation over Trumper's run blitz. When he was caught by

Fletcher fielding next to the fence, 162 of his 215 runs had been compiled with boundary hits.

In our day and age it is difficult to grasp fully the importance that cricket played in Australian society in Trumper's time. When one studies primary documents of the period a real feeling is grasped for what it was like to be involved in the wonderful game during this exciting era. The following newspaper extract may assist in conveying some impression:

> On land cricket is monarch of summer sports, adored by thousands of all ages and both sexes. Both sexes, mark you, and as players as well as spectators. In proof of this there may be occasionally seen some teams of strapping lasses, clad in blue serge, close-fitting frocks, wearing the conventional white linen hats, and carrying bats, and balls, and stumps, wending their way crease-wards. Such a team the other day excited the admiring curiosity of passers-by on Circular Quay, and moved them almost to tears by descending in all force on a pastrycook's shop from which they emerged laden with delicacies. One requires a little refreshment at times in between runs. All cricketers know that. But, that is by the way. Nearly every Australian is a cricket enthusiast of a more or less pronounced type, and it is in sunny New South Wales that the proportion of cognoscenti is greatest. It would be interesting to set the census-taker to work to let the world know just what of our population plays cricket or watches it being played. The roll of actual players must be, without hyperbole, prodigious ... But real cricket! Is there any marvel in its unmeasured power of attraction? It is an abiding joy to the participants, and a picture of grace and skill to the spectator. All its surroundings are delightful to the eye, and refreshing to the brain. Its geometric precision and the flashing celerity of polished movement are blandly exhilarating, and, without any extra charge at all, every onlooker may be a critic. And he generally is. For the players themselves—well, we all know that the greatest victories of the nation have been won on the cricket field. (*Sydney Morning Herald*, 22 October 1904.)

Trumper did not make the customary trip south for the Sheffield Shield engagements during the Christmas–New Year period due to his new business commitments. His contributions to his State's fourth Shield victory in as many years were his scores of 28 and 76 against South Australia in early January 1905 and his sparkling 81 and 13 in the Victorian fixture at the end of January, prior to the departure for New Zealand. In the South Australian engagement Trumper's 76 out of a total of 108 for the first wicket included 13 fours and he was only at the wickets for 65 minutes. After stumps in this match Clem Hill packed his bags bound for Launceston to be married to the petite, grey-eyed brunette Florence Hart.

In the Victorian clash Trumper hit up 81 in 88 minutes, producing one five and 9 fours on a biting wicket. Albert Cotter was responsible for a devastating spell of fast bowling taking 5 for 83 in the first innings and thus justified his selection in the Australian touring team.

Just before the voyage Victor agreed to be interviewed for the New Zealand publication, the *Young Man's Magazine* in his Market Street store one Saturday in late January 1905. Significant portions of the article by C. A. Redgrave are reproduced below:

> In view of the approaching visit of the Australian XI to New Zealand, I thought the readers of the *Young Man's Magazine* would appreciate a chat with one of their representative men.
>
> I therefore took advantage of my stay in Sydney to call upon Victor Trumper, and solicit an interview on behalf of New Zealand's young men.
>
> Trumper is without doubt the most popular cricketer in Australia to-day, and is generally recognised to be the best batsman in the world. Twenty-six years of age, well proportioned, standing over six feet in his socks, with square shoulders, well-made limbs, and a bright open face, he strikes one as being a fine type of the young colonial. I fell in love with him at once. The most striking thing about him, however, is his manner. Cordial, frank, and absolutely unaffected, he charms you and commands your friendship at once. He put me at ease straight away with his warm handshake and entire absence of "side." "... the proudest moment of your cricketing career?" I enquired. "Oh, I don't know" he replied evasively, "I know I've felt jolly wild very often when I've got out for a 'duck' when I should have made a score, but I don't remember ever feeling too pleased with myself."
>
> "Do you ever suffer from nervousness, Mr Trumper?" I asked. "Yes, when starting an innings. It is a bit of an ordeal meeting the first ball or two and knowing there are 20,000 pairs of eyes watching you. I never feel safe for the first half dozen strokes, and have often lost my wicket to a ball that I could confidently have got a fourer off when properly set. After the first couple of overs, however, one forgets all about stage fright and forgets almost that there is an audience; his only thought then is to make a score."
>
> After thanking him for his interview, I took my leave. As I looked

into those clear blue eyes and heard his cheery voice bidding me farewell, I felt that I had been conversing with a true man, one whom success had not spoiled and of whom Australia may well be proud.

On the day that Victor and his fellow team-mates left for New Zealand he received a letter from an unknown woman asking why he had not kept his arranged rendezvous the previous night. At first sight this appeared to be a prank carried out by members of the Eleven, but on closer investigation the episode was found to have been caused by the actions of a young gigolo posing as the great cricketer to win the woman's affections. Before the departure the Hordern Shield was presented to the Paddington Club for permanent safe-keeping, the club having won it three time previously in 1894–95, 1897–98 and 1900–01. The current trophy, the Rawson Cup was won this season by the North Sydney Club.

The *Sydney Morning Herald* in a leading sports article entitled "From a Cricket Notebook," when reviewing the prospects of the colts in the touring team stated: "Three years ago no name was sounded through England like that of Trumper, and any colt who goes to England and does as well—but, alas, we have no such expectation yet awhile—may know that cricket fame in England is a rushing, roaring flood, that has swept away the ballast of some promising young players. But not Trumper's—personification of modesty through it all."

The *Manuka* was delayed for four hours while a result was reached in favour of Trumper's team in the Victorian match. Finally as the Australians left for New Zealand, cries of "Bring back The Ashes" rang over the water from those clustered at the pier to witness the departure.

Several days later an equally large gathering met the travellers at Auckland Harbour and they were driven in motor transport by New Zealand Cricket Association officials to their rooms in the Central Hotel. Inside, the President of the Association gave the customary welcome and proposed a toast to the visitors from glasses bereft of alcoholic contents. Being a Sunday the licensing laws forbade liquor to be dispensed, even to cricketing notables from Australia. Having two days at their disposal they elected to explore the thermal region of Rotorua. They decided to travel in rowing boats, with their Maori oarsmen negotiating the white water at breakneck speed. During the trip Victor Trumper had

Trumper behind the oars in New Zealand, 1905.

his turn behind the oars and Frank Laver captured such moments with his camera.

The night was spent at the Geyser Hotel at Whakarewarewa and after dinner a long walk by torchlight had the sightseers adhering closely to the pathway between the steaming ponds of boiling mud and water. Before retiring the young cricketers disported in the specially constructed bath house at their hotel.

Leaving Rotorua the tourists returned to play the local Fifteen of Auckland, winning the three-day fixture by an innings and 160 runs. Once again in a match for his country, Trumper top-scored

139

The Australians jump for thrown coins in the Bath House at Whakawerawera in New Zealand in 1905. Trumper (centre) is making the highest leap.

with his 92. Ten thousand were present to see him but were very nearly deprived of seeing the genius in action. Batting at second drop he received one ball from Stemson and was then clean bowled by the next, a no-ball. The *New Zealand Herald* described his eventual dismissal:

> When Trumper had scored 92 he mis-hit Hay and was caught by H. B. Lusk. The Australian champion had batted for an hour and 40 minutes, and hit 11 boundaries. His strokes were clean and well-timed. He placed the bowling almost as he pleased. One feature of his innings was his carpet-driving. He seldom, if ever, lifted a ball, being satisfied to see it travel to the boundary along the ground.

After a picnic launch excursion to Waiwera the tourists travelled for two days down the picturesque Wanganui River. Frank Laver told how some of the party attempted to smuggle liquor into King County; a prohibition officer inspecting a gladstone bag was bypassed as the culprits slipped past him in the gloom, avoiding investigation.

At daybreak the following morning Victor Trumper and the Australian party took a canoe and small launch down the two hundred and ninety-three rapids on the Wanganui River and at noon ate lunch on a houseboat. Some team members attempted to shoot ducks, pigeons and wild dogs, but their aim was not comparable to their cricket skill. After a night at Pipiriki, followed by a further launch journey and a train trip the tourists finally arrived in Wellington. The next night they were honoured at a smoke concert in the capital city at which the Prime Minister Richard Seddon was in attendance.

Against the Wellington Fifteen the visitors secured 433, Clem Hill hitting 95 and Monty Noble taking 10 for 63 in the home side's first innings of 183 as the match was drawn. Trumper scored 10. In the next game his 87 not out in the tourists' second attempt at Lancaster Park, Christchurch against Canterbury, was the highest score of the match. He was omnipotent on the sodden pitch described by one journalist as "a quagmire":

> Trumper then took a hand. After making two or three beautiful cuts he proceeded to hit repeatedly over the heads of the in-field. Three men were placed on the boundary but this only had the effect of causing the champion to change the direction of his strokes. (*New Zealand Mail*, 3 March 1905.)

Victor and his fellows, having triumphed by eight wickets, were presented with gold cufflinks of New Zealand greenstone by the Lord Mayor. In the next game at Dunedin against Otago "the champion" again top-scored with another 87 as the Australians won by an innings and 173 runs:

> When Trumper and Duff made their appearance the spectators settled down to see good cricket. The pair started off at once. They made the bowling seem very simple, scoring freely all round the wicket, with beautiful clean, crisp strokes, always out of reach of the field. (*New Zealand Mail*, 8 March 1905.)

Immediately after this fixture the tourists treated the crowd to a batting display with the home side bowling, Syd Gregory hitting six balls over the boundary in his 114 made in sixty minutes.

The scene was now set for the internationals, the first of which took place in Christchurch starting on 10 March. Winning the toss, Monty Noble sent his openers out to bat and although Duff was out at once without scoring, Trumper batted maturely for his 84:

> He was the same Trumper of the Canterbury match. There was the same excellent timing and crispness, with his runs got in quite a different manner from his great performance at Lancaster Park. This time there was none of the powerful well-placed driving and no play so characteristic of his innings against Canterbury. On Friday he made some lovely off drives but more prominent was his cutting. His timing and placement were perfect. (*Canterbury Times*, 15 March 1905.)

The Australians set their hosts a massive 533 runs to chase but they managed to stave off defeat despite some prodigious bowling by Warwick Armstrong with 5 for 27, and 5 for 25.

The two nations again met at the Basin Reserve in Wellington three days later. New Zealand were asked to bat by Noble on a wicket made soft by three days of light rain. Cotter, Howell and McLeod sent the home team back to the pavilion for just 94 runs. Australia were next and Trumper did not come in until four wickets had fallen. He and Clem Hill were responsible for a partnership of pure and sustained batsmanship that is still remembered in Wellington to this day. So many runs were scored in such little batting time that the journalists and scorers at the Basin Reserve could barely keep up with the action:

> The spectators at the second day's proceedings of the test match were treated to the finest exhibition of batting ever seen in this city. Trumper and Hill punished the bowlers unmercifully, and their clean and forceful hitting was hugely enjoyed by the crowd. The partnership produced 269 runs, and an idea of the rapid rate of the run-getting of this redoubtable pair may be gauged by the fact of their putting on 100 runs in thirty-five minutes and 150 in fifty-six minutes. The bowling was slammed all over the field, boundary hits being as common as blackberries. Trumper executed all those strokes for which he is world famous, while Hill's hitting and driving were superb. (*Canterbury Times*, 22 March 1905.)

Trumper's hundred was posted in 85 minutes and the partnership put on 269 in a mere 110 minutes. This still remains in 1984 the record for the sixth wicket in first-class matches played in New Zealand. Hill hit 26 off one over from Ollivier including three sixes and two fours, and Trumper hit two consecutive sixes from Upham. At the time balls hit over the boundary in New Zealand were registered as six.

The reporter for the *New Zealand Mail* was in raptures over Trumper's awesome display of controlled power and precision:

> Trumper then started hitting hard and high; he sent Upham away over the fence three times for six each. Fifteen was knocked of one of the Wellington bowler's overs. It was batting!

Trumper's 172, which was the highest score in any match on the 1905 Tour of New Zealand, was made in only 145 minutes including four sixes and twenty fours. Finally the Sydney genius decided it was time to give others valuable practice for the impending English tour and he gently lofted the ball to Mason from Bennett's bowling. Thus Trumper laid the foundations for an Australian victory by an innings and 358 runs. He made 538 runs from 7 innings at an average of 89.66 on tour. Soon after, Charles Bannerman who umpired in both internationals, and who had been for the last two seasons resident coach at Christ's College in Christchurch, was interviewed by the *Sydney Morning Herald* in Sydney on his return home: "That must have been a brilliant exhibition of batting by Trumper and Hill during their partnership in the Second Test?" "Yes, it was a display the equal of which one very seldom witnesses."

After six eventful and pleasant weeks in New Zealand the Australian cricketers sailed for Fiji on the *Navua* and four days later arrived in Suva. Among those on the landing to welcome the tourists was the Fijian prince, Kadavu Levu. Immediately on landing Victor Trumper and his companions were taken to the Prince's residence where toasts were drunk and community songs of welcome performed.

Despite ten days of torrential rain in Fiji before the arrival of the visitors, the one-day game against an Eighteen of Fiji went ahead as scheduled on the Albert Park ground. Cricket enthusiasts from neighbouring islands travelled great distances to see Trumper play, some taking many days to make the trip. The *Western Pacific Herald* takes us back more than seventy years: "The pavilion was crowded, every available inch being occupied, whilst the grounds round about were well patronised. The parade was one living mass of natives with whites here and there and the gay coloured sulus and dresses of the natives must have made an interesting picture for our visitors, many of whom were busy with their cameras."

Fiji batted first and made 91. Bill Howell took five wickets for 6 runs. For Fiji, Pope took five Australian wickets for 51 runs as

Part of the crowd watching Trumper play in Suva, Fiji, 1905.

the visitors ran up 212 with thirteen of the Eighteen fielding. Albert Hopkins made 54 and Victor Trumper 40 on the coconut matting pitch as the Australians won on the first innings by 121 runs:

> Trumper, the champion batsman of the world, and Duff batted first for Australia. The exhibition of batting by the former was a treat to witness and a revelation to our young players of what can be done with the ball by a skilful player. (*Western Pacific Herald*, 28 March 1905.)

At sea once more, this time on the *Miowera*, Trumper and his companions settled in their new quarters on the long run to Hawaii. Cricket practice on the games deck was common and at one session Philip Newland, the understudy wicket-keeper to Jim Kelly, was hit in the eye and was in considerable pain for several days. After a few days at sea the team divided into two distinct groups, one favouring the sea air on deck mixing with

144

the other passengers, and the other group retiring below to the smoking room for long card sessions. Victor Trumper often sat on his own reading or sifting through copious quantities of letters. Two wives accompanied their husbands on this trip to England, Mrs Clem Hill and Mrs Philip Newland. Annie Trumper joined Victor during the tour (Bill Ferguson makes mention of the fact in his daily diary), and it was while Annie was in England that their daughter Anne Louise was born.

Joe Darling, who was later to be elected captain of the Twelfth Australian Eleven at a team meeting, was by this time on his way to England via the more conventional route through Suez and Gibraltar. Bill Ferguson, who was to begin a lengthy and colourful period as official Australian scorer also travelled separately to England to begin his duties, his position having been arranged while sitting in the dentist's chair in Monty Noble's surgery.

Meanwhile the main touring party was approaching Honolulu. After a day's stopover, which included a trip to the top of the Pali precipice, they steamed toward Vancouver, where on disembarking they climbed aboard the Canadian Pacific mail train which was delayed for half an hour to await their arrival. Victor Trumper and his companions were impressed with the alpine scenery that unfolded before them during the journey across Canada. They had an entire carriage consisting of sleeping compartments and a smoking and living room specially reserved for their exclusive use.

At one stage the train stopped for lunch at Glacier House high up in the Canadian Rockies and the Australians and their champion batsman threw snowballs and tried to walk with snow shoes. Later Reg Duff covered himself with snow and clambered onto the train surprising the unwary with his ghostly impersonation.

Winnipeg was the next stop and here a fleet of cars provided a motorcade through the ice-covered city to a mayoral luncheon. Back on board the cricketers raced past the Great Lakes to Buffalo where Trumper and his party boarded another train to visit Niagara Falls before returning to Buffalo to speed down the Atlantic Coast to New York City. Here they climbed aboard the *Majestic* for the final leg to Liverpool to begin the 1905 Tour of England.

On landing the Australians were mobbed by reporters,

145

The Australians frolic in the snow in the Canadian Rockies, 1905. Trumper is fourth from th
right.

cameramen and souvenir hunters. Nearly two dozen photographers spent one entire morning at work, among their number being a silent movie technician. The result of his labour was later screened in a local music hall much to the embarrassed mirth of the visiting cricketers. Some unscrupulous cameramen, despite guarantees to the contrary, made faked postcards with slightly enlarged heads placed on incorrect torsos. These are still used today in some cricket books and are only revealed on close scrutiny.

The first engagement with the Gentlemen of England, led by the Grand Old Man, W. G. Grace, was at the Crystal Palace during early May. In the 1905 match Trumper did not continue his New Zealand form making only 2 and 7. L. O. S. Poidevin, who was studying medicine in the Old Country, made 18 against his countrymen in the drawn fixture. At Trent Bridge versus Nottinghamshire Trumper hit 10 scorching boundaries in his second innings score of 61 compiled in sixty-five minutes. In the

146

The Australians in England, 1905.
*Standing: Howell, unidentified, Gehrs, Kelly, Newland, unidentified, Laver, Hopkins, Ferguson (scorer), Armstrong, Cotter.
Seated: Duff, Hill, Darling (Captain), McLeod, Trumper, Gregory.*

Notts. first innings the first three batsmen, Jones, Iremonger and Gunn, were all brilliantly caught by Trumper; Jones in the slips and the other two batsmen deep on the square-leg boundary. The match was drawn with the honours equally shared by both teams.

Having scored 31 (he hit three fours in one over from Knox) and 25 against Surrey, Victor Trumper and his fellows were presented to the Prince of Wales, the game being specifically stopped for that purpose. The future King was deeply interested in cricket and the Australians' visit. During their stay the Prince of Wales sent invitations for them to attend functions such as the Albert Hall concert featuring Nellie Melba. Unfortunately this clashed with the previously scheduled Surrey Cricket Club banquet and the tourists were instead represented by Annie Trumper and the other two wives.

Against Oxford University Trumper made 77 and 45 and contributed greatly to his team's easy win. During his 77,

147

top-score for the match, he hit ten fours and in his second stay he and Reg Duff rattled up 40 runs from three Oxford overs.

Returning to London, Trumper and his fellow tourists were eager to accept the invitation from Nellie Melba to hear her performance of *La Traviata* at Covent Garden. At the final curtain the Australians presented their countrywoman with a bouquet arranged to represent cricket stumps with the word "Australia" spelled out in green and gold flowers underneath the floral wicket. The legendary singer was also handed a cricket bat with the signatures of the entire Eleven and the inscription, "To Madam Melba wishing her many happy returns of the day. That she may score as many successes off her own bat as we collectively score runs off ours is the wish of the undersigned members of the Australian Cricket Team of 1905."

Trumper's 85 against Yorkshire in the grimy Sheffield light was a superb exhibition against the champion county, made under extreme adversity as fog rolled in and dark clouds filled the morning sky. As they walked to the wicket Victor said to Reg Duff, "We must leave the off stuff alone for awhile." The ball was promptly sent racing to the boundary from a square cut during the champion's first few scoring shots and as they met at the end of the over Reg said, "When do you think we should start punishing the off stuff, Vic?"*

The pitch was soaked but the crowd, which increased to more than 12,000 when news spread that Trumper was batting, was treated to some wonderful cricket as the Australian openers totalled 76 in thirty-five minutes. After rain halted play for half an hour Trumper was bowled by Hirst with a no-ball and then moved to 50 made in forty-five minutes. He abandoned any attempt at driving on the soggy surface, concentrating his powers on a series of late cuts, glances and pull shots off his stumps all around the field. Finally after 90 minutes he was caught in the slips when on 85, having extracted 13 fours from the sloppy pitch in a display of awesome panache and daring. Here was yet another example of Trumper not reaching the century but making a contribution for his team which was easily worth twice as much, as Yorkshire collapsed on the wet wicket and the Australians won by 174 runs. Frank Laver took 8 for 75 in the

---

* Eric McElhone, unpublished address for the Waverley Historical Society, 9 June 1975.

first innings, Bill Howell 6 for 38 in the second innings and Trumper was acclaimed man of the match by the British press for his top score of 85.

Bill Ferguson, who scored in all the fixtures in 1905, and whose career stretched for more than fifty extraordinary years, wrote:

My favourite batsman was Vic Trumper. Probably the neatest and most elegant bat in the world at that time, Vic was anything but neat when he was in the dressing room, or at an hotel. He was the despair of his charming wife, and the not-so-charming baggage master, because he simply refused to worry about the condition of his clothes or equipment. Any old bat would do for him, whether there was rubber on the handle or not, and I can still see him now, after slaughtering the best bowling in England, taking off his flannels in the dressing-room, rolling them in a ball and cramming them into an already over-loaded cricket bag—there to remain until they were worn again the next day. Mrs Trumper used to say to me, "Just look at Victor's clothes. Whatever does he do with them?" On such occasions I would often fold his clothes neatly and re-pack his bag, but, within twenty-four hours, chaos again reigned supreme.

The Trumpers were real aces, for my money. If Victor caught me packing his bag, he would say, "Don't bother about that, Bill. You have enough to do, without me causing you extra trouble."*

When he was a teenager, Leonard Hutton, having practised with George Hirst at the Leeds nets and carried the veteran cricketer's bags to the tramstop, was amazed to be told, "Make sure that you never get like Vic Trumper." When asked for an explanation Hutton was informed, "He was so superstitious that he made life a misery for himself. His favourite creams were so well used that their resemblance to the original was purely imaginary." Monty Noble in *The Game's the Thing* wrote:

He hated display of every description and took very little pride in his own appearance either on or off the field (the privilege of genius). His cricket bag was a byword among his team mates. Held together by a strap at each end, the lock being broken, it was invariably full to bursting with clothes pushed in and jumped on. It was as funny as a circus to watch his futile efforts to close that bag. It did not worry him in the slightest that his cricketing uniform was disgracefully creased, neither did the jocular epithets hurled at him ruffle his composure.

---

* W. H. Ferguson, *Mr Cricket*. Nicholas Kaye, London, 1957.

At times, however, the Paddington genius did appear at the crease in immaculate condition as Annie Trumper invaded the privacy of that legendary bag. Arthur Mailey reported in *10 for 66 and All That* that when he played against Victor in Sydney First Grade cricket he was "beautifully clad in creamy, loose-fitting but well-tailored flannels." Mailey also wrote, "Although slightly pigeon-toed in the left foot he had a springy athletic walk and a tendency to shrug his shoulders every few minutes, a habit I understand he developed through trying to loosen his shirt off his shoulders when it became soaked with sweat during his innings." Mailey recorded that Trumper when taking guard from the umpire usually asked for "two legs", and when the leg-spinner deceived his hero in a Sydney match, having had his best deliveries hammered all over the field, the outgoing champion, "... smiled, patted the back of his bat and said: 'It was too good for me!' I felt like a boy who had killed a dove."

Disposing of Lancashire by 244 runs (Hill 149, Trumper 36 and 14), the scene was now set for the First Test of the 1905 Tour at Trent Bridge. Stanley Jackson won the toss, as he was to do in all five Tests that year and England batted first for 196; Laver with 7 for 64 and Cotter, 3 for 64, bowled with considerable hostility. Trumper and Duff opened for Australia with Duff scoring a single before being caught by Hayward low down close to the wicket. Unperturbed, Trumper from Gunn's second over hit three slashing fours, an on-drive and two cuts backward of point. Then the gallant cricketer suddenly reached behind his body clutching at his back as he tore a muscle close to the spine. He had to be helped from the field hobbling with great difficulty, retiring hurt for 13. The heart seemed to go out of the Australian side although Armstrong and Cotter hit out strongly just before stumps, the Victorian lifting Bosanquet out of the ground over the pavilion for 6. As Trumper could not leave his bed the next morning the Australian innings soon closed at 9 down for 221.

Archie MacLaren batting with all his old power made 140 in England's second innings allowing Jackson to declare at 426 for the loss of five wickets. Chasing more than 400 runs Australia were soon struggling and could manage only 188 in reply, Bosanquet dismissing eight batsmen. The ninth wicket having fallen the wan face of Trumper appeared at the visitor's dressing room door. Gilbert Jessop clearly captured the scene in *A Cricketer's Log*:

One does not usually associate cricket with pathos, but the sight of poor Victor Trumper being assisted by two of his companions to shuffle down the pavilion gangway in an attempt to gain the crease which McLeod had recently vacated struck me as a pathetic spectacle. We had been told on the first day that there was little probability of him taking any further part in the game, and after McLeod had lost his wicket we were preparing to leave the vicinity of the pitch when we saw spectators who were clustering around the entrance to the dressing room, brushed aside and Trumper appear in their midst. He got as far as the last step, then nature gave way and he could go no further, and with a wave of the arm from Joe Darling we trooped from the field as lucky a winning team as ever fought out a Test Match.

Trumper did not play in the next three matches, consulting the London specialist Sir Alfred Fripp for physiotherapy to the ruptured muscle fibres in his back. He returned to cricket on 12 June at Leicester scoring 14 and 70. This second total was described by Bill Ferguson, who was watching from the scorers' box: "Trumper gave a beautiful display, his cutting being a treat, ball after ball flying to the boundary like a shot. But when 70 he cut one from Odell on to his off stump. Some of the Leicester chaps said to me afterwards that they never saw such a beautiful display of cutting in their life before."* Trumper's innings of an hour included eleven fours and the result was a draw.

The Second Test Match at Lord's was eventually rained out with the contest in England's favour and the pitch a swamp; England 282, and 5 for 151, Australia 181. Bill Ferguson described the start of play on the second day, Friday 16 June: "Our chaps started with Trumper and Duff and on the wicket which was wet and tricky, hitting was the best thing to do. The batsmen were soon at it, Trumper playing splendid cricket, one stroke of his being wonderful—picking the ball off the off stump and lifting over the square-leg boundary, everyone agreeing that it was a wonderful stroke, calling it the Trumper flick. When 31 Trumper was bowled by Jackson after a dashing innings (1–57). C. B. Fry said it was the finest he had ever seen played."

For the second time an Australian eleven travelled to Ireland, going by rail from Euston Station to the port of Holyhead, by sea on the Irish steamer *Ulster* to Kingstown and from there by train to Dublin. Monty Noble captained the team in the Dublin

---

* The diary of W. H. Ferguson, Scorer to the Australian Eleven, 1905.

University Past and Present encounter as Joe Darling stayed in London. The match played in the University grounds was handsomely won by the Australian tourists by 231 runs.

Before resumption of play on the morning of the second day the team accepted an invitation to visit the Guinness Brewery. They were shown all around the premises and then driven back to the University in jaunting cars, the one-horse light vehicle so prevalent in Dublin in Trumper's time.

Trumper's scores of 22 and 65 provided the Irish spectators with a glimpse of his renowned vivacity and dash. Bill Ferguson wrote, "Trumper was next out lbw. to Meldon for 65, a perfect innings, which delighted the spectators who wished to see him make a good score. Some said to me that they never wished to see better."*

Victor's first century in England in 1905 occurred towards the end of June at Bristol. He and Duff opened and in 33 minutes made 72 runs. Trumper's 50 came up in only 35 minutes. With the Australian score at 132 Duff was caught and Trumper really opened up, cutting and driving in all directions. He was caught at the second attempt by Townsend fielding near the long-on boundary a few minutes before lunch. His 108 took 110 minutes and he thus emulated his feat of the previous tour of England when he raced to a century before lunch on the first day of the memorable Manchester Test of 1902. The only other Australian to achieve this in a match in England was Hugh Massie at Oxford in 1882; now Trumper had accomplished it twice as his team drew with Gloucestershire.

Trumper and his team-mates were always guests of honour whenever they attended the music halls and theatres. They were usually admitted free of charge, special boxes being set aside for their exclusive use. Introductions to the leading stage personalities occurred after each performance and one music hall gave each member of the Eleven a green and gold metal pass for permanent use. At one performance the outside of the theatre glittered with green and gold lights.

Against Hampshire, Trumper's 92 runs were some compensation for his scores of 8 and 0 in the drawn Third Test at Leeds. He hit a six clean out of the ground and smote 14 fours (six runs for a ball merely hit over the boundary was not introduced in

---

* The diary of W. H. Ferguson.

Trumper faces Brearley in the Fourth Test at Old Trafford in 1905.

England until 1910). Australia won the Hampshire match by an innings and 112 runs, Cotter taking nine wickets in the match and Hill, Noble and Gregory each scoring centuries, yet the Fleet Street press rated Trumper's effort as the innings of the match. Bill Ferguson wrote: "The scoring went on at a great rate by Trumper, but Duff after giving two chances was caught by Hill off Persse for 13 (1–39). Hill was now in and I had a fine, large box to score from. Trumper got 50 runs in 25 minutes and the 100 runs went up in 45 minutes, and when 92 Trumper was caught by Johnston off Persse, 2–162. It was a beautiful innings, scoring off nearly every ball, the time being 77 minutes."[*]

Some weeks later at Manchester in the Fourth Test Match a youthful Neville Cardus was watching his hero bat:

> I sat on the grass at Old Trafford when Victor made 30 for Australia in 1905. Walter Brearley sent him a fastish inswinger. Trumper played late and, with a turn of the right wrist and forearm, sent the ball past forward square-leg at such a pace that I couldn't get out of the way, as I hopped up from the turf. The ball struck my ankle; and for days I showed the bruise to my friends, young and old. And when

---

[*] The diary of W. H. Ferguson.

153

Trumper demonstrates his superb batting stance in England, 1905.

Trumper pulls forward of square leg, 1905 Tour.

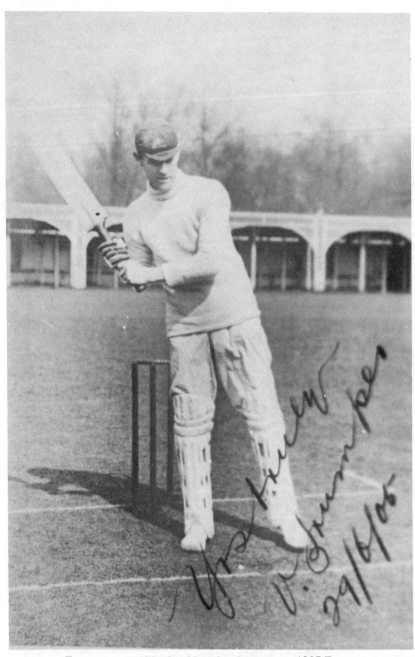

Trumper opens his shoulders for the camera, 1905 Tour.

Trumper cuts backward of point, 1905 Tour.

Trumper demonstrates his superb lofted drive, 1905 Tour.

the discolouration began to fade I tried to perpetuate it by application of a blue pencil.†

Trumper scored 11 and 30 as England destroyed Australia's hopes of recovering The Ashes, winning easily by an innings and 80 runs.

Trumper's only other century innings of the tour was in early August at Worcester. The wicket was drying out after heavy rain precluded play on the first day, and the ball was kicking viciously as Trumper and Duff made an opening stand of 25. Trumper was struck on the body several times but continued to hit out and at lunch was 59 not out. The wind was so strong that the bails were not used. Despite the howling wind and the poor light Trumper hit fourteen boundaries and after he registered 110 runs in 165 minutes, he was bowled off his pads by Wilson. Scudding showers on the last day ensured that the match remained unfinished; Australia 330, Worcester 78 and 5 for 51. Tibby Cotter had the admirable figures of 7 for 15 and 5 for 19.

The final Test Match at The Oval was drawn; centuries by Charles Fry with 144 and Reg Duff contributing 146 enlivened proceedings. Trumper made 4 and 28 and England retained The Ashes winning two Tests, the remainder being drawn. Despite this the Australians lost only one other match during the tour, versus Essex. They won sixteen engagements, lost three and drew the remaining nineteen, and received admiring praise for their demeanour on and off the field.

Trumper's aggregate from 51 innings on tour was 1798 runs with an average of 35.96. He was fourth in the Australian's batting aggregates and fifth in the averages of the fifteen tourists, a commendable and courageous effort from a player who was crippled for almost a month with a torn back muscle. He also took 28 catches in all matches.

The day after the final match with a South of England eleven the Twelfth Australian Cricket Team convened its final meeting and then dispersed. They did not return together to Australia but broke into groups, some returning immediately and others, such as Victor and Annie Trumper, remaining behind to rest and visit the Lakes district and Scotland before returning home. Frank Iredale, reporting for the *Sydney Morning Herald*, recalled the voyage:

---

† John Arlott (ed.), *Cricket: The Great Ones.* Pelham Books, London, 1967.

I came out with him and his wife from England in 1905, and it was in communion with him on this trip day after day that I got to know him so well. It was only his real friends who knew him, and I am sure the cricket world knew nothing of the real man. He looked upon his cricket as a duty more than as a sport. If he punished a bowler he felt sorry for him afterwards.*

Sydney Pardon wrote in Trumper's obituary, *Wisden*, 1916:

Under all conditions Trumper was a fascinating batsman to watch. His extreme suppleness lent a peculiar grace to everything he did. When he was hitting up a big score batting seemed quite an easy matter. He took so many liberties, however, and scored from so many good balls, that in order to do himself justice he had to be in the best possible health and condition. The strokes with which he drove even the best bowlers to despair demanded a marvellous union of hand and eye. His game at its highest point of excellence could only be played by a young man.

---

* *Thirty-three Years of Cricket.*

"A White-flannelled Knight"

On returning to Australia Jim Kelly, acting on medical advice decided to retire from representative cricket after serving behind the stumps for thirty-three consecutive Tests against England plus three in South Africa. Trumper's brother-in-law had one of his fingers badly injured in England taking a hard return from Reg Duff early in the English tour but played on in considerable discomfort. Later in the tour he was struck over the heart by a sharply rising ball from Walter Brearley. Kelly's successful benefit match on the Sydney Cricket Ground in January 1906 saw the Australian Eleven (Trumper 15 and 60) defeat New South Wales by 79 runs.

Trumper's first foray with the willow for Paddington after his return took place at Manly in the Middle Harbour match, yielding him 101 runs. His season with Paddington earned 363 runs at an average of 51.86 during 1905–06. On 20 January 1906 in a social match with Middle Harbour, he rattled up 124 not out in only 55 minutes and from the last over of the day he scored 24 runs.

In Sheffield Shield matches he occupied the crease four times for 175 runs, his most powerful display being in Sydney while facing the Victorian bowlers in late January on a very wet wicket:

> On being joined by Duff, Trumper, who was on 23, did all the scoring as he laid about in all directions. Laver he lifted grandly, a straight hit high upon the roof of the northern pavilion, a magnificent stroke. Duff ordinarily is very little, if at all, a slower run-getter than Trumper, yet he looked on while the Paddington man smashed the bowling. Trumper ran to 67 in half an hour, the last over from Saunders yielding 11. At the luncheon adjournment the total was 130,—Trumper 73, Duff 9. (*Sydney Morning Herald*, 27 January 1906.)

Trumper scoring 50 while Duff made 9, raced to his 100 in an astounding 58 minutes and ensured that his State retain the Sheffield Shield for the fifth consecutive year, his 101 setting the seal on Victoria's defeat by 145 runs. Charlie Macartney, experiencing his first Shield season recalled:

161

In the game against Victoria, Victor Trumper made such a magnificent 100 on a sticky wicket that it was worth being in the side for that alone. Laver and Saunders were a pretty rich pair to bat against on a wicket of this kind.

Saunders nearly bowled Trumper with the first ball, but Vic, after remarking that he would just as soon be caught off him as bowled, set about the job properly, and with beautifully executed strokes, belted every bowler all over the Sydney Cricket Ground.

Trumper brought off the best big hit I have ever seen. A yorker from Frank Laver was the ball he selected for the hit, and with no apparent effort he seemed to pick it up with the bat and it finished on the roof of the northern pavilion at straight hit. I have seen bigger hits made by lunging, but this was a fast-footed one, necessitated by the pitch of the ball.*

Trumper's services to world cricket are generally common knowledge, however his efforts in promoting the game in rural areas of his own country are not as well known. His willingness to travel long distances at short notice to popularise the summer spectacle and to share his vast knowledge of skill and tactics was amply demonstrated in the autumn of 1906. On 14 April he led a Sydney team to Goulburn to play the local Eighteen who made 206 against Cotter (11 for 45) and Trumper (2 for 5). Trumper's top score of 182, which had the thousand-strong crowd enthralled, consisted of 6 sixes and 22 fours, and at one stage on the matting pitch he blasted 50 runs in 15 minutes as the Sydney Eleven totalled 383. J. J. Giltinan, who was to later join with Victor in introducing Rugby League football in Australia, was team manager for this trip.

Upon returning to Sydney, Victor barely had time to share his experiences with Annie before sailing the following day on the *Wodonga* for Queensland with his team of Sydney cricketers, "The Victor Trumper Team". The party comprised: V. T. Trumper (Paddington), A. J. Hopkins, S. J. Redgrave (North Sydney), A. Cotter, E. R. Bubb, C. R. Gorry (Glebe), W. McIntyre (Middle Harbour), A. L. Newell (Waverley), J. C. Barnes, T. H. Foster (Redfern), and R. N. Hickson (Gordon).

At Charters Towers Trumper's team faced the local Eighteen in perfect autumn weather on Saturday 28 April 1906. On opening with Ernest Bubb, Victor helped add 100 runs in half an hour, his contribution in that short space of time being 75. He

---

* C. G. Macartney, *My Cricketing Days*. Heinemann, London, 1930.

The Victor Trumper Team, Queensland Tour 1906.
Back row: C. R. Gorry, A. Cotter, R. N. Hickson, V. T. Trumper, E. R. Bubb, A. J. Hopkins.
Front row: W. McIntyre, T. H. Foster, A. L. Newell, S. J. Redgrave, J. C. Barnes·

then retired to give others a turn at the crease. He injured his left hand while fielding and declined to bat in his team's second innings, and the match was drawn.

Travelling to Townsville Trumper's team scored 478, Redgrave, who later in his career became a Queensland coach, made 168 and Foster 155. Although he reached only 23 at his first attempt the Townsville Eighteen closed their second innings prematurely to allow Trumper to display his skills in an exhibition innings. He obliged with 75 runs in a mere 25 minutes, sending five of his twelve boundary hits soaring over the fence and scattering the delighted crowd.

Returning to Charters Towers for the contest with a North Queensland Fifteen, the Sydney cricketers played their third drawn game in as many matches, but at Mount Morgan Trumper really opened out with a slashing 179 not out in eighty minutes which consisted of 33 fours and 2 sixes. He and Bubb amassed 272 runs and then the Sydney skipper retired having captivated the crowd with his dashing batsmanship. In an exhibition innings he hit 85 after the southerners had won by an innings and 138 runs.

163

Although the Sydney men won easily at Bundaberg, they batted again so that their captain could entertain the onlookers, which he did by smashing 85 not out in half an hour, at one stage executing 40 runs from twelve balls.

The tourists were welcomed in the gold town of Gympie at a smoke concert and during a newspaper interview Trumper said, "I find the class of country cricket in Queensland much better than I expected. We have seen some really good individual cricketers who are competent to represent Queensland in any interstate match. I strongly urge the formation of a North Queensland Association as soon as possible." Wherever he went in the north, his suggestions and initiatives were acted upon for the ultimate good of cricket as a game and a spectacle. The following quote from Hutcheon's *A History of Queensland Cricket* supports this view:

> "After some weeks of negotiations a match has definitely been arranged between the North Queensland Association and the Q.C.A. to commence on the Brisbane Cricket Ground on New Year's Day. It will mark an epoch in the history of cricket in this State . . ." This announcement in a Metropolitan newspaper was an indication of the influence Victor Trumper's tour had upon cricket in the North of the State. The North Queensland Association was formed as a result of that tour.

After the Gympie fixture, which was drawn because of the rain, Trumper's team returned to Brisbane for two matches against a Brisbane eleven. In the first match Victor top-scored in atrocious conditions with 30 runs, and in his side's second stay at the crease he was 16 not out ensuring victory by ten wickets. His display of awesome power in the second match was sensational as one drive went soaring over the fence at the Stanley Street end of the Woollongabba Ground, the first time that such a hit had been made. Trumper's innings of 207 not out which included 4 sixes and 25 fours was to be a talking point among those present for more than fifty years as he led his team to victory by nine wickets.

The whirlwind tour of the coastal districts of North and Central Queensland was a triumph for Trumper and for cricket. Queenslanders flocked to see the legendary champion in full flight, some station stockmen riding for days through swollen creeks and rough country to witness his artistry. In all he made 1044 runs in ten matches, with an average of 104.40, his side winning six encounters and drawing four, usually against odds of up to eighteen opponents. At that time Guy Eden included the following Irish-Australian style ballad, "Victor Trumper," in his *Bush Ballads and Other Verses*:

I.

There's a gintleman I'd spake of, Victor Trumper is his name,
He's a striplin', but bejabers, he's already known to fame,
For to see the darlin' battin', well, it's simply just a drame,
When me Victor cocks his eye to take the bowlin'!

II.

Did ye see him in Ould England, in the year o' grace '03?*
It was just about the swatest sight a man could live to see,
For he took iliven centuries, the spalpeen, glory be!
'Twas tremenjous how me Victor flogged the bowlin'!

III.

He began wid poor ould Surrey, in a frindly sort o' way;
Then, thinks he, the bould Oxonians must be taught me style o' play.
I'll reserve the MCC to have me fun another day,
When I get me invitation to the bowlin'.

IV.

As I trate the bould Oxonians, so at Cambridge I will do,
They're as innocint as babies, and I'll bate them black and blue;
And wid Essex, poor ould Essex, I'll remain a day or two,
For I'm told there's somethin' tasty in their bowlin'!

V.

So before his mighty powers fell the valiant and the brave,
And full many a reputation found a most untoimely grave,
As me Victor tramped the country, like a divastatin' wave
Makin' ivry kind of wreckage wid the bowlin'.

VI.

Oh! he's just a dandy batsman, he's a rajah, he's a toff,
Wid out any fancy feelin' for the "on" or for the "off."
He just takes his bat, and thin, wid one apologetic cough
Sets to work to play the divil wid the bowlin'.

VII.

Oh! It's Killarney to him, if they shoot, or if they bump.

---

* Poetic licence—actually 1902.

By me soul I've sat and watched him till me heart wid joy would
  thump,
Just to see the saucy darlin' hook 'em off the middle stump
Wid contimptuous indiff'rence to the bowlin'.

VIII.

Misther Duff's a slashin' batsman tho' his figure's not so tall,
And I hail the little hero wid his swate moustache and all,
But there's no one at the wicket can the ladies' hearts enthral
Like me Victor when he starts to clump the bowlin'.

IX.

He's as modest as a daisy, and as gentle as can be,
So I take me hat off to him, wid this message frank and free,
That his rivals in ould England think a match well lost, to see
Victor Trumper spind an hour wid their bowlin'!

While Trumper was in Queensland the seeds were sown for the
serious disruption to Australian cricket which was to occur in
1912 when "The Big Six" refused to back down from their stand
against the Board of Control.

At the meeting of the New South Wales Cricket Association on
Monday night, 14 May 1906 it was ordered that the members of
the State team withdraw their promise to the Melbourne Cricket
Club to play under its direction during the forthcoming 1907–08
English tour of Australia. In essence the Association was
attempting to force obedience to the newly formed Board of
Control. The players refused and were suspended by the
Association.

On returning from Queensland Trumper, Cotter and Hopkins
were also suspended when they refused to withdraw their
promise. Trumper and his State team colleagues then released
the following statement to the press:

1. There is no disloyalty to the NSWCA in the act for which the
   cricketers have been suspended.
2. The Cricket Association has not the right to make an innocent act
   disloyal by calling it so, and the cricketers who intended no
   disloyalty have certainly justice on their side in resenting such
   procedure, and in refusing to submit to it because the pistol of
   suspension is held at their heads.
3. The Cricket Association's charge against the cricketers amounts
   to this: That in giving their promise to play against any English
   team brought to Australia next season by the Melbourne CC the

166

cricketers have hindered not the Association but the Board of Control. This cannot be disloyalty to the Association since it does not manage international cricket. But no loyalty to any board of control for international cricket can reasonably be demanded from any individual cricketer until such a board is in existence fully clothed with free power to manage international cricket.

In retaliation for the role played by Victor Trumper and Monty Noble in masterminding the above press release the Association gave the Paddington Club one week in which to suspend both players. Failing this the Club would itself face suspension. Trumper's Club resisted and disqualification seemed imminent until Trumper and Noble eventually resigned from Paddington. At its meeting on 16 July 1906 the Association decided that this was not to its liking and ordered the Paddington Club to suspend both players. The Club baulked at doing this and was suspended. Finally in early August 1906 the Club was reinstated when it finally suspended Trumper and Noble. The Association bureaucrats soon relented, however, and Trumper and Noble turned out for Paddington in the opening matches of the new 1906–07 season.

The winter months of 1906 meant business as usual for the firm of Trumper and Carter, at 108 Market Street in the heart of Sydney's retail shopping area. Anecdotes exist concerning Trumper's compassionate responses to needy individuals entering the precincts of his store. Monty Noble in *The Game's the Thing* described how a group of newspaper boys entered the shop to buy cricket equipment and, having assisted the youngsters to select the necessary items, he looked down at the few pieces of silver placed in his hand then sent them away with gloves, bats, balls and money. Just before Christmas those boys bought a pair of vases with that same money and presented them to their idol. Victor always kept these on his mantelpiece and one day while her husband was at work Annie rearranged the living room and its contents. On returning home Victor noticed the absence of his precious mementoes. Their return was immediate and permanent. This incident helps to reveal one facet of Victor's personality: his keen humanity for others less fortunate than himself. It should not be construed as an example of a man who gave everything to others because he was a soft touch or cared nothing for worldly goods.

Hanson Carter inherited his father's Yorkshire business acumen and it is extremely difficult to visualise him standing by while his partner lavished sporting goods with philanthropic abandon on all and sundry who came into the shop with a tale of woe. Equally preposterous is the scenario of Trumper, an aware and intelligent family man mindful of his responsibility towards the material needs of his own young family, squandering profits on complete strangers. Victor now not only had a wife to support in the extended family quarters of the Trumper house in 112 Paddington Street but a bonny baby daughter as well, Anne Louise or "Nancy" as Victor affectionately called her. Indeed evidence suggests that he was as mindful of the value of a pound as the next family man in Edwardian Sydney. In April 1906 he wrote the following letter to the New South Wales Cricket Association, having previously requested the £5 playing fee owed to him under Rule 19:

> In reply, I beg to state it must be well known to the executive of your association that I am interested in a sporting business in this city, which supplies all cricket requisites. Considering that it is ten years since I first represented the State and that I am still playing and probably will do so for a while yet, I find it very strange that the firm of Trumper and Carter has not been favoured with the orders at the disposal of the association. Had this been done I should have been very pleased to continue playing for your association, under your rule 18, as I have done in the past; but, under the above circumstances, I feel justified in playing under your rule 19. Mr Carter and myself are representing the State and we are the only two players actually interested in a sporting business and whilst this is so I consider that Trumper and Carter should receive the favour of your orders, but till it is done my services are at the disposal of your association under rule 19.*

The Secretary, Percy Bowden, sent off a cheque for £5 with the following curt reply, "Note your remarks re orders at the disposal of the association, and beg to inform you that your firm has been given more orders than any other firm."

The Trumpers' neat Victorian terrace house with its first-floor bedroom windows decorated with lacework wrought iron, was only a short tram ride from the sports store at the conclusion of

---

* Rule 19 related to the payment of a player whose business was disadvantaged while he played for the State.

Victor's working day. It was also within easy walking distance of Paddington Town Hall where Victor and his father Charles walked through balmy midsummer evenings to attend cricket meetings, Victor in his role of first-grade selector and Charles as a vice-president of the club. During the remainder of the interval during which he remained with Paddington Victor regularly attended these monthly meetings as a member of the club committee, yet throughout them all he remained enthusiastically alert but singularly silent. Once when questioned about this he quietly considered the query and then replied with his disarming smile, "If I don't talk, you know there are others who make up for it."*

H. V. "Ranji" Hordern, the North Sydney dentist, so named because of his swarthy complexion, recalled in his autobiography, *Googlies* his first encounter with Trumper at Hampden Park:

> He collected 17 off my initial over, four fours and a one, which latter, by the way, was stopped by Reg Duff on the boundary. That night I dined with three cricketing friends, all bowlers of first-class standard, and during the meal I became very enthusiastic about Trumper; said what a marvel I thought he was, and what he had done to me. One of my friends said: "How many did he get off your first over?" I promptly said:
> "Seventeen."
> They all three became thoughtful, and after a minute or two confessed their own secrets—my seventeen was the best performance of the four of us!

In his autobiography *My Cricketing Days*, Charlie Macartney recounted an incident which took place when he wore the pads for Gordon against Paddington before Trumper changed to the former club. Monty Noble delivered a fast lifting ball outside the off stump which was deflected by the diminutive batsman into Jim Kelly's gloves. The unanimous appeal by Trumper and the rest of the Paddington team was ignored by the umpire. Unsettled by the reprieve Macartney slashed wildly at the next ball sending it sailing over the fence. At the end of the over Victor Trumper approached the batsman and advised in his soft yet vibrant voice, "Don't throw it away, slogger, you'll be given

---

* *The Referee*, 14 July 1915.

'out' many more times when you're not out than you will 'not out' when you are out."

During the period before Christmas in 1906 Trumper indicated his intention to travel south to Melbourne and Adelaide for the impending Sheffield Shield matches. However, when the departure date was brought forward by two days it meant that he and Hanson Carter would have had to leave an assistant in charge of their sports depot on the Saturday before Christmas and on Christmas Eve—the two most important retail shopping days of the business calendar—so Victor declined to join the team, although Carter went as State wicket-keeper.

New South Wales's loss was Paddington's gain as he elegantly annihilated Burwood on the Sydney Cricket Ground in late December 1906 with 172 scorching runs in 105 minutes, hitting 3 sixes and 22 fours. On Boxing Day before a good crowd on the Number Two ground he hit a debonair 92, including 3 sixes and a four from 4 balls, before he was run out while batting for Mr Macarthur's XI against a Western Districts side. He also took 2 wickets for 36.

Trumper spent some days in the Blue Mountains over the New Year period visiting the Three Sisters Lookout and other scenic locations with Annie and Nancy, consequently he did not play against South Australia in Sydney.

The Western Districts match precipitated a return encounter at Easter 1907 when Monty Noble led a side over the Blue Mountains by train to play at Lithgow and Bathurst. The main drawcard for the spectators was of course Trumper and he did not disappoint anyone. On Good Friday Trumper delighted the local coal miners and their families with his skill as he made 93 not out in just under the hour on the Lithgow Showground, the visitors scoring 281 and the locals 146. The guests were entertained at dinner that night before moving on to Bathurst where Trumper pleased the spectators with 130 sparkling runs, again top-scoring for his side.

Trumper's consistent form for Paddington in the 1906–07 season was largely instrumental in the club gaining the coveted Rawson Cup. He hit an aggregate of 945 runs at an average of 85.91. His last display was documented by the *Sydney Morning Herald*:

> There was a big crowd at the Hampden Park Oval to see the Paddington–Central Cumberland engagement, and the people left in

170

the gloaming thoroughly satisfied with the cricket they had witnessed. They saw Trumper out on one of his bowling annihilating expeditions. The cricket was steady until Trumper was about 125; then he opened his shoulders and batted with his best brilliance. He was in two and a quarter hours for 212 out of 317.

Trumper had his final innings for the season on the first day of the final competition round, and Charlie Macartney in his autobiography told a typical tale about the great cricketer. With only one Saturday remaining to conclude the Sydney Grade competition, all five feet four inches of the Gordon all-rounder sauntered into Trumper's shop enquiring, "Vic, how many runs will I have to make on Saturday to beat your average for the season?" With paper and pencil the Golden Cricketer swiftly calculated the precise figure, and that weekend at Chatswood Gordon went to the wickets and Macartney blasted 224 not out. Victor was the first to offer his congratulations on the following Monday, "Well, you did it Charlie, and with a bit to spare after all!"

The Market Street store was a popular rendezvous for many of Sydney's leading sporting personalities, one of these being James J. Giltinan, who with Trumper was the co-founder of Rugby League football in Australia. He became a partner in Victor's George Street Sports Depot after the 1909 Tour of England when Hanson Carter began working with his father's undertaking business at Waverley.

It was the great cricketer's friendship with the master Rugby exponent, Herbert Henry "Dally" Messenger which expedited negotiations completed during August 1907 leading to the latter's first game in the professional code against the touring New Zealanders in Sydney. Besides sitting on the committee of the newly instituted Australian Rugby League as its founding treasurer, Trumper also made his premises available for the league's initial meetings.

The 1907–08 Australian cricket season was dominated by news of the English touring team, yet one innings by Trumper for Paddington had the cricket world agog; it even reached the English press. Monty Noble recalled in *The Game's the Thing*: "Victor had a particularly keen dislike for the boaster. He was not resentful, never harboured ill-feeling, and seldom retaliated. If the fate of the match had been decided he would occasionally allow a young bowler to get him out so that he might derive some encouragement thereby; but, if he deemed it necessary, not to show his own superiority, but to administer a corrective to an over-confident opponent, he would drive home the lesson with all the force of his wonderful ability."

Tommy Rose, an impetuous young leg-spinner from the Waverley Club eagerly revealed to his team-mates that he had perfected a ball that would keep Victor quiet when they next confronted Paddington. Hanson Carter casually let this news hang in the air when the two business partners were conversing in their shop. It was decided that Tommy needed reminding that success in Sydney cricket was not won by boasting.

Fortunately for Rose he did not face Trumper in the first innings when Waverley and Paddington met in late October 1907 as the Australian batsman was bowled by Hill for 24. On the second Saturday, 26 October, cricket fans travelled to Hampden Park by every available means, even though the local team had already won on the first innings. The *Sydney Morning Herald* reporter at the match filed this description:

> The Australian Eleven man and N. Winning opened Paddington's second innings, and in 35 minutes 120 runs were obtained. Trumper, revelling in his work, punished Rose to the extraordinary extent of 32 off one over, and 50 off nine balls, which is a record in this class of match in Australia. In one over he hit two fours and four sixers, and facing the Waverley leg-break bowler at the fourth ball of his succeding over he hit three more sixers. His hitting was magnificent and naturally the Paddington crowd were delighted. It may be mentioned in connection with the time occupied over the runs that several minutes were lost in recovering the ball from the back yards of the residences into which the drives of Trumper had despatched it.

The sublime cricketer was eventually stumped by Hanson Carter going down the wicket to Howard when on 89. Rose's figures for the day were 1 wicket for 77 runs.

An unusual incident during Trumper's bombardment of the terrace houses on the ground's perimeter provided additional copy for those reporters present. One policeman standing inside the boundary fence was continually forced to change position while dodging Trumper's off-drives. The policeman just managed to avoid fifteen youngsters and the fence on which they were leaning as they were precipitated into the field of play. Fortunately no one was injured. The incident did not bother Trumper in the least as he continued to pound the ball sweetly in all directions before Carter stumped him.

Trumper was soon at it again when the New South Wales First Eleven met the Next Fifteen to determine the State side to play the English tourists. In early November 1907 he totalled 160 in 110 minutes before becoming stranded between the wickets. His score included 3 sixes and 20 fours. The touring MCC Eleven humbled the home State later in the month, winning easily by 408 runs, Sydney Barnes snaring 6 for 24 on the soggy pitch, and Trumper reaching 38 in the New South Wales first total of 101. Against Petersham, five days later, he and Monty Noble gathered 206 runs in 65 minutes, Trumper's contribution being 136 (3 sixes and 19 fours). One week after, versus South Australia, his 135 made in 179 minutes did not prevent the visitors winning in a high scoring match by just 20 runs.

All interest was now fixed on the First Test in Sydney in which Monty Noble led the Australians to an exciting two-wicket victory. Trumper, who opened, made 43 and 3. A. O. Jones's illness caused him to miss the first three internationals as captain, the tourists being ably led by F. L. Fane.

In Melbourne for the Second Test Trumper and Macartney gave the home team a sound start with their opening stand of 84, Trumper losing his wicket one run short of his half-century. Opening with his captain in the second innings 126 appeared for the partnership until he was trapped in front of his stumps for an invaluable 63. Chasing 282 runs to square the series, England scrambled home by one wicket, aided by good cricket from Hobbs, Fane, Hutchings, Braund and Barnes. G. R. Hazlitt misdirected a throw to Carter which would have ensured cricket's first tied Test; this of course was to occur almost 52 years later in Brisbane between Australia and the West Indies.

Australia won the next two Tests easily, by 245 runs in Adelaide and 308 in Melbourne. Trumper's contribution of 4 and 0 in Adelaide was followed incredibly by his making "a pair of spectacles" in the latter Test. This was the first occasion that he was forced to retire without scoring in both innings in any match of his entire career. That such a calamity should befall their hero was viewed as a national disaster by cricket followers throughout Australia, and treated as such by the nation's press.

Having avoided the dreaded duck—he made 10 in the first innings—the dashing cricketer completely regained his composure in his last Test innings for the series at Sydney in late February 1908. The ball was kicking viciously when he came in to bat with Australia five wickets down and in trouble. The first two deliveries he faced from Barnes rose abruptly, the second rapping him on the gloved hand. Trumper usually batted without gloves or with just one on his right hand when playing on a truculent pitch. He preferred bats without rubber handles, delighting in the direct contact his fingers made with the string which he usually roughened with a piece of glass. He often shaved the back of the blade of the bat to raise the centre of gravity as he held his hands very high on the bat's handle.

The third ball from Barnes rapped Trumper on the pads and the voices of all the close-in English fieldsmen went up in a unified appeal as Umpire Hannah's stentorian, "Not out!" rang around the Sydney arena. After he made his first run he was missed by Rhodes from Barnes at silly mid-on as the ball popped viciously. That was to be the only chance he gave as he gradually gained ascendancy over the English bowling. He reached his 50 in 94 minutes and brought up his three figures by characteristically driving Barnes to the off pickets, having taken two hours and 54 minutes. His next fifty occupied only 50 minutes with a series of flashing pulls and drives. J. C. Davis portrayed his eventual dismissal:

> He [Trumper] tried to hit Rhodes to the on, but the ball flew high over and behind the bowler's head, and Gunn took the catch. He batted 4 hours and hit 18 fours. It was in every way a great innings, played at a critical time uphill, and fully merited the zestful applause that greeted him as he retired.*

Australia won this Fifth Test by 49 runs and the series by four matches to one. Victor Daley penned the following tribute in the *Bulletin* to the hero of the hour:

TRUMPER

Ho Statesmen, Patriots, Bards make way!
Your fame has sunk to zero;
For Victor Trumper is today
Our one Australian hero
High purpose glitters in his eye,
He scorns the filthy dollar,
His splendid neck, says Mrs Fry,

---

* Trumper scored 166 in his second innings.

Is innocent of collar.
Is there not, haply, in the land
Some native-born Murillo
To paint, in colours rich and grand,
This Wielder of the Willow?
Nay, rather let a statue be
Erected his renown to,
That future citizens might see
The gods their sires bowed down to.
Evoe Trumper! As for me
It all ends with the moral
That fame grows on the Willow Tree
And no more on the laurel.

The above poem was inspired by a gushing article in the English magazine, *V.C.* written by Mrs C. B. Fry, wife of the future England captain which began:

There is something peculiarly satisfactory in his having such a suitable name. Victor Trumper, with a real healthy, fresh, pink skin, a long muscular neck, and small, keen, bright eyes. Nothing sad about those eyes, not for one moment. A pair of very fine arms, splendid forearms, wrists, and hands; the whole together makes up a very perfect telephonic communication between his eye and bat. Rather sturdy legs, which never are between the wickets or on the edge of a very wide boundary, but try all day.

When Trumper, chasing the ball, comes towards you, the air seems to divide; he makes a buzz of power, something like you associate with a very first-rate motor-car. When he bats, if you are fond of cricket in the right sort of way, to you then will Trumper's batting be like reading Robert Louis Stevenson's description of some great granite rocks. "There they stand, for all the world like their neighbours ashore; only the salt water sobbing between them instead of the quiet earth, and clots of sea-pink blooming on their sides instead of heather; and the great sea-conger to wreathe about the base of them instead of the poisonous viper of the land."

It is good and pleasant to watch cricket, with the same mind's eye that glories in a beautifully written description. His timing has the exactness, rhythm, and fit of the ocean-going ship's piston-rod—true. Quite naturally his bat hits the ball. Owing to the fibre of the hit a beautiful stroke is the outcome, and this to almost every ball which is bowled. He shifts his feet, steps across, over and back with infinite variety and ease, he can play any bowling on any wicket, not from any particular luck, but just sheer natural ability. He is a poet of cricket; he has a poet's extra sense, touch and feeling.

Trumper can play, with his bat, a cricket ball as Paganini played his violin; to him it is alive; he plays his strokes by nature, in the easiest possible way, to do it well, and get all there is to be got out of that particular stroke, a note. Trumper, is an artist. Some day someone will paint his portrait: it will be hung in a National Portrait Gallery; he will be dressed in white, with his splendid neck bared to the wind, standing on short green grass, against a blue sky; he will be waiting for the ball the orchestra to strike up. Not even a bowler need go away regretfully from this healthy, strong picture; so easily imagined—a white-flannelled knight.

The 1909 Tour of England

The summer of 1908–09 was marred by Trumper catching scarlet fever which prevented his participation in any of the Sheffield Shield matches. Just before his illness he smote 2 sixes and 19 fours in his 128 runs made on St Lukes Park, Burwood at the end of November, Paddington winning by 153 on the first innings. During December and January 1909 he played no cricket and some doubted if he would be able to tour England with the Australian Eleven. Speculation regarding his selection for the tour was widespread. *Cricket: A Weekly Record of the Game* mirrored the concern regarding Victor Trumper in Australia and England:

> Somewhat alarming rumours which everyone will hope have been much exaggerated, have recently been circulated respecting his health. The loss of such a player to the game would be nothing less than a tragedy.

The Australian Eleven played two matches against the Rest of Australia in Sydney and Melbourne before it departed for England. Trumper did not take the field in the second game and in the first he opened in his only appearance in first-class cricket for the season. He was given out before he had scored, caught at the wicket, after the ball apparently touched the pad and not his bat.

Almost four weeks later he showed a welcome return to form at Waverley blazing 10 sixes and 29 fours in his total of 260, the *Sydney Morning Herald* reporting:

> Many roads led to Waverley on Saturday, where Paddington were meeting the local club. The former required 129 to win, and had ten wickets to fall. Trumper was one of the not out and something big was expected of him. Nor were the spectators disappointed, for he played what is easily his best innings of the season. Waverley's 199 was left behind with only a couple of wickets down, the winning stroke being a six by Trumper off Meagher. Australia's most brilliant batsman was very quiet at first, but when he warmed up he dealt out severe punishment to the bowlers.

177

Trumper's 260 occupied 210 minutes and his second hundred was made incredibly in only 45 minutes.

Before their departure the Paddington Club farewelled Victor Trumper and Monty Noble at Bateman's Hotel where the Right Honorable G. H. Reid implored the Australian captain to make more use of Trumper's bowling in England, "Trumper has such a beautiful style," said the ex-Prime Minister of Australia, pausing in his speech to gather a picture in his mind's eye of the dashing cricketer in action. Victor replied, "I think that in Australia there may be something in Mr Reid's advice to our captain to use me as a bowler. Here where our international matches are played to a finish, were I to bowl, it would prolong the game and afford Mr Reid an opportunity of getting his 'forty winks'. In England, however, where matches are restricted to three days, I am of little use with the ball."

After a rousing welcome in Fremantle and dinner at the Orient Hotel the tourists steamed for Colombo where they were invited to play the local team at the Galle Face ground, but declined to do so until after the series in England. Frank Laver said, "We were sorry we could not arrange a match today, the only reason being that we wanted to see as much of Colombo as possible." (*Ceylon Observer*, 8 April 1909.) Thus Victor Trumper was never seen in action on the Galle Face complex. When the *Orontes* docked in Naples, nine of the Eleven travelled to Pompeii to inspect the ruins, they then travelled overland to France and then London. Armstrong and Laver visited Monte Carlo and Trumper spent three days in Paris.

English cricket enthusiasts awaited the summer with relish and the coming of Trumper was anticipated eagerly. The following appeared in the publication, *Cricket at the Breakfast Table*:

> Vickery, Vickery Vock,
> The ball went over the clock,
> The knock was Vic's,
> He scored a six,
> Vickery, Vickery, Vock.

In the same publication a cartoon depicted an unblemished and glistening Crystal Palace before Trumper arrived at the crease. A second picture showed the glass structure after he had batted half an hour with 166 glass frames shattered.

In the opening tour match at Trent Bridge the supreme

Trumper at Colombo in 1909, inscribed on reverse:
    To Victor Trumper as a memento of a few hours' chat in Colombo, from
    his Ceylon friends,

                                            S. P. Foenander

The tourists inspect a Roman Senator's house in Pompeii. Trumper is third from the right.

batsman reassured those critics who considered he should not tour because of the severity of his illness. His sixth-wicket partnership of 142 with Warwick Armstrong took only 90 minutes and he contributed 94 to the score carving a dozen boundaries to all corners of the field, frequently cutting square and late and driving through the mid-wicket region. The tourists won the Notts. match by an innings and six runs, the above partnership ensuring victory. *Wisden* stated that "Trumper gave a delightful display."

A sound win by nine wickets in the Northamptonshire fixture a few days later was assisted by stylish batting from Armstrong, Bardsley and Trumper who scored 79, 76 and 56 respectively. Trumper hit 8 fours as he and Armstrong put on exactly 100 for the seventh wicket.

In the third match at Leyton Trumper hit freely and his contribution of 74 made in 65 minutes was by no means overshadowed by Bardsley's 219 or Ransford's 174, all three innings being a delight to the eye. Charlie Macartney in his second game on his first England visit made a useful 48 not out as Essex just managed to stave off defeat. The Gordon player was to distinguish himself by taking eleven wickets in the Third Test at Leeds on a wet wicket later in the tour.

Trumper's first century came in the ninth match versus Cambridge University after England's crushing victory in the First Test at Birmingham by ten wickets in which he could manage only 10 and 1. At Cambridge he opened with Bardsley and the first 25 minutes produced 50 runs, while the first-wicket partnership realised 122 runs in an hour and a quarter before an enthusiastic crowd. They saw Trumper reach his century after only 135 minutes stroking 19 fours with extreme grace, and he registered 133 out of 228 in 160 minutes. It was, as *Cricket: A Weekly Record of the Game* described, a "faultless and excellent innings." In the University innings he brought off a brilliant catch to ensure the follow on and although one whole day plus one hour was lost through rain, the Australians almost achieved a remarkable win.

In the next encounter at Southampton with Hampshire, he scored only 9 and 4 on a very wet ground; Australia 83 and 4 for 155, Hampshire 131 and 106. Charlie Macartney in his autobiography told how Trumper, having been dismissed late on the first day decided to walk to the docks past the warehouses after breakfast the following morning. One of the large ships berthed in the harbour was the White Star liner *Adriatic*. An official of the company recognised the famous cricketer and showed him over the vessel. By the time he arrived back at the ground it was almost lunch time and his team was in the field with several of the opposition back in the pavilion. Next day the Australians spent an enjoyable morning on that same liner before travelling to Bath.

Inclement weather which was a feature of the 1909 Tour of England was responsible for twenty-two of the thirty-nine matches remaining inconclusive. Nevertheless the visit remained highly successful financially, as a spectacle for lovers of cricket, and in the quest to retain The Ashes.

Many writers have tended to overlook Trumper's contributions to the fortunes of both Australian Elevens in England after his sublime successes in 1899 and 1902. His services to cricket as an ambassador and participant are beyond price. One anecdote, so aptly portrayed by Neville Cardus, illuminates this point superbly:

A famous cricketer, who, by bad luck, saw only one innings of Trumper in his life, raved about him. "It was against Surrey at The Oval in 1909," he said, "I'll never forget him"—he was recalling the

The Australians inspect the upper recreation deck of the Adriatic. *Trumper on the extreme left wearing a bowler hat.*

event forty years later—"never". "How many did he get that day?" I asked. "Oh about 20." We can no more get an idea of Trumper's batsmanship by looking at the averages and the statistics than we can find the essential quality of a composition of Mozart by adding up the notes. . . . Time after time he gave his wicket away usually to some hard-working unlucky bowler. Moreover he was constantly throwing down the gauntlet to fortune. He was really the living embodiment of the game; cricket incarnate, in an age when cricket was played as a game and loved for its glorious uncertainty.*

Trumper's second century which was scored at Derby in late July occupied just over two hours. Whilst partnering Gregory he hit 40 of the 50 runs made and with Hopkins put on 100 runs during the final 50 minutes of the afternoon's play. On the second morning he quickly cracked three fours but, having added 113 runs out of 201 in 125 minutes he was caught at the

* Cricket: The Great Ones.

wicket. *Wisden* commented, "Trumper late in the afternoon batted with quite his old brilliance." Australia's win at Derby by ten wickets owed much to Trumper's contribution.

Moving to Old Trafford for the Fourth Test with the international series at Australia 2, England 1, the visitors went in first and could muster only 147. Trumper managed just 2 before skying a ball from Barnes, and England replied with 119, Frank Laver taking 8 for 31. At lunch on the third day the "Cornstalks" were in the happy position of being unable to lose with Trumper and Ransford adding 89 in 80 minutes for the sixth wicket. Shortly after lunch Trumper hit an enormous drive off Blythe straight over the sightscreen and clean out of the ground for six. *Cricket: A Weekly Record of the Game*, commented, "Trumper set himself to score quickly and the play, with runs coming at a good rate, was interesting." This Test ended in a draw after Australia had declared at 9 for 279, Trumper 48, and England played out time to be 3 for 108.

Despite the fact that Noble's tourists had maintained their grip on The Ashes, interest throughout the country for the final Test Match at The Oval exemplified the extreme love for the game in England, 53,000 spectators paying admission money during the three-day contest.

Carr, the Kent leg-spinner, with help from Barnes had the tourists reeling at 4 for 58 and the scent of an England victory pervaded the warm London afternoon. Bardsley, who had been the only visiting player to show any aplomb against the spinners, was joined by Trumper who set about to compile one of his most underrated innings in Test cricket. He reached his 52 out of 87 in 80 minutes and scored 3 fours and a five from an over by Sharp. Just before that he off-drove in the air to Barnes from Carr's bowling when on 48, but the difficult chance was put to the grass. Nevertheless, the display was that of a batsman playing delightful cricket, not only for the enjoyment of Prince Edward and Princess Mary of Wales and the crowd, but for his team and country. *Cricket: A Weekly Record of the Game*, stated: "At 176 Trumper made a bad stroke and was caught at mid-on. He played a most valuable innings at a very critical time and of the 118 runs put on for the fifth wicket in 105 minutes made 73. His chief strokes were a 5 and eight 4s, the majority of them either off-drives or cuts."

Warren Bardsley made history in this Test with his 136 and

Trumper faces Barnes at Kennington Oval 1909.

130, with great assistance and encouragement from Trumper, becoming the first batsman to score two separate centuries in a Test Match, this final international ending in a draw.

Trumper's final century innings occurred at Blackpool versus an England eleven. He posted 49 in his first stay, dancing down the wicket to claim 6 fours, all drives. In the second innings he blasted one six clean out of the ground, made a five and stroked 21 fours in compiling 150 gifted runs in just 115 minutes without a single chance. He was bowled by the last ball of the game when attempting to hit Reeves over the fence. A player interested in preserving his average would have played out that last over. Altogether 1283 runs were made for the fall of 27 wickets at Blackpool, and at one stage Australia were in real danger of losing until Trumper's athletic figure graced the playing area.

At Cheltenham he captained Australia, won the toss and registered 48 runs but the game was drawn as Gloucestershire came close to vanquishing the tourists. Having made 80 at Lord's versus the MCC Trumper top-scored for Australia at Leyton with 71. Following the game against Mr Bamford's Eleven at Uttoxeter in early September, and with three fixtures remaining, he sailed alone for Sydney on the *Macedonia*. While returning home two separate parties of Australians took part in one-day games at the Galle Face ground in Colombo.

Trumper's 1909 Tour of England was a success: he realized 1435 runs in 34 matches with an average of 33.37 and took 19 catches. All this from a player who, six months previously, had been seriously ill. Due to the fiasco which was to rend Australian cricket asunder in 1912, English crowds had seen the last of the sublime cricketer, but as one aficionado stated, "I'll never forget him, never."

Trumper attracts an admiring audience, 1909 Tour.

The South African Visit and Trumper's Testimonial

Early in 1909 Charles Thomas Trumper, Victor's father, purchased from George Morgan Bales Lots 52, 53 and 54 situated between Help Street and Brown Street in Chatswood close to the railway line on its western side. Each block was 200 feet by 50 feet and the land, complete with a small orchard, was part of that originally allocated to an Isaac Nicholls by Crown grant in 1805. Charles Trumper used the land as collateral for a mortgage from a school teacher, Miss Annie Holten of North Sydney. With this money he had several cottages built on the Help Street land; the dwellings were named "Auckland" (in recognition of Charles's early boyhood life in that New Zealand city), "Louviana" (a combination of the names Louisa, Victor and Annie), and "Gunyah", an Aboriginal term for dwelling or house. Victor, Annie and Nancy lived in "Auckland", while Charles, his wife Louisa along with the other sons and daughters, occupied the other two houses. Una Margaret was now 23, May Louisa 17, Sydney Charles 13 and Charles Ernest Love had turned 11. Alice Mary Trumper had died tragically from tuberculosis at 112 Paddington Street on 27 October 1908 at the age of 24. She was unmarried and her death caused the Trumpers considerable grief, and expedited the move away from the Paddington home.

Charlie Macartney was a regular visitor to the Trumper property on Sunday mornings and practised cricket with Victor and young Sydney and Charles, who were to both later play with their illustrious brother for Gordon Cricket Club.*

Victor had by this time, late 1909, in partnership with J. J. Giltinan, opened a new sporting goods store which included a men's mercery department. The firm, Victor Trumper and Company, was situated at 317 George Street, opposite Paling's store and besides selling cricket equipment the shop catered for devotees of boxing, football, golf, tennis, bowls, croquet and

---

* Eric McElhone, unpublished address the Waverley Historical Society, 9 June 1975.

186

hockey. On his daily journey to the city, by train from Chatswood to St Leonards station and then by tram to the Milsons Point ferry, Trumper chose to sit in an unobtrusive position to avoid public scrutiny.

His first tilt at the bowling for his new club Gordon was unremarkable and took place at Chatswood Oval late in November 1909. He was bowled in both innings, scoring 6 and 13. On one occasion while he was batting on Chatswood Oval the great batsman began violently waving his bat in the air. Nobody in the crowd knew what troubled him until he pointed the bat at the scoreboard, over which young Nancy was about to disappear. The Trumper's new property in Help Street adjoined Benjamin's Store and stables and when Victor noticed a groom mistreating a high-spirited horse he severely remonstrated with the employee who was dismissed for his actions. When he heard of this Victor spoke to the management and pleaded the groom's case. Subsequently he was reinstated to a different position.

Just before Christmas in 1909, Monty Noble formally announced his retirement from first-class cricket. His position as New South Wales captain would soon be filled by Victor Trumper, but not before a clash with the Cricket Association prevented his appearance in Sheffield Shield matches during the 1909–10 season. Like all men of high principle Trumper could be extremely stubborn, as his letter to Percy Bowden in January 1910 suggests:

> In reply to your notice of the 4th instant, I must state that I am not available for the forthcoming match against South Australia. Your selectors will not be surprised. For the first time in the history of Australian cricket your Association has adopted the English custom of appointing the captain of their State team but has not followed that custom and appointed a senior player, providing he could play in a majority of matches. Your association in not doing so is an injustice to me, and leaves me only one course to adopt, and that is to withdraw from the eleven. On my arrival from England the First Eleven was selected to play against the Second Eleven, and a captain other than myself appointed by the selection committee. I immediately withdrew from that team, and a similar action of the committee regarding the team for South Australia and Victoria necessitated me dropping out of the teams also. Had the selection of the captain been left to the different teams, I would have no objection whatever to playing under any captain, no matter even if he be the junior member, and (if necessary) giving him any advice at my disposal. I

would like to state that Mr Diamond is a very dear friend of mine, and this action I am taking must not be construed as being against him. Under usual cricket conditions I would have been pleased to have made the trip to South Australia and Victoria in accordance with my promise to some of the leading cricket people in South Australia, but, owing to your committee's new action in appointing the new captain I could not possibly do so. I greatly regret that the treatment of your association leaves me no other course but to retire from the team to meet South Australia.

Trumper's stand achieved the desired result as he was appointed captain for New South Wales for the following 1910–11 season. He led his State splendidly on twenty-four occasions during his career for 15 wins, 4 draws and only 5 losses.

During the C. T. B. Turner Testimonial in which the renowned bowler lost his wicket to Frank Laver for 8 in the first innings, Trumper made a dazzling 105 compiled in 120 minutes at his only appearance in first-class cricket for the 1909–10 season. He did not bat in the second innings of the match as he had a heavy cold. He quickly recovered his health with an energetic display against Glebe at Chatswood in early February, falling to Albert Cotter, after making 87. At the end of the month at Birchgrove Reserve he was in devastating form, as the *Sydney Morning Herald* report suggests:

> The feat of scoring centuries in two separate innings in a first grade match was accomplished by Trumper for Gordon *v.* Balmain. The difficulty accompanying such an achievement may be understood when it is remembered that only two afternoons, and short ones at that, are allotted for the matches. This performance is seldom enough accomplished when the time is unlimited, but to do so when the play does not exceed about eight hours, and, besides, the opposite side must have an innings, make the accomplishment one of very great merit. As might be expected Trumper met with an ovation on returning to the pavilion. His two scores were 105 and 103, and on each occasion he was out caught Walker, bowled Sullivan.

Trumper scored for Gordon in his first season with that club an aggregate of 518 runs at an average of 47.09.

He greeted the new 1910–11 season characteristically, leading Gordon to a 62-run win at Parramatta Oval during the October long weekend. His vigorous 105 had the Central Cumberland fieldsmen constantly retrieving the ball from its resting place next to the boundary. Trumper's batting in grade cricket that summer ensured that Gordon won its first Sydney premiership. Excitement in cricket circles was high in Sydney as the first South African team to visit Australian shores prepared to face New South Wales under Trumper's leadership in the Springbok's third tour fixture.

He scored 70 and 78, on both occasions making opening stands exceeding one hundred with Warren Bardsley, and led his State to an exciting victory by three wickets. Trumper's batting against the South African bowling this season was extraordinary, and lest the strength of the visitors be underestimated, the opinion of the Australian selector, Frank Iredale, is reproduced from the *Sydney Morning Herald*: "They are a magnificent bowling team, and they have shown a variety of attack which has never before been witnessed in Australia. We heard that when these googly bowlers were on our billiard table pitches, they would not be able to turn the ball. We saw them in this match, and we saw three of them do so—Faulkner, Vogler, and Schwarz. Their off-breaks were as big as any we have seen since the days of McKibbin. Of course, so far as their success or failure against our players is concerned, it must not be forgotten that they had in both innings to open against two of the finest batsmen in the world, who have always shown ability to play any bowling."

The First Test on the Sydney Cricket Ground in early December, 1910 saw Trumper run out for 27, while Bardsley 132 and Hill 191, registered a second-wicket partnership of 224 to boost Australia's total to 528. Scoring 174 and 240, the South Africans succumbed to Cotter and Whitty, the opening bowlers taking eight wickets each in the match.

Moving to the Melbourne Test, Trumper, bowled by Pegler for 34 at his first attempt, replied with 159 glorious runs at his second, when his team seemed certain to lose. The *Sydney Morning Herald* reporter in Melbourne described his dismissal on the fourth day:

Trumper and Kelleway resumed to the bowling of Faulkner and Sinclair. The Gordon champion did not take long to get his eye in. Right from the jump he went at the bowling, his late-cutting again being magnificent. Faulkner was bowling better than on the previous day, but his short ones were smashed to the boundary. Several times the "Incomparable" placed the ball between the five men clustered between cover and Sherwell (the wicket-keeper). Kelleway

189

was playing the rock and letting his more brilliant partner do the scoring. Trumper moved rapidly to 159, and then took his quietus from Faulkner. He tried his favourite late cut, but the ball kept low, and just touching the bat found its way to the wicket. Trumper had compiled his runs in 171 minutes. It was a magnificent display, brilliant right from the outset, sparkling with beautiful strokes. Fifteen times he found the railings, and once he belted a sixer. It was an innings worth coming a long way to see, and it proved that Trumper is still the same old Victor, and the brightest star in the cricket firmament.

South Africa, set 170 runs for victory, again fell to Cotter and Whitty making only 80 as Australia won by 89 runs.

While Trumper was annihilating the bowling of the visitors, far away in an English winter, newspaper posters emblazoned with "Trumper Victorious", "Trumper Again" or just simply "Trumper", conveyed some impression of the carnage he was wreaking on bowlers on the other side of the world.

The Adelaide Test began on 7 January 1911 and after Clem Hill lost the toss South Africa registered an impressive 482. Australia were soon 3 down for 111 when Trumper left the pavilion amid tumultuous applause. Llewellyn the left-arm slow to medium pace bowler had taken three wickets for 15 runs. Unruffled by the extreme moment of the occasion Trumper and Bardsley scored freely by sharp running between the wickets whilst Faulkner fielded faultlessly on the square-leg boundary. At lunch Trumper was 11, Bardsley 26 and the Australian total 141 for the loss of three wickets. After the interval Trumper registered his first four of the day, all run, by straight driving the giant South African Sinclair just wide of his outstretched hand. In Llewellyn's next over he pulled two successive good length deliveries to the cycle track bringing his score into the thirties. Bardsley was scoring mainly on the leg side with Trumper hitting freely all round the wicket, taking 15 from a Sinclair over which was to prove the most expensive in the match.

With Faulkner bowling from the river end, the champion reached his 50 in just thirty minutes with an elegant late cut and an off-drive, both strokes sending the ball racing to the boundary. Australia then reached 200, the last 50 of which occupied only 26 minutes. Among the elated spectators present was the youthful A. G. Moyes, who recalled the experience in his book, *Australian Batsmen*:

190

I was a schoolboy at Adelaide at that time, saw the innings, can still picture the majesty of it all: the amazing range of strokes, the footwork, the certainty with which he beat the field, finding gaps, forcing changes in the field, and then hitting the ball into the open space just created. This was perfection of cricket, the Master creating a masterpiece for all time, for eternity.

Trumper ran into the sixties by cutting Sinclair for four and then driving him for three. Nourse was swinging the ball prodigiously in the air but Trumper continued with his feast of runs even after Bardsley left the arena, trapped in front by an in-swinger. Trumper was now glancing the ball with fascinating precision to the leg boundary under his upraised left leg, a stroke of sheer originality and daring which only he could create and master.

Trumper executes his "yorker shot".

Trumper himself called his invention the "yorker shot" and he played the stroke by lifting either the right or the left leg at the moment of impact. Sir Hector Clayton related how Trumper while coaching schoolboys at Sydney Grammar School practised the "yorker shot" for three months before including it in his repertoire. Alf Jones, former Sheffield Shield and Test umpire, told E. W. Kann of the Sydney *Sun* that he saw Trumper play the ball under either leg depending on the direction and trajectory, usually a yorker on the leg stump being dispatched under his upraised right leg.

The Adelaide crowd continued to roar its approval as Trumper raced into the nineties by taking nine runs from a Faulkner over with a succession of straight drives which umpire Crockett just managed to avoid by leaping in the air. With Clem Hill now at the crease, Trumper drove Faulkner to bring up his century and when he was on 109 tea was taken.

During the interval Bill Ferguson who was scoring in the Test overheard the following conversation in the visitors' dressing room, Llewellyn gently rebuking Pegler, "What are you playing at, Syd? Isn't it time that you removed Victor for good?" The bowler replied gravely, "I have never bowled any better in my life, but he seems to make me put the ball exactly where he wants!"

Resuming his innings the Gordon genius repeatedly jumped down the pitch to Schwarz and Llewellyn, seemingly unconcerned about the danger of a stumping. Schwarz in desperation turned to his captain and exclaimed, "It's no use, I just can't bowl to him." Sherwell said incredulously, "You're not trying to get him out are you?" "Yes, of course, Percy, what do you think I'm trying to do?" the bemused bowler replied. Sherwell, with worldly wisdom, retorted, "Forget it. Victor will get himself out when he is ready."

Hill departed, caught in the long field, and Armstrong joined in to see Trumper reach 150 after 175 minutes at the crease; he was now scoring off virtually every ball. Drinks were taken and Sinclair soon bowled the big Melbourne cricketer for 30 and Carter, taking his place, looked on as Trumper exceeded his Melbourne score of 159 amid prolonged applause. He now went after Pegler driving him to the long-on fence, grandly lifting the next ball to the cycle track and late-cutting the very next to the pickets to bring up Australia's 400. Carter, attempting to emulate

192

his brilliant partner, misread a Schwarz top-spinner and was trapped in front of his stumps. Despite the excellent performance of the Springbok googly bowlers in tying up most batsmen in the series, the visitors' attack relied equally on medium pace and fast medium bowling.

As "Tibby" Cotter made his entrance to the Adelaide ground after Carter's departure, the crowd hummed approvingly in anticipation of his cutomary big hitting, but he played solely for his more illustrious partner who now had reached 192 by glancing Schwarz to the boundary. As time approached 6 o'clock Trumper brought his score to 197, then a single made him 198. Amid a tumultuous roar the next delivery went racing away for four to bring up his double century, only the fifth batsman in Test cricket history to reach this mark. Soon afterwards stumps were drawn and the *Sydney Morning Herald*'s representative at the scene wrote:

> To the mathematician it may be of interest to know that Trumper scored 208 not out, that he batted for very nearly four hours, that 25 boundaries punctuated his figures, and that not one single chance marred the symmetry of the exhibition; but the cricket enthusiast likes to know that it was a graceful and brilliant exposition of the national game. Trumper took length balls on the off peg and hooked them to the leg boundary. He forgot that the best wicket-keeper in the world was crouching behind him, and drove fast and slows indiscriminately. Off theory that the cautious tyro leaves alone, Trumper tackled vigorously, and cut and drove hot-footed to the railings. There was no orthodoxy about his display. The *summum bonum* was runs, lots of them, and Victor got them in superb style. One after another the champion bowlers of Africa came up to the scratch, each time to be repulsed disastrously. Schwarz came with his googlies, Faulkner with his wrong 'uns, Pegler with his fast ones, Sinclair with his perfect length and nasty yorkers, Nourse with his swerves, and Llewellyn with his mixed left-hand deliveries, but it was all the same to Trumper. One after another they retired baffled, but the "Incomparable" went on as if for ever. The crowd cheered his fifties and his centuries. They cheered him when he left behind his Melbourne 159, when he passed W. G. Grace's 170. Syd. Gregory's 201, and Aubrey Faulkner's 204. A few numbers more and he would have eclipsed Murdoch's 211, when 6 o'clock mercifully gave respite to the poor trundlers. The crowd rushed the ground, and Trumper fought his way to the pavilion amid a seething and cheering multitude.

The Adelaide *Advertiser* remarked:

> His had been one of the most brilliant exhibitions ever seen at the
> Adelaide Oval. His freedom and forcefulness all round the wicket
> were wonderful, and his precision in placing the ball between the
> fieldsmen at will was loudly applauded. During his innings he did
> not give a single chance, which makes the big score all the more
> meritorious. Six bowlers were tried during the day, but all were
> treated in the same manner by Trumper. Keen work in the field
> prevented many runs.

Indeed Sherwell behind the stumps allowed only one ball past
him all day and it went for four byes. On leaving the ground
Trumper returned to his hotel, enjoyed a hot bath and a leisurely
meal and retired early, having completed a most successful day's
toil.

Early the following day he was left without partners as
Australia were all out for 465. His 214 not out placed him among
those immortals who had reached two hundred in a Test Match:
W. L. Murdoch, 211 at The Oval in 1884; S. E. Gregory, 201 at
Sydney in 1894–95; R. E. Foster, 287 at Sydney in 1903–04; and
G. A. Faulkner, 204 in the Second Test at Melbourne in January
1911. Among the five only Trumper remained unconquered at
the finish.

Despite this heroic innings the South Africans went on to win
the Adelaide Test in a thrilling finish by 38 runs, Faulkner
making 115 in the second innings and Schwarz taking 4 for 48 to
help dismiss Australia for 339, Trumper being bowled by
Llewellyn for 28.

The home side now led the rubber by two matches to one as
both teams journeyed back to Melbourne for the Fourth Test.
Sherwell won the toss, and rain during the night tempted him to
field first, yet despite his strategy Australia reached 328,
Trumper making only 7. H. V. Hordern, the North Sydney
dentist, with uncanny flight and control of googly and top-spin,
joined with Bill Whitty in limiting the Springbok score to 205.
Opening in the second innings Trumper was this time dominant
again as he stroked the ball where he willed in his dashing 87.
The home side made 578 and South Africa could not master
Hordern who claimed 5 for 66 and Australia won easily by 530
runs.

In the last Test in Sydney, Australia won by seven wickets,
Trumper's contribution being 31 and 74 not out. Charlie

The Australian Team for the Fourth Test Match v. South Africa in Melbourne, 1911.

Horden	Kellaway	Gehrs	Ransford	Matthews
Armstrong	Cotter	Hill	Trumper	Whitty
Carter				Bardsley

Macartney, omitted from the side in Melbourne, came back with a grand 137 and 56. Altogether in the series Victor Trumper amassed 661 runs in nine innings with an average of 94.43, well ahead of any other Australian batsman; Bardsley's average was 63.66, Hill's 53.12. In all Tests against South Africa in 1902 and 1910–11, Trumper's aggregate now stood at 900 with a 75-run average. A patron of Lord's on reading of Trumper's triumph, exclaimed, "I'd willingly sail round the world just to see him bat!"*

As he had done so often in the past, Trumper greeted the new 1911–12 season with a century; 112 not out for Victor Trumper's Eleven versus the Marrickville District Eleven in late September

---

* Town and Country Journal, 29 January 1913.

1911. In the Sheffield Shield contests he was to captain New South Wales to ultimate victory for the second successive year. This was the jubilee year of international cricket in Australia, the first English team arriving in Melbourne on Christmas Eve 1861, led by H. H. Stephenson.

Pelham Warner who captained the MCC in 1911–12, was struck ill after scoring a breezy 151 in Adelaide against South Australia, and enjoyed no further participation in the tour. On the train to Melbourne he suffered a ruptured duodenal ulcer which resulted in serious complications. J. W. H. T. Douglas, who had out-punched "Snowy" Baker to win the final of the middleweight boxing in the 1908 Olympic Games, took over team leadership. At a civic reception in the Melbourne Town Hall, Douglas, quoting another famous boxer, Bob Fitzsimmons, said amid laughter, "I ain't much at making speeches, but I'll fight any man in the room."

At the annual meeting of the Board of Control for International Cricket in Australia, held at the headquarters of the Victorian Cricket Association, Clem Hill was unanimously elected captain for Australia during The Ashes series. Victor Trumper was nominated for the position of Australian selector along with Hill, Frank Iredale, Peter McAlister and Hugh Trumble. Trumper and Trumble missed out on the position, but Trumper, who gained four votes from a possible eleven for the selector's spot, was instead made vice-captain of the Eleven.

For an Australian eleven versus England in Brisbane in early December 1911, Trumper registered 30, caught J. W. Hearne, bowled Iremonger. Two days after the game's conclusion, Trumper's swash-buckling partner of numerous grand opening partnerships for New South Wales and Australia, Reg Duff, died suddenly from heart disease at the age of 33 in Sydney's Royal North Shore Hospital. He was survived by two brothers and two sisters, and Victor Trumper helped the family make the arrangements for the burial at the Gore Hill cemetery and persuaded his State team-mates to contribute towards the cost of the funeral. Their contributions came to only half the total required and the chivalrous cricketer paid the other half himself.

Trumper's classic 113 made in the First Test in Sydney, just after Reg Duff was buried, was at that time a record as he became the first to score six centuries in Anglo-Australian Tests, and the only Australian to register a hundred in that series. Seventeen thousand spectators packed the Sydney Cricket Ground to see their hero, batting at third drop, end the day needing 5 runs for his record century. He joined the contest with the score at 3 for 121 and began his display with a scorching on-drive to the pickets. Apart from an occasional flash of his wizardry he was content to wait for the loose ball, his first fifty taking him 98 minutes which was unusually slow for a Trumper Test innings, but which would be applauded today for its speed of compilation.

He was in for 25 minutes for his first 5 runs and when he finally took a single from Douglas the crowd burst into ironic applause as he shrugged his shoulders and smiled good-naturedly. He reached his half-century with a flashing straight drive from Foster's bowling, which sent the ball hurtling up the cycle track. He moved into the seventies by hooking Barnes for 2 and then on-drove him to the boundary. Taking few risks in the deepening gloom he reached the eighties with a series of neat cuts and off-drives, and when the umpires halted play he was 95 not out.

Strong westerly winds on the Saturday caused clouds of dust to envelop the arena but this did not divert Trumper from his goal. With Minnett batting strongly, the New South Wales captain late-cut Foster to the fence for his century amid wild applause. One elderly gentleman remarked, "I wouldn't have missed seeing him get the record for a five pound note." His dismissal occurred soon after when he swung hard at a short ball from Woolley and it lofted gently to Hobbs in the covers. His 113 took 226 minutes and included 12 fours, 3 threes, 9 twos and 38 singles.

Trumper's classic innings laid the foundation for an Australian win in this Test but England had won the initial international ten years previously and then lost the series. In 1911–12 the batting of Hobbs and Rhodes combined with Barnes's and Foster's brilliant bowling was to win back The Ashes for England. Despite his wonderful start to the series, Trumper did not regain his usual form until the final innings of the Fifth Test in Sydney, his last Test appearance for Australia. He opened in both innings making 5 in the first. Arriving at the wicket with Sydney Gregory, he got off the mark in the second attempt with a late cut for 3 through the slips from Barnes. He then hit four successive square cuts from the Staffordshire bowler, with Vine charging up and down the boundary in desperate attempts to intercept the ball. A bumper from Barnes added four to the sundries, then Douglas came into the attack and Trumper late cut one of his deliveries to the fence. Hitch relieved Foster and five men clustered in the slips only to see Trumper twice hook the Surrey speedster to the leg-side pickets. At lunch with the score at 70 without loss the ground began to fill as news of the opening stand reached the city. Whenever Trumper warmed to his task in Sydney grandmothers died in their thousands as the "bereaved" rushed from their places of work to the Cricket Ground to see him in action.

When play resumed Gregory was out to Barnes who was swinging the ball very late and utilizing some accurate bouncers. Hill partnered Trumper who continued to attack with some wristy cuts. The sky soon became cloudy and the light uncertain when Hill played the ball on to his stumps while facing Foster. The *Sydney Morning Herald* described Trumper's dismissal:

> Trumper pulled Barnes to square leg, where Rhodes stopped it, and then glanced one prettily to the boundary. Then he made the crowd happy by lifting Barnes high to the grandstand reaching 50. But this was his limit. He was dismissed by a fine spectacular catch by Woolley at short square leg.

Despite local optimism Australia succumbed for 292 and England won by 70 runs to complete a lesson in cricket to the host nation, winning the series by four to one. Trumper's final display was described by George Gunn, who was in the field, as a "perfect peach".

By this time the infamous fiasco involving Trumper, Hill, Cotter, Armstrong, Carter and Ransford and the Board of Control had erupted and the "Big Six" had withdrawn from the team to tour England for the Triangular Tournament in 1912. The problem largely revolved around the "Big Six's" desire to select their own manager, Frank Laver, but the Board of Control insisted on its own nominee.

Public sympathy for Trumper and his associates was widespread. In this biography it is not intended to dwell excessively on this issue except to reproduce an interesting comment from M. A. Noble:

> I say that the Board of Control has acted unjustly and dishonestly, and has violated its own constitution. I am a strong supporter of the board as a board, and I believe in the principle of board control, but

I am strongly against its present personnel. They have had six years now to bring everybody into line, and to legislate for Australian cricket, and they have absolutely failed. In these six years they have not been credited with one single act of conciliation or forbearance. They have held the pistol of coercion at the heads of the players the whole time, and gradually taken from them all their privileges. Where a happy issue and solution of the present crisis might easily have resulted, we now have the spectacle of a non-representative team going to England. (*Sydney Morning Herald*, 29 February 1912.)

Mayors Parlour,
Town Hall,
Adelaide.

2nd March, 1912.

V. Trumper, Esq.,
    George Street,
        SYDNEY, N.S.W.

Dear Sir,

        I have, by direction, to convey to you the following Motion which was carried unanimously at a Public Meeting held in the Town Hall, Adelaide, last evening:-

        "That we extend to Messrs. Hill, Armstrong, Cotter, Carter, Ransford and Trumper our deep sympathy in the treatment they have received at the hands of the Members of the Board of Control, our recognition of the straightforward and manly attitude they have adopted all through the dispute with the Board, and our appreciation of the great services they have rendered to Australian Cricket."

        Yours faithfully,

M A Y O R.

One of many expressions of support for the "Big Six".

199

In April 1912 an Edward Charles Clifton advanced the sum of £1040 to Annie Trumper and her business partner Dudley King. Repayment with interest was guaranteed by Victor Trumper. When the joint business venture, a clothing store in Wynyard Square, failed in 1913, Victor requested that the two partners be released from responsibility of payment. Clifton released Annie and King from any further debt, and accepted a sum of £268 from Victor and his personal guarantee for the balance payable plus interest accrued. Monthly payments by Trumper of £10 commenced but at the time of his death in 1915, £826 was still outstanding. Meanwhile his own business, his sporting goods and mercer's store in George Street, continued to flourish, although much of the profit was being consumed by the above repayments.

During the progress of the 1912–13 season Sydney Charles Trumper began playing for Gordon while Charles Ernest Love Trumper turned out for the Sydney Grammar School's First Eleven. Early in November the first visit by a Western Australian State team to Sydney was highlighted by Victor Trumper's brilliance in the atrocious batting conditions. He registered 51 and 55 in the drawn game. The Western Australians when questioned by Johnny Moyes while returning home, said, "He batted on the wet wicket in a manner we wouldn't have believed possible if we hadn't seen it with our own eyes!"

In January 1913 the New South Wales captain produced yet another dazzling display in the South Australian fixture in Sydney which was documented by the *Sydney Morning Herald*.

> Graceful off-drives, neat leg-glances, lofting on-drives, powerful pulls, wristy square and back cuts, all came from the bat of Trumper, made with less brilliancy than of yore, but nothing more perfect in stroke play has been seen on the cricket ground in recent years. And Trumper's style was as beautiful as ever. He is a glorious batsman. It is a pity that such a cricketer as Trumper will age, for it is only once in a hundred years that such a genius appears on the cricket horizon.

He and Macartney in this match added 142 runs in only 75 minutes. At the conclusion of the New South Wales innings Trumper was unconquered with 201 and he hit 21 fours. Johnny Moyes, who played in the contest for South Australia appealed for bad light when visibility deteriorated during the visitors' second innings. At the finish of the over Trumper approached and enquired, "What's the problem slogger?" Moyes pointed to the darkening clouds to the south and explained that he was losing sight of the ball. Victor looked himself and then in his role as home team captain approached the umpires and said, "I agree with the batsmen, I think it's too dark to continue." The umpires did not agree, however, and the host State, despite the chivalrous gesture from its captain won handsomely.

During the match post-mortem, Moyes explained to his captain, Clem Hill how spellbound he had felt while fielding against Trumper:

> On the way back to Adelaide Clem Hill said to me, "I suppose you think that you have seen Vic bat?" I thought I had, and told him how fascinated and amazed I had been. "Yes," said Clem, "they reckoned I was pretty good, but I used to be fighting for my life in England, and that fellow would be hitting fours at the other end. If you've not seen Vic bat on a bad pitch, then you've never seen real cricket."*

Moyes did have the opportunity of seeing Trumper bat on a difficult pitch during his Testimonial Match in Sydney one month later in early February. The Citizen's Committee formed to collect monies suggested that the funds be invested by trustees nominated by the New South Wales Cricket Association; W. P. McElhone, H. B. Jamieson and E. A. Tyler.

Monty Noble agreed to return to first-class cricket for this one important match as Trumper was very keen to play just once more with his former comrade of so many games with Paddington and the Australian Eleven. Charles Bannerman umpired in the big match and on the first morning even before the captains walked out to toss, £1000 had already been collected in Sydney. Trumper led the New South Wales Eleven and Clem Hill the Australian Eleven. Dr Leslie Poidevin wrote in the *Sydney Morning Herald*:

> Trumper is one of the few batsmen who might score an innings of 400 odd and perhaps eclipse Archie MacLaren's record score (424): with opportunities offered by regular English county cricket the probability is that he would have done so had he cared to. However, great and all as Trumper's performances have been, it is safe to say that, in the matter of reputation, no other batsman is so completely independent of statistics, and Trumper's name will go down to cricket posterity as, if not "the greatest ever," as "great as ever". The

---

* A. G. Moyes. *Australian Batsmen*. 1954.

wish is unanimous that this testimonial match commencing on Friday shall be a fitting tribute to his well-known popularity as a man and a good fellow.

The Testimonial had as its official patron, the State Governor, Lord Chelmsford, and Wolfe's Schnapps offered incentives of a sovereign to any batsman making 50 runs in either innings and one guinea for the bowler disposing of the top-scorers for each side in both innings.

Unfortunately a fine day did not occur during the duration of the match, intermittent rain falling in Sydney from the Thursday before the game's commencement through to its conclusion. A souvenir scoring card designed by T. J. Houghton for the Citizen's Committee, and autographed photographs of Trumper were sold by the New South Wales team members as they moved among the crowd. Monty Noble busied himself among the onlookers in the outer reserve with his collection box. Leslie Poidevin remarked, "I hardly saw any play but I thoroughly enjoyed myself among the spectators who were very kind."

As their hero emerged from the pavilion with bat and cap held in his right hand, the crowd, as if triggered by a rehearsed signal, roared a mighty welcome which continued for three minutes. The sound of the band performing, "For He's A Jolly Good Fellow," was barely audible above the din as Clem Hill and the Rest of Australia team members gave Trumper three rousing cheers. He was understandably moved by the reception and wiped a sleeve across his face as if to remove tears. When Bill Whitty sent him a full toss at the start of his innings he missed it completely but it was wide of his leg stump. After a slow and hesitant beginning in the murky light Trumper went on to record a splendid 126 not out on the difficult pitch. The press lauded his exhibition as "brilliant," as he carved out 16 fours in 165 minutes. *The Referee* remarked:

> Every imaginable stroke was used. Cleverly placed back cuts, forceful shots past cover, hard off drives, cheeky pulls, were blended in a manner that made up delightful cricket. It was no wonder that the comparatively stolid occupants of the member's stand cheered again and again as the clever batsman ran in ahead of the others, as though bent on quickly seeking the seclusion the dressing room affords. Behind followed the other players applauding him.

During the second innings in his Testimonial, Trumper crafted

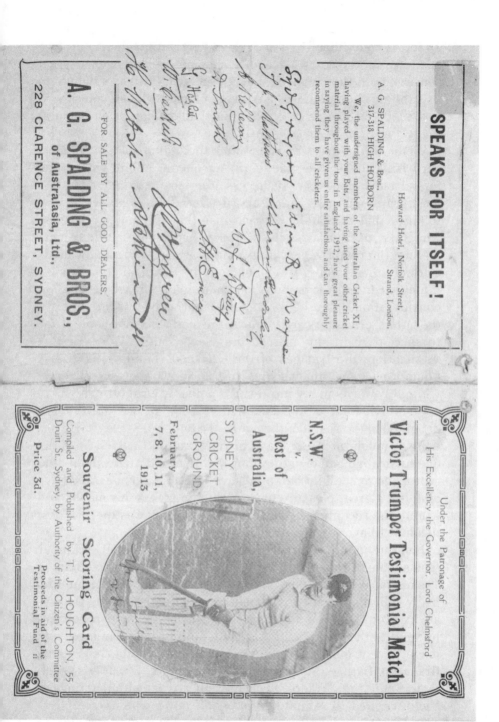

Under the Patronage of
His Excellency the Governor, Lord Chelmsford

Victor Trumper Testimonial Match

N.S.W.
v.
Rest of Australia,

SYDNEY
CRICKET
GROUND.

February
7, 8, 10, 11,
1913

Souvenir Scoring Card

Compiled and Published by T. J. HOUGHTON, 55 Druitt St., Sydney, by Authority of the Citizen's Committee

Proceeds in aid of the
Testimonial Fund ::

Price 3d.

The cover of Trumper's Testimonial "Souvenir Scoring Card".

10 fours, compiling 61 runs in exactly 61 minutes with carefree abandon in the knowledge that the match had been a great success, both financially and as a spectacle. Sydney's tribute to its sublime champion was a triumph of goodwill and generosity, as £2950 13s 3d was realized, a particularly handsome sum at that time.

Victor in the dressing room after the match said, "It is most surprising to me the manner in which the public have come forward and made a great success of my testimonial match. It is most gratifying to me, and I am sure it will be to others as well to know that the public do recognise that the majority of men who take part in first-class cricket regularly sacrifice commercial interest to a very large extent. A trip to England sounds a grand thing—and so it is—but from the financial point of view it may mean ten times more to a man taking his whole life into consideration, than the recompense he receives at the time. To the public, cricketers, particularly the men who have come so far to take part in my match, the New South Wales Cricket Association, the trustees of the Cricket Ground, the Citizen's Committee, and other bodies that have worked so diligently without rewards in my interest, I am deeply grateful."

Clem Hill added his comment, "Well, all we players are delighted at the result of the match. Trumper deserves it. He has done as much for Australia as anyone, and in England he is the one Australian batsman they long to watch. They rave about him; crowds go to see him bat, and leave when he gets out. We have all felt it a great pleasure to turn out and play in his match, and I think the reception he received on Saturday was the grandest incident I have seen on a cricket field."

Just one month after the finish of the Testimonial, Trumper took a team of New South Wales cricketers to the island State of Tasmania. While fielding in the slips on the Hobart ground he badly split his finger while making contact with the ball. Despite advice from his men not to bat against the Tasmanian bowlers he went to the wicket with his right hand heavily bandaged and made 87 not out in 55 minutes, batting at number six in the first-class fixture. Sir Norman Gregg, one of Trumper's teammates implored, "You're surely not going to bat with that finger." Victor replied, "I cannot let the people down who have come to see me bat." Indeed some spectators had travelled for days to catch a glimpse of the immortal figure at the crease and left the ground completely fulfilled as the visitors defeated Tasmania by an innings and 298 runs.

In early May 1913 a strong team including Charlie Macartney, Warren Bardsley, Herbert Collins and John Crawford, boarded the steamer *Niagara* in Sydney to tour North America. Trumper was booked to sail with the team, his passport was issued, dated 3 May 1913 and a letter of recommendation from State Premier McGowan was written on 2 May 1913 bearing the State seal. Yet two days later, because of business and family commitments, the *Niagara* sailed without the star attraction.

Victor and Annie, who by now had almost despaired of another child, were overjoyed when Victor junior was born on Wednesday, 7 October 1913 at their Chatswood home. (He was to later play with distinction for the Manly club and for his State as a fast right-arm bowler who could swing the ball prodigiously. A tall and striking man with blue eyes, he worked for the Rural Bank at the Sydney headquarters and was respected by all for his courtesy and kindness.) Victor celebrated the following Saturday on Manly Oval leading his team to a win, in the Middle Harbour engagement, by an innings and 150 runs.

Austin Diamond, the Western Suburbs skipper, sympathetic but strict and meticulous in the placing of his fieldsmen, altered his style completely whenever Trumper left the dressing room. Knowing that it was impossible to predict the strokes that the Gordon captain would choose from his fabulous repertoire, Diamond instructed his men, "Spread around the field boys, anywhere will do."

It was during the summer of 1913–14 that Arthur Sims, a much travelled wool dealer and a representative for Canterbury and New Zealand, persuaded Monty Noble and Frank Laver to bring a group of Australian players to his country early in the New Year with Victor Trumper as the star attraction. The Australian Board of Control was at first unhappy about the tour but the venture eventually went ahead as planned.

The 1914 Tour of New Zealand

Trumper did not participate in the first three fixtures in the North Island in early February. Arriving on the Sydney boat on the first Wednesday of the month he waited in Wellington for the rest of the team. He could manage only 0 and 16 during the fourth match played by the touring Australians against the Wellington Eleven which the visitors won easily by 7 wickets. He improved in the next engagement at Hastings against Hawkes Bay with scores of 42 and 23, the home side losing the two-day encounter by 9 wickets.

At Gisborne against Poverty Bay in late February the Australians played a draw and Trumper registered 48. He was now starting to find his usual form and in the next match at Wanganui he top-scored with a sparkling 94 at just under a run per minute,

The 1914 Australian Cricket Team in New Zealand.
Back row: I. A. Cody, L. Black, F. J. Laver, C. E. Dolling, A. A. Mailey, W. McGregor, W. Ferguson (scorer), V. T. Trumper, C. McKenzie.
Middle row: Mrs Noble, M. A. Noble, Arthur Sims, W. W. Armstrong, Mrs Armstrong.
Front row: J. N. Crawford, E. L. Waddy, V. S. Ransford, H. L. Collins.

but another draw resulted. Trumper and the Australian Eleven were treated handsomely throughout this visit, "Long Slip" of the *Otago Witness* commented wryly:

> The members of the Australian team are having a royal time in New Zealand, and everywhere the glad hand of hospitality is being extended to them. It is almost a finer thing, indeed, to be an Australian cricketer than it is to be a genius. It is almost a more glorious thing to have played in a test match than to have invented wireless telegraphy . . . to have captained Australia than to have led the army at Waterloo. I left one man happy who had shaken the hand of Victor Trumper!

In between the tight schedule of two- and three-day cricket matches the tourists found time to visit Lake Taupo and landed an impressive catch of rainbow trout which were consumed with much relish the next morning. On the Waitomo with the aid of hand-held lanterns and small dinghies they negotiated the inky darkness of the glow-worm caverns.

Moving to the South Island the touring party were guests at the stud farm "Kinloch" to inspect the champion sire Martian

erguson (scorer), Black, Waddy, and McKenzie admire the catch of Lake Taupo trout, 1914 Tour.

before returning by motor transport to Christchurch. The following day Canterbury won the toss at Lancaster Park and elected to bat, and were soon back in the pavilion for 92. The Australians started poorly against Bennett and Carlton, both renowned for their ability to bowl tirelessly for hours keeping an almost perfect length while moving the ball off the seam. The visitors were soon 3 for 28 against the opening bowlers and at the day's end were 105 for the loss of 5 wickets.

Trumper was deliberately kept for the Saturday to draw a large and profitable crowd which he did, as 5000 paid gate money. They had to wait until after lunch before he came to bat with the score at 7 for 209. The fact that he was batting at number nine did not deter the champion in the least. He opened his display with a single from Bennett and then late-cut Carlton, who later played for Victoria and South Australia, to the fence. Double figures soon appeared next to his name and he raced to 35 in 22 minutes, sending one ball flashing to the off-side fence and placing others at will with masterly leg-side strokes. He reached 50 in 26 minutes and rapidly approached Sims who had been just over the half-century when Trumper opened his innings.

Passing his partner's total with a cracking pull to the boundary he proceeded at great pace to his century which he reached in 73 minutes with a scintilating on-drive. The *New Zealand Herald* described Trumper's play following his 100:

> He kept scoring rapidly with hard, clean strokes, mostly on the off, but Bennett steadied the scoring when he came on again. Sandman was hit for two boundaries, the Australian crack hitting out to the slow balls in brilliant style. Trumper reached 150 in 92 minutes. He hit Whitta for 6, almost into the scoring box, and Bennett for another 6, over the square-leg fence.

Afternoon tea was taken with the score at 7 for 423. On resumption Trumper on-drove another four and then lifted a delivery from Bennett on top of the pickets. Wilson replaced the speedster and Trumper greeted him with a massive on-drive which soared over the fence and landed with a great splash into the frog-pond well behind the main ground. After 152 minutes of power-laden cricket he registered 250 and a little later the 600 was attained, the last 50 runs occupying only 12 minutes. Finally as the superb batsman neared his triple century he skied Bennett to Sandman fielding at point and he was out for 293. The

Trumper, on 80, faces the Canterbury bowlers at Christchurch as he and Sims compile the world record for the eighth wicket, 1914 Tour.

eighth wicket partnership by Trumper and Sims of 433 has stood as the world record in first-class cricket for seventy years. At one stage they put on 100 runs in an astonishing 21 minutes. Trumper's exhibition included 3 sixes and 44 fours and the Australians won this remarkable match by an innings and 364 runs.

Trumper was active again in the next game at Temuka versus the South Canterbury Fifteen. In this match the Australians aided by a splendid innings from J. N. Crawford, the talented Surrey all-rounder who had settled in Adelaide, replied to their hosts' 180 by gathering 922 runs for the loss of 9 wickets. Crawford grossed 354 runs in five and a half hours in the two-day encounter. His score included 14 sixes, and he and Trumper, who again batted at number nine, put on 298 runs for the eighth wicket in an unbelievable 69 minutes of withering batsmanship. At one stage they took the total from 450 to 550 in just 23 minutes. Trumper made 60 in 32 minutes and reached his century in 54 minutes. He struck one six and twenty fours in his 135-run display.

The *Otago Witness* commented:

> Trumper played a characteristic innings scoring all round the wickets by pretty strokes. There was a good attendance in anticipation of seeing the crack Australian batsman, and while Christchurch spectators are congratulating themselves that they witnessed Trumper at his best, the southerners are more than ever jubilant, for they have seen the great batsman make a century—perhaps not so much as they would have liked, but quite enough to show them his marvellous ability.

After Trumper departed Monty Noble came in and he and Crawford made 50 in 9 minutes. Crawford's combination with Trumper and Noble produced 200 runs in the last hour of play.

The first International of the 1914 Tour was scheduled for the Carisbrook Ground in Dunedin on 6, 7 and 9 March. Weakened by the absence of several key Auckland players, New Zealand batted first with Monty Noble leading the Australians. With the home team all out for 228 Australia replied with 354, the partnership by Trumper and Armstrong salvaging what would have otherwise been a moderate total. The *Canterbury Times* described the performance:

> The Australians had now lost five wickets for the miserable total of 33, but the big guns were then brought into requisition. Trumper the classiest of them all, joined Armstrong, and the spectators were treated to the finest exhibition in the test match, Trumper and Armstrong playing beautiful cricket. The placing of the incomparable Victor, the perfection of his timing and the easy grace with which he hooked the off ball to the on boundary raised the spectators to a pitch of enthusiasm.

When he reached 72 Trumper failed to connect properly with a Sandman delivery and played it to Bennett at mid-on. He batted for 69 minutes and struck 11 fours. The partnership with Armstrong was the highest of the match and realized 144 runs in 69 minutes. "Long Slip" of the *Otago Witness* analysed Trumper's play:

> Trumper's innings was an education less than a spectacle. The champion had gone out to give an exhibition of cricket in its highest sense, and not a display of cricket pyrotechnics. His strokes all round the wicket were marked by rare craftsmanship, perfection of

timing, and celerity of execution. Whether it was the drive, the back cut, the flick past the right hand of point, or the hook, all the strokes were masterly. His footwork was clever, and the manner in which he jumped in front of his wicket and hooked off balls to the boundary was an exhibition seldom seen.

The Australians went on to conquer New Zealand by 7 wickets, Arthur Mailey capturing 7 wickets in the home side's second innings.

The next engagement, a two-day match at Invercargill versus a Southland eleven, took place following the long train journey from Dunedin. On the way the tourists alighted from their carriage to view the rugged scenery. At Invercargill on Rugby Park the host team batted first for 156 and the visitors responded with 709. The reporter for the *Otago Witness* filed this report:

> The feature of the innings was the brilliant display given by Trumper (211). He scored freely all round the wicket. He gave a chance of a catch early in his score but thenceforth the home team was given an afternoon's leather-hunting.

Trumper's scores leading up to the final International were as follows: 34 *v.* Canterbury at Lancaster Park, Christchurch; 54 *v.* Nelson at Nelson; 67 *v.* Wellington at Wellington; 76 *v.*

Trumper and Laver clown for the camera. Trumper is fourth from the left, Arthur Mailey is second from the right, 1914 tour.

211

Trumper, Cody, Waddy, Ferguson, and Mailey, 1914 Tour.

Manawatu at Palmerston North. Clarrie Grimmett played against Trumper in both Wellington matches but failed to take a wicket in either encounter.

The final meeting of Australia and New Zealand began at Eden Park, Auckland on Friday 27 March 1914, New Zealand batting first registered 269. At lunch on the Saturday, Australia were 1 for 76. During the break farewell speeches were offered by the various officials and then Frank Laver presented the secretary of the New Zealand Cricket Council, F. C. Raphael, with a silver rose bowl inscribed with the engraved signatures of the touring cricketers. Victor Trumper proposed the toast to the Council with these words, "Cricket in New Zealand is certainly on the up grade, and I trust that before long a team will be sent from here to Australia which will more than double the gates of the previous team. I would also like to thank Mr Raphael for his many kindnesses to us and while the Council remains as it is presently constituted there is nothing to fear for New Zealand cricket."

Later in the afternoon while batting at number five Victor gave the final display of his art in the international arena. Arriving from the pavilion with the scoreboard reading 3 for 231 he swept the attack before him and his classic off-drive to the fence saw the New Zealand first innings total surpassed.

Following the tea interval he took the long handle to the bowling. He cut, hooked and drove with majestic precision and soon reached 40. Dolling was bowled by Robinson for 104 and Armstrong joined Trumper who continued to execute strokes with great gusto. He reached his half-century with a lovely late cut for four from Robinson and lifted a ball from Hemus over the mid-wicket fence. Robinson received similar treatment, for in the fast bowler's next over the ball was driven out of the ground into the backyard of a house adjoining Eden Park. During the following over from Hemus, Trumper slammed another six and a four. Finally Sneddon, with his third ball of a new over, trapped the champion leg before wicket as he attempted a leg glance. His unconventional innings of 81 took just over the hour and his team went on to make 610 for the loss of six batsmen. New Zealand at their second attempt could muster only 228. Although Waddy, Dolling, Armstrong and Crawford all scored centuries,

Trumper, on the extreme right, is showing the effects of an arduous tour, 1914 Tour.

the connoisseurs of the press wanted only to talk of Trumper's display. One of them wrote, "Although his cricket was far from orthodox his exhilarating innings was much appreciated by the spectators."

Trumper easily had the highest tour batting aggregate with 1246 runs from 15 innings for an average of 83.07, yet he missed the first three matches. Warwick Armstrong took 89 wickets and Arthur Mailey captured 48. The weary party, before sailing home, enjoyed a well-earned few days' rest in the thermal district of Rotorua. By the time the next southern cricket season resumed the two allies of Great Britain would be inexorably plunged into a bloody conflict which would decimate the ranks of young men from the cricket fields of the world.

The Last Summer

On the first Saturday in October the New South Wales Cricket Association officially opened the new 1914–15 season under blue skies. However, the pitches throughout Sydney, and those close to the Harbour in particular, were rain affected and difficult, some of them being under water during the night. Large scores were scarce as the bowlers easily reaped the honours for the day. Albert Hopkins took twelve Petersham wickets for North Sydney, J. D. Scott 5 for 13 for Petersham, and P. W. Dive 5 for 23 for Western Suburbs against Paddington.

By far the most prominent batting perfomance was at Wentworth Park where Victor Trumper, mustering all his old flair and skill stroked 123 charming runs at just under a run per minute, leading Gordon to a first innings win over Glebe. His was the first century innings of the season and the only one registered that long weekend. The *Sydney Morning Herald* reported:

> It was eminently appropriate for the long-established champion to be the first centurion of the season, especially as the task was one calling for superior skill and tremendous resource. Those characteristics, of course, have always been prominent in Trumper's displays, many of the best of which have been achieved in the face of considerable difficulties. He batted for two hours on Saturday, hitting sixteen 4s and two 6s, and although several of his strokes were not entirely without risk, evidence of his wonted artistry was abundant, as the wicket was in favour of the bowlers. This innings in itself should be a reassuring answer to the oft unspoken query: "What will Trumper's form be this year?"

Despite this promising start to the season, Victor was gradually sickening, as his subsequent scores of 19, 13, and 4 suggest. On the Sunday after the Round 4 match with Petersham at Chatswood Oval, Annie noticed that Victor's ankles were swollen. Worried, she persuaded him to seek medical advice and to please her he consulted an old school friend. Fretfully Annie awaited Victor's return home. After his usual sunny entry he told her that there was nothing to worry about as he probably had a chill on the kidneys and he needed only to watch his food intake for the illness to pass.

The encounter with Petersham was to be the last game of cricket in which Victor ever participated but it is interesting to note that Victor's younger brother Charles began playing for Gordon at this time.

A patriotic match which was played in late November 1914 between the New South Wales First and Second Elevens, was arranged by the Cricket Association to augment donations for the Lord Mayor's Patriotic Fund. As captain of the State First Eleven Victor was too sick to participate, the *Sydney Morning Herald* stating, "Victor Trumper is not well, and did not play, his place as captain being taken by Warren Bardsley."

At this time an impressive memorial service was held in Martin Place for Lord Roberts who had died in France. The ceremony was presided over by Archbishop Wright and the Lord Mayor, Alderman Richards, and over 5000 assembled to hear the Professional Musician's Band play Chopin's Funeral March.

When there was a temporary lull in the carnage, French soldiers at the front were astonished to see their British allies during the warmer months playing with leather balls and wooden bats near the fighting lines. In the Australian War Memorial in Canberra there are photographs showing the Australian Light Horse at Gallipoli playing cricket near the trenches. In England teams from HMAS *Australia*, on duty in the North Sea, playing against the cricket clubs of the ships of the Grand Fleet only experienced one defeat from sixteen matches.

Back in Australia an announcement from Adelaide declared that Clem Hill had decided to retire from first-class cricket. In an interview following the decision he was asked to give an opinion on the greatness of his contemporaries. He replied, "I place Victor Trumper as the first among the batsmen that I have known. Trumper is the champion on all wickets—fiery wickets, good, sticky, and slow—and that is the true test. Ranjitsinhji was wonderful on a good or fiery wicket, but on a sticky wicket there was no comparison between the two."

At the end of November 1914 the New South Wales Cricket Association called for nominations to fill the position of secretary and received over seventy applications. Having reduced the candidates to ten the committee chose Frank Iredale and in so doing paid a graceful compliment to an accomplished international and a tireless worker for the game. The State selectors,

216

V. T. Trumper, Dr L. O. S. Poidevin and T. H. Howard met and chose the team to play South Australia and Victoria over the Christmas period. Trumper stood down from the team but he decided to attend practice at the Sydney Cricket Ground nets on Thursday 3 December and on the following Tuesday and Thursday, advising and coaching and having an occasional hit.

New South Wales were to run second to Victoria that season, but the presence of Trumper may well have reversed the result. After this 1914–15 season the Sheffield Shield competition was suspended for the duration of World War I.

During March 1915 the Trumper family booked holiday lodgings at Collaroy on Sydney's northern beach front for two weeks, but after only two days they returned home to Chatswood as Victor began feeling unwell again. This time a specialist was consulted and he confined Victor to bed to reduce the swelling in his ankles. Despite his obvious dislike of physical inactivity he was in good spirits, and improvement was noted under Annie's loving care. He caught up on his reading and before Anne Louise went to sleep at night she was allowed in to her father's bedroom to listen to a story. During the daytime hours Annie brought young Victor into the room so that he could be near his dad. Frank Iredale, Victor's Gordon club-mate, often visited the Trumpers in their Help Street home. He wrote:

> To see him at his best, one had to go into the sanctuary of his home, his wife and child, and there the man who the world saw but never knew, was at his best. How much he loved this life one may never know, but one felt that if all homes reflected the glory that his did, it would indeed be a world worth living in. I met him on many occasions out walking in the cool of the evening with his wife, whom he loved with a tenderness which one knew was so real, and it was on these evenings that Victor enjoyed his real pleasure in life.

M. A. Noble in *The Game's the Thing* supplied evidence which provides a possible explanation as to the cause of Victor's chronic illness:

> Although very strong physically, Victor had not a robust constitution, and when, at the age of thirty, he contracted scarlet fever, it seemed to undermine his health. Yet he never complained. He continued to play, and occasionally we got a glimpse of his real genius.

One of the side effects of scarlet fever is kidney inflammation,

217

and it usually occurs insidiously. If the condition is not overcome by the body's defences the foundation for chronic Bright's disease is laid. In late June *The Referee* reported:

> Victor Trumper's health is still not as satisfactory as could be desired. He is again confined to his home. He has the sympathy of a very wide circle of friends and admirers, whose sincere wish is that he will shake off his trouble and emerge with all his old health and strength.

Growing impatient with his bedridden status Victor persuaded his specialist, Dr H. H. Bullmore, to permit him to get out of bed and move around the house, but the swelling returned. On 21 June he was admitted to St Vincent's Private Hospital, Darlinghurst for steam treatment in an attempt to revive his ailing kidneys. Among those allowed in to visit Victor was Frank Iredale who reported that he was cheerful despite his obvious discomfort. A meeting was convened by Iredale and other close friends to plan a voyage to England in the hope that this might assist the great batsman's convalescence.

The weather towards the end of June grew cold and bitter. On the Friday after Victor entered hospital snow began to fall on the Blue Mountains west of Sydney. The fall was heavy at Blackheath where local residents threw snowballs. City visitors, arriving on the Saturday morning train, were entranced by the glittering white scenery as the thermometer dropped to 28 degrees Fahrenheit.

The minimum temperature in Sydney on the Sunday was 42.1°F as heavy clouds obscured the morning sun. Annie Trumper arrived at the hospital in the late afternoon with the sun shining, and she discussed with her elated husband the plans for the proposed visit to England in March of the following year. Victor told Annie that he still had much to accomplish for her and the children, and that he would do everything in his power to send young Victor to study at Oxford when he was older. Despite the emergency use of oxygen equipment, two hours before midnight Victor became desperately ill and lapsed into a coma from which he never awoke. At 10 o'clock the next morning he died in Annie's arms.

After the autopsy, Dr H. H. Bullmore, who signed the death certificate, stated that the extinction of life was caused by uraemic convulsions brought on by chronic nephritis. Annie placed the following obituary notice in the *Sydney Morning Herald*:

TRUMPER—June 28, 1915, at St. Vincent's Private Hospital, Sydney. Victor Trumper, dearly loved husband of Annie Trumper, of "Auckland", Help-Street, Chatswood, aged 37 years.

Despite the constant news of war, the daily newspaper stories and portraits announcing the fallen at Gallipoli, a distressed Sydney paused to pay homage to the departed genius of the cricket field. Every newspaper in the country relayed the sad news. Jack Davis, who followed and reported the dead cricketer's entire career, wrote:

Victor Trumper dead! It is so hard to realize. But alas! It is true.

He was removed from his home at Chatswood last week to St Vincent's Private Hospital, Darlinghurst, where he died on Monday from Bright's disease.

Sad news that one so great, so gifted, so popular in our national sport, so exemplary in his life should go so early; he was in his 38th year, born November 2, 1877. The war hits us hard; but this blow has a sadder touch than any we have felt when our other heroes of the athletic world have died on the field of battle. Those whom the gods love die young.

Trumper's name in cricket will never perish. He was the artist of cricket from toes to finger-tips. He was a man of bright winning personality, upright, and generous to a fault, as was recognized by those responsible for placing the proceeds of his testimonial match under trustees, for himself, and after him for his widow and children. I cannot conceive of his having had any enemies, for he was a spotless youth in character and habits. May the turf rest lightly over his head.

He brought into cricket a new conception of the batsman's art. He was original, with the polish and grace of the ideal, in style. He was matchless in brilliancy and with the power of a limitless variety of strokes, which depended on hairline accuracy and timing. The word genius may be often mis-applied to men who achieve wonders in sport and art, but Trumper was an absolute genius in cricket.

Frank Iredale the new secretary of the New South Wales Cricket Association composed the following tribute:

The death of Victor Trumper was a great shock to his old comrades. To those of us who were privileged to visit him during his illness, his cheerfulness under great suffering was amazing. Just as in his cricket, so in his illness, he refrained from choosing the middle way,

219

but fought the foe face to face. His was a noble nature, free, unrestrained, and open. He made no foes, his opponents always recognised the fearless fighter and the generous friend. Australia has lost her greatest batsman, and the most glorious and brilliant she ever had. . . .

As an old comrade of his, I deeply deplore his loss. It was my pleasure to know him well, and during the years of our friendship, I had many opportunities of knowing his worth as a man. His nature was frank and loyal, and always inclined to kindly feeling. He made many friends, and in every country that he visited his popularity was, apart from his cricket, unquestionable. One could write miles of paean in praise of him as a cricketer, and yet never exhaust his subject. As he lived, so he died, a true and honoured man. One may well ask, "Shall we ever see his like again?"

News of Victor's death was cabled to London and was received with regret among cricketers and lovers of the game. The stark headline "Death of Great Cricketer" displaced the news of the battlefront from the evening editions of the London newspapers. Pelham Warner in an interview on 29 June 1915 said, "Trumper was the most unassuming cricketer in the world, and at one time was its finest batsman; but he spoke as if he had never made a run in his whole life."

The press was unanimous in its praise:

Mr Trumper's hitting was unique in its boldness. He hit all round the wicket and seldom left a ball alone. His off-drive was superb, and so was his power of stepping almost on the wicket and forcing the ball anywhere. (*The Times*)

No other batsman has played cricket with greater grace and more attractiveness. Even his shorter innings were masterpieces of artistic cricket. (*Sporting Life*)

No one among the famous Australians had such remarkable powers. His ability to make big scores when orthodox methods were unavailing lifted him above his fellows. (*Daily Chronicle*)

He was Australia's greatest batsman. Certainly he was the most brilliant, particularly on bad wickets, when his skill and daring enabled him to score. (*Daily Mail*)

The Melbourne *Argus* noted that at the time of his death Trumper had shared in more century partnerships than any other Australian player, the total being 72. The *Sydney Mail* stated in its obituary:

220

Dear Mrs Trumper,

      I cannot say what a shock it was when I saw on a poster outside the war office "Death of Victor Trumper"—and I beg to offer my most sincere sympathy with the great loss you have had. Everyone liked Victor; he was so nice, modest and unassuming. Not an ounce of "side" in him—he might never had made a run he was so modest. What a batsman! I am sure that there has never been better, and many pleasant hours have I had watching him bat. Even his opponents rejoiced at his success. How popular he was in England you may, perhaps, know. There was always a big cheer for him when he came out to bat. I shall never forget my first match at Sydney at the end of March 1903 when playing for Lord Hawke's XI versus N.S.W. Victor and poor Reggie Duff going in first. What a welcome they had from the big crowd—it was a Saturday afternoon—and what cricket they showed! 72 in half an hour and then Victor bowled by "Bose" with a googlie. I shall never forget that bit of cricket. What a pair Victor and Duff were—and now alas both gone. But you may be sure as long as cricket is played Victor's name will be remembered among the immortals of the game. His generation of cricketers will never forget his charming personality and delightful modesty.

         I am

          Yours sincerely,

          P. F. Warner

Now the gifted youth has gone. He was more than a genius of the bat and ball. Perhaps that was not so important to him as it was to others. He was a modest, good-living young man. His success on the field had no effect on him, save to strengthen him in Spartan restraints. His courage in his illness was the natural revelation of a Christian character.

When Albert "Tibby" Cotter heard of his friend's passing he broke down and wept. (Cotter himself was to die heroically as a stretcher-bearer at Beersheba on 31 October 1917.)

Sydney Smith speaking on behalf of the New South Wales Cricket Association said, "It is with deep regret that we learn of the death of our friend Victor Trumper. Only a few months ago he was playing in the game and selecting teams to represent the State, so that the sad news comes as a shock to all. His retiring and kindly disposition made him a great favourite, and the cricket world can ill afford to lose him. His name stands out as the greatest batsman of his or any other day, and the pleasure he afforded to the cricket-loving public will never be forgotten. The sympathy of every true lover of sport throughout the whole world will go out to his widow and children and parents in their sad bereavement."

Victor's fellow New South Wales selector, Dr Leslie Poidevin, wrote with heartfelt grief:

Accustomed as we have lately grown to tidings of sadness and sorrow, the news of the calling away of Victor Trumper on Monday morning last came as a great shock to the whole cricketing community. Australian cricket without Victor Trumper is almost unthinkable. That we shall see him no more, the accepted master with the bat amongst Australians, is a contemplation laden with profoundest regret and weighty sorrow. By the magic of his skill he carried delight and entertainment into the hearts of devotees throughout the entire cricketing world, and his displays provided friend and foe alike with unforgetable memories and masterpieces. His best was the best. It has been described as the champagne of batting, and, in real truth, it proved a most stimulating and invigorating tonic to all. His batting was the model of finished excellence and artistic efficiency. Not infrequently excellence loses its effect on the mind by custom, as light after a time may cease to dazzle; but there was always a sparkling novelty about Trumper's play that simply dazzled and amazed all the time. By common consent, he was regarded as the most attractive batsman Australian cricket has ever produced—attractive not only because of the natural grace of his style, but also because he possessed the power of achievement almost to an unprecedented degree.

The majority of great Australian batsmen have been run-getters rather than stylists; they have made their reputations as batsmen of the highest class by making good scores in the big matches rather than by exceptional brilliance in the style and methods of play. Trumper was the grand exception. Like them, he was first and foremost a "doer" of great things, but the elegant style in which he did them was rather the gift of nature than the result of studious endeavour. For that reason his batting was *sui generis*—and unforgettable.

Though this is but a simple appreciation of Trumper the cricketer, I cannot let pass the opportunity of paying a small tribute to Trumper the man. Dazzlingly brilliant, versatile, and unconventional with the bat, he was the very antithesis off the field, being of a most modest, retiring, kindly, and unaggressive disposition. A staunch teetotaller and an exemplar in conduct, he was equally staunch in his friendships and comradeship. His easiness of approach and suavity of manner won him more than is expressed in the words "universal popularity." He was just "Vic" to all—the idol of the crowd. Such popularity was not undeserved. His early demise will kindle the spark of sadness in every follower of cricket throughout the world. His loss to Australia is a loss indeed, irreparable and altogether premature. His name and fame, however, will always be a cherished memory. The most gifted of cricketers, the hero of many of the most historic battles of the greensward, and withal the most modest of men, having "played the game" all his life, he has at last answered the final call all too soon, but his name will live in the imperishable annals of the game, and his memory in the hearts of his compatriots.

At 12.30 p.m. on Wednesday 30 June, Victor's family and his closest friends and the members of the Gordon Electorate Cricket Club, who had gathered at "Auckland" in Help Street, followed the horse-drawn hearse to Milsons Point where the coffin was taken by water to Fort Macquarie, present site of the Sydney Opera House. The cortège was timed to leave Fort Macquarie for Waverley Cemetery at 2.15 p.m. and many gathered on the southern shore of the Harbour to await the principal group of mourners. Among those watching from Fort Macquarie as the line of funeral craft made its way slowly over the water, were the umpires of the NSW Cricket Association and those of its kindred leagues in Sydney, plus members of the City and Suburban Cricket Association.

The procession stretched nearly three miles as it made its way up Macquarie Street from the shore, watched by more than twenty thousand citizens who stood with heads bared as the Australian flags fluttered from the skyline at half mast. Jack Davis of *The Referee* described the solemn proceedings:

> The funeral of Victor Trumper on Wednesday was one of the most impressive ever accorded a sportsman in Sydney. It left his residence in Chatswood, and was met at Fort Macquarie by many hundreds of cricketers and friends of the deceased, who marched four abreast, thence along Macquarie Street and Oxford Street. Near Regent Street, Paddington, the procession halted and those who had marched joined special trams, and went as far as Charing Cross. There they left the trams and formed in line again, leading the procession to the cemetery and down through the winding paths to the beautiful spot chosen for the grave, on a height not far from the cliffs, overlooking the broad, blue Pacific—a very beautiful scene.

At Waverley a substantial number of veteran cricketers led by Charlie Bannerman, Victor's old coach, headed the two hundred who walked with measured step in front of the flower-covered hearse. Among these were Alec Bannerman, Tom Garrett and Albert Gregory. At the sides of the hearse and immediately in front marched M. A. Noble, F. A. Iredale, S. E. Gregory, C. T. B. Turner, Dr L. O. S. Poidevin, A. Cotter, C. G. Macartney, W. Bardsley, Dr H. V. Hordern, A. J. Hopkins, C. Kelleway, J. D. A. O'Connor and H. Webster; an imposing list of prominent Australian cricketers.

The chief mourners were Charles Thomas Trumper (Victor's father); his brothers, Sydney and Charles; his uncle, Thomas Trumper; and his three brothers-in-law, W. P. Briggs, J. A. Briggs, G. Smith plus J. J. (Jim) Kelly. Among the countless politicians and dignitaries present were the great H. H. "Dally" Messenger; the Minister for Railways, Mr Briggs, representing the Premier; Senators Gardiner and MacDougall representing the Prime Minister; and R. F. Wyley, the secretary and manager of the Sydney Cricket Ground.

> Cricketers and sportsmen generally were represented in very great numbers. This may be interpreted not merely as an expression of the admiration they felt for him as a cricketer, but as a token of the affection he inspired among all classes of men who knew him. Mere words cannot tell those who come into sport in Australia's future the feeling which Victor Trumper's personal charm and batsman-

ship inspired in the hearts of men and boys of his time. (*The Referee*, 7 July 1915.)

The funeral was directed by Walter Carter, Hanson's father, and the Reverend George Harvard Cranswick of St Paul's Church of England in Chatswood who had conducted the private early morning family service at the church near Victor's home, delivered the graveside eulogy. His moving tribute included these words: "We exalt Victor as a son, as a husband and as a father. He was the hero of all assembled here to pay the last honour to his memory, and of thousands of others who are not present. Victor possessed many noble qualities. These made him the great sportsman that he was all through his career. He played the game of life as it should be played, and although he will be remembered for many things, nothing could be greater than his wonderful spirit of sportsmanship."

Among the many wreaths sent to Waverley were those from the Australian Board of Control, the Cricket Associations of New South Wales, Victoria, Queensland and South Australia, the Melbourne Cricket Club, the New South Wales Rugby Union and Rugby League, various district and suburban cricket clubs, and numerous personal friends and admirers. Telegrams arrived from the Tasmanian and Western Australian Cricket Associations as well as from overseas bodies such as the South African Board of Control and various cricket clubs in New Zealand.

At a meeting of the Gordon Cricket Club a few days after the funeral, the secretary, J. T. Hartigan said, "Victor Trumper greatly endeared himself by his unassuming and cheerful disposition, which success failed to alter." From Hobart the following was received: "Very sincere regret is expressed in Tasmania at the news of the death of the peerless Victor Trumper. Islanders who met him speak highly of his qualities as a man and a cricketer, and those who had the good fortune to play against him never concealed the pleasure they felt in watching him."

The Melbourne journalist David Scott said: "As one who has followed the career of Victor Trumper, I should like to add my opinion of the greatest cricketer in the world. In his prime we never had a batsman with his variety of strokes and his great faculty of scoring off all kinds of bowling and on all wickets. He was also a magnificent field, and such a quiet, unassuming man that he was a general favourite with all. He was the means of filling all grounds whenever he played. To his wife and friends I send my deepest sympathy in this their great loss. One and all in Victoria are with me in this sympathy."

Two weeks after the Waverley funeral a meeting of teachers and ex-students of Crown Street Superior Public School opened a fund to raise money for a memorial tablet in the school and to erect a tribute over Victor's last resting place.

Those visiting Waverley Cemetery today may notice the names of other famous people such as Dorothea Mackellar, Henry Lawson, Henry Kendall and Lawrence Hargrave, but one cannot help but be moved by Victor's humble grave superbly placed on the middle of the hill overlooking the sweeping blue Pacific Ocean with its backdrop of distant clouds, blue-grey horizon and golden sandstone cliffs.

The inscription at the head of the grave says simply:

> VICTOR THOMAS TRUMPER
> DIED 28TH JUNE 1915, AGED 36.
> AND HIS WIFE
> SARAH ANNE
> DIED 1ST APRIL 1963, AGED 85.

It is puzzling to note the age discrepancy as the death certificate indicates that Victor's age was 37.

Anne Louise and Victor junior lie side by side with their parents at Waverley.

Years after Victor's death those who recalled his genius and personal charm wrote with real loss concerning his passing. In 1921 Pelham Warner said, "His death did not go unnoticed even in the midst of war. His name is held in veneration by all cricketers. Trumper stood alone. He was like no one and no one was like him, and he was as modest as he was magnificent as a batsman. No one ever played so naturally. Batting just seemed a part of himself."[*]

Charlie Macartney wrote: "I have one great satisfaction regarding Victor Trumper—I never saw him grow old as a cricketer. I say, without hesitation, that he was the best batsman I ever saw. He excelled on any wicket, and against any bowling, but beyond all his cricket he was a *man*, a fighter on the cricket field, and a thorough gentleman at all times. Everybody who

---

[*] P. F. Warner, *My Cricketing Life*. Hodder & Stoughton, London, 1921.

knew Vic loved him, and when his death came they felt that they had lost a friend. A wonderful sportsman, a clean liver, and generous to a fault was Trumper, and he was a true example to any cricketer. He was the idol of every follower of the game, and his memory is green to-day to those who watched him throughout his career."

Daniel Reese, the New Zealand captain commented: "There was a charm about Trumper that won a warm spot in the hearts of all who knew him. He was one of the most modest and unselfish of players. He accepted umpires, decisions as a matter of course, and no one ever heard him say there was a doubt about any ruling that sent him back to the pavilion. Australians and Englishmen alike honour the memory of Victor Trumper. He was to die at the early age of thirty-seven, but left behind him a record and a reputation that shone like a planet in the history of the game."

A. G. "Johnny" Moyes, who played against Victor in Sheffield Shield matches for South Australia wrote: "When he came he opened the windows of the mind to a new vision of what batting could be. He lifted it to heights never before known, gave us thrills we had never before experienced. He was the originating genius of a new outlook in batsmanship, and those of us who saw him in his most gracious days can never forget. Then all too soon he passed over, and I am sure that all the trumpets sounded for him on the other side."

Neville Cardus penned this eloquent tribute: "The grand manner of MacLaren, the lyrical grace of Spooner, the lion energy of Jessop, the swift opportunist spirit of Tyldesley—all these excellences were compounded proportionately in Trumper.... When Trumper got out, the light seemed to go for a while from an Australian innings. 'The eagle is gone, and now crows and daws.' We make an artist's immortality by thinking upon and loving his work; Trumper was an artist-cricketer; let him live again in the mouths of men whenever Test matches are in action."[*]

Appropriately, Victor's long time friend and Gordon club-mate Frank Iredale wrote in 1920:

> I cannot speak of him as a cricketer, because I realize that nothing I could say would do him justice. He is comparable to no one

---

[*] Neville Cardus, *The Summer Game*. Rupert Hart-Davis, London, 1948.

because he was the first of his line. .... He was the beginning and the end of a new life in cricket, and when he died—all too soon—his cricket died with him. His memory, however, lingers and will for ever, so long as this grand old game of ours is played.

He was the master and himself the standard. In his prime he could play any game in any old way he liked. Nothing worried him at the wickets, and bowlers had no terrors for him. He was never perturbed at a crisis in the game, and could play a side himself. There was no one to compare with him because he stood alone. He could hit or defend just as it pleased him. His defence was his attack, and no one could emulate his deeds. There have been many good batsmen in the world, but only one Trumper. His death was a tragedy, and cricketers throughout the world have mourned the loss of the greatest cricketer Australia—if not the world—ever knew. In future years we may develop great players who may achieve great deeds, but one feels somehow or other that we shall never see a man like Victor again.*

What a void would exist in cricket lore if Victor Trumper had never graced the earth! But he did, and we are the more fortunate for his presence among us. His charisma is perpetuated by John Arlott's immortal poem, "On A Great Batsman,"

> As the gull conceals in easeful glide
> The inborn gift to curb and ride
> The gale—merging the sea-wind's force
> With lovely movement on a chosen course—
> So, in timed swoop he moves to charm
> The ball down-swirling from the bowler's arm
> Along some glissade of his own creation,
> Beyond the figure's black and white rotation.
>   Recorded centuries leave no trace
>   On memory of that timeless grace.†

---

* *Thirty-three Years of Cricket.*
† Frewin, L. (ed.), *The Boundary Book.* MacDonald, London, 1962.

Postscript

The memory of Victor Trumper's extraordinary panache lives on through the minds of those who witnessed his grandeur and compassion.

Hanson Carter, his Australian team-mate and business associate for five years, told Jack Fingleton, "You must never compare Hobbs, Bradman or anybody else with Trumper. If you want to try and classify the great batsmen in the game, put Victor way up there—on his own—and then you can begin to talk about the rest."* To clarify his point the veteran wicket-keeper pointed a gnarled index finger heavenward.

After his outstanding century before lunch on the first day of the 1926 Leeds Test Match, Charlie Macartney was congratulated by a club member who likened the innings to one from Trumper, the first to achieve this feat twenty-four years earlier. The "Governor-General", not one to be beguiled by silken words, acknowledged the compliment then asked, "As a point of interest what would Vic have done today that I didn't?" The member whose initial aim had been to praise the diminuitive batsman replied, "Nothing at all, except that he did it more gracefully."

Macartney would have been the first to acknowledge Trumper's superior grace as he himself recalled his partnerships with his hero, "I would have been proud just to carry his bag."

H. L. Collins, an Australian captain reminisced how Trumper, endowed with exceptionally strong fingers and wrists of steel, could pick up any bat and bend the handle to breaking point. Said Collins, "He'd rather die than become subservient to any bowler. There'll never be another Victor!"

When Clem Hill, also an Australian captain, was congratulated in Adelaide on a beautiful innings just completed, he commented, "As a batsman I am not fit to lick Trumper's boots!"†

---

* *Sporting Globe*, 15 October 1958.
† Eric McElhone, unpublished address for the Waverley Historical Society, 9 June 1975.

During the early 1930s Wilfred Rhodes, when asked by Alan Kippax who was the greatest batsman that he ever faced, after a slight pause, replied, "There was only one; Victor Trumper." Kippax noted that before Rhodes uttered the name he could see the words forming in his mouth.

In a conversation with Neville Cardus, Pelham Warner, when asked to describe Trumper's worth as a cricketer stated, "He was of blood royal; you couldn't set a field to him, and when he hit the ball it struck the fence before the bowler had recovered his balance." Cardus also told of his talk with a fellow countryman, a respected Test batsman of the fifties, in the pavilion at The Oval. As both lingered over their drinks, gazing with awe at the famous Beldam photograph of Trumper dancing down the wicket to drive, the international player asked, "Was he really as good as you claim?" The reply came back, "Of course, why do you ask?" Incredulous in tone, the England player pointed to the framed picture, "Look where he is, no crease in sight and stumped yards out of his ground if he misses the ball!"

Once at a dinner at Lord's, Sydney Barnes, arguably the greatest bowler of all time, replied with a far-away look in his eyes to a question concerning his Australian Test adversary, "Victor, well he always gave you a chance, almost daring you to bag his wicket."

The celebrated singer John McCormack, who used to watch Test encounters as Trumper's personal guest, once said, "I wish some of my American friends who dismiss cricket as an old man's game could have seen Victor. Sticky wicket or plumb, crumbling wicket in Manchester or billiard table in Sydney, it was all the same to Victor. Here was a combination of eye and foot and wrist that I have never seen approached. I have seen Fry's late cuts, I have watched Ranji drive a slow googly from Albert Trott into the pavilion at Lord's; I have seen Jessop pull a fast bowler from the off stump to the square-leg boundary. But Victor Trumper was the master of them all. From the moment he left the pavilion with his cap pulled over his eyes, until he came back after making 10 or 200, he was my ideal batsman and my ideal sportsman. When people say of something that it is 'not cricket', I think they must have seen Victor Trumper."

On 15 January 1947 Lock Walmsley, the president of the Sydney Musicians' Club was buried. He recorded his last will and testament on a gramophone record. "They can't argue about that," he said. Walmsley was from a very old cricketing family and in the will he stated, "I would like to record for posterity that Victor Trumper was the best batsman of the lot."*

Dick Whitington spoke to the author in the NSW Cricket Association offices of an incident in the members' bar of an Adelaide club. A devotee who had witnessed all the great Australian batsmen between 1920 and 1970, said, as the conversation inevitably turned to the Golden Cricketer, "I would have given my right arm just to see him bat with my own two eyes." Standing next to the speaker drinking in the conversation was the imposing but sightless figure of John Davey, himself an ex-cricketer of some repute. As embarrassed silence hung over the small gathering the unperturbed Davey uttered these words, "Heard melodies are sweet but those unheard are sweeter."

Archie MacLaren years after the Manchester confrontation of 1902 which Australia won by three runs, was chided by friends for allowing the young opener to score that immortal century innings before lunch on the first day. Neville Cardus who was present described the conversation as the dinner progressed:

> "Why, Archie, you must have slipped a bit when you allowed Trumper to win the 1902 rubber on a turf nearly water-logged in the outfield. Did you place too many men deep, and allow Victor to pick up the runs through the gaps near the wicket?" MacLaren, who adored an argument, rose to the bait; he took lumps of sugar out of the basin and set them all over the table, saying, "Gaps be damned! Good God, I knew my man—Victor had half a dozen strokes for the same kind of ball. I exploited the inner and outer ring—a man there, and another man covering him." (He banged the lumps of sugar down one by one, punctuating his luminous discourse.) "I told my bowlers to pitch on the short side to the off: I set my heart and brain on every detail of our policy. Well, in the third over of the morning, Victor hit two balls straight into the practice ground, high over the screen behind the bowler. I couldn't very well have had a man fielding in the bloody practice-ground, now could I?†

During the Second Test Match at Lord's in 1905 when Australia were dismissed for only 181, the early return of Trumper to the pavilion was expedited by an oversight on the part of Stanley Jackson who failed to position his customary

---

* The *Sydney Morning Herald*, 16 January 1947.
† *Autobiography*.

third man. The Sydney genius, batting with all his customary flair, noticed the weakness in the field placement and attempted to late cut a good length ball from the England captain past his off stump, only to see the symmetry of his stumps disturbed. This was the innings that C. B. Fry and W. P. Hone both described as the finest they ever saw. Trumper made 31.

When the Australians batted in the final Test of that series at The Oval early on the second day, Trumper opened as usual with Duff. When on 4 he took block to face Brearley. As the fast bowler released the ball it seemed to be a loose one wide of the off stump. Archie MacLaren in the slips complained, "What a bloody useless ball—Oh, well bowled, Walter!" The ball had taken a divot on the soggy turf and broke back sharply, dislodging the off stump.

While he attended Crown Street Superior Public School Trumper was an outstanding young cricketer and the story is often told in Sydney of his scoring a century every Saturday followed by avid crowds up to five thousand strong. As pointed out in the first chapter of this book, Victor played his school cricket on Fridays and his highest score was 86 not out*. The source for this unfortunate twisting of fact into inaccurate legend appears to be the *Official Souvenir About Trumper's Team, Queensland Tour, 1906*. Printed in Brisbane by R. S. Hews and Company, it states, ". . . he began scoring his hundreds at Crown Street Superior Public School where he was educated."

Trumper's parents were eager for him to round off his education by attending Sydney Grammar School but he was reluctant to leave Crown Street. His younger brothers, Sydney Charles and Charles Ernest Love, did enrol at Sydney Grammar and the champion cricketer helped as coach while his brothers were students there. He did not teach in any of the State schools of the period as is clearly revealed by the historical files of the New South Wales Department of Education.

Close to the foreshores of Sydney Harbour, across the waters from where the white-shelled Opera House sails reflect the fading afternoon sun, lies Loreto Convent at Kirribilli. Some time before the First World War the nuns decided that bedside prayers would consist of those usually said in each girl's home.

---

* The *Sydney Morning Herald*, 27 October 1893.

As the teachers moved from bed to bed to hear each prayer finish with the customary "God bless Mummy and Daddy" and "God bless this family," one tiny lass caused some wonder with her, ". . . and please God, bless Victor Trumper."*

During his 1905 English tour the Australian hero went out to do battle against the might of Yorkshire. A young talented collier playing in his first major match for the county was brought on to bowl and understandably took a while to find his length. Trumper, instead of pounding the ball all over the field, paid his bowling uncharacteristic respect. When questioned by his team-mates after the innings Victor replied, "Would you have preferred me to destroy his chance of making an easier living than working down the pit?"

Soon after he married in 1904, Trumper opened his Cricketing and Sports Depot in Market Street, Sydney in partnership with Hanson Carter, destined to become Australia's wicket-keeper when Jim Kelly finally retired in 1905. Once, before a Test Match Trumper was supposedly working in the shop and suddenly realizing the time, he grabbed a brand-new bat, dashed outside and hailed a passing horse-drawn cab which took him to the Sydney Cricket Ground, where he made a large score. A member, anxious to buy the bat as a keepsake of the historic occasion, approached the "Incomparable" and humbly asked him if he would be willing to part with the piece of willow, which by now had had its elegance altered. "Yes of course I would," said the chivalrous champion, "You can have it for nothing." The embarrassed member insisted on paying two gold sovereigns for the priceless relic. To the end of his days Trumper could never understand why anyone would pay such money for a battered cricket bat.

Despite similar anecdotes which depict Trumper as a compassionate but unsuccessful businessman, Victor did manage to support his young family from his sports goods ventures for ten years from 1904 until 1913 at which stage he formed a partnership in a mercery venture, importing and manufacturing men's ties and formal wear at his George Street address.

"Johnny" Moyes was present one day when the proprietor replaced a damaged bat which had been used in a game by a

---

* J. H. Fingleton, *The Immortal Victor Trumper*. Collins, London, 1978.

youngster who had not prepared its face correctly beforehand. Without a word of reproach Trumper took the mutilated implement and replaced it with a new one explaining, "The poor lad, he couldn't afford another one." Moyes also told how interstate cricketers who often dropped into Victor's Sports Depot and Mercers at 317 George Street, just to be near him, were forced to discontinue this practice as he always insisted on giving away neckties to the entire team. A modern chemist shop now occupies the George Street site.

Roy Johnson, a friend of Eric McElhone, won a cricket bat as a prize for his efforts at scholastic achievement, but being much more interested in tennis, he approached Victor in his shop and enquired if he could exchange the bat for a tennis racquet. The compassionate cricketer then exchanged the bat for a Doherty racquet that was considerably more expensive than the bat. As the items changed hands Victor said gently to the boy, "It is not the sport that is important but how you play it that counts. Be fair and be a sportsman."* This was, in essence, Trumper's philosophy of life.

Other friends of McElhone told him how they had taken their tennis racquets to Trumper's George Street shop to be restrung or otherwise repaired and if they were not ready on time Victor would loan them a new racquet until he had completed the work. Charles Trumper told McElhone how Victor would, when arriving early for a match at the Cricket Ground, be beseiged by an army of small boys waiting for him to hand them threepenny pieces for the entrance admission to the Shilling Stand. (One shilling for adults, threepence for children.)

Vernon Ransford recalled the second innings of the Fourth Test in Melbourne during the South African Tour of Australia in 1910–11 when a young man knocked at the dressing room door asking to see the Crown Prince of Cricket. As Trumper opened the door he noticed that the visitor was holding a large bat. He explained that he was beginning his own sporting firm manufacturing cricket bats and would be eternally grateful if Victor would give him an opinion as to the bat's worth. Trumper took the implement into the dressing room to show his team-mates. It was heavy and ungainly and weighed just on three and a half

* Eric McElhone, unpublished address for Waverley Historical Society, 9 June 1975.

pounds, a large bat by any standard. On inspecting the plank themselves the other members of the Eleven exclaimed, "Surely Vic you're not going to use that cudgel out there!" He replied with conviction, "There's nothing wrong with this bat, it's a perfectly good one." To prove his point he delighted the spectators with the finesse and delicacy of his strokes before finally succumbing to Vogler for 87. He then handed the bat to its delighted owner with an approprate inscription on the shoulder.

Aubrey Faulkner recalled another incident during this series which also involved celestial batsmanship. One day while shopping in Sydney he called in to the George Street shop to chat with Trumper and inspect his merchandise. Despite his protestations he was given a large bat as a memento of the visit and on using it in the nets for practice found that it was unwieldy and rock-hard. On hearing of this Trumper volunteered to use it himself and in the following Test, Faulkner watched spellbound from his place near the stumps as the ball was despatched to all corners of the field with a harmonious tune ringing from its broad surface. After the game it was returned to its new owner, "I've played it in now Aubrey, it's as good as gold." Alas, the piece of willow continued to behave like a barge-pole when not in Victor's gifted hands.

While Faulkner was himself attempting to dislodge Trumper during the same series, Warwick Armstrong at the non-striker's end decided to amuse himself. He confided to the bowler that Victor's only real weakness was the yorker. The very next ball was pitched up into the block-hole and was sent racing away to the boundary under Trumper's upraised left leg. Next a similar delivery was tried and the ball careered across the turf just wide of the fieldsman who had been moved to negate the stroke. Another yorker, and the red leather sphere rebounded from the pickets with a sharp crack. On each occasion Armstrong leaned on his bat with a wide grin creasing his face, until Faulkner realized he had been duped. Trumper had no weakness.

Shortly before Trumper's benefit match in 1913, H. V. Hordern thought his bowling was unplayable on a saturated spinner's wicket at Chatswood Oval. With the ball kicking and turning viciously, all the batsmen except one had the utmost difficulty in protecting their bodies, let alone scoring runs. From Hordern's first over to him Trumper hit 12 runs. The second to Frank Iredale was a maiden. During the third the bowler delivered a perfect length leg-break outside the line of the leg stump turning back sharply to the wicket. Trumper by now had stepped well away towards square leg and bringing the blade of his bat down late with a chopping motion of the wrists sent the ball hurtling to the fence between point and gully. Turning to the bowler Frank Iredale complained, "You don't bowl that rubbish to me when I'm facing you." Hordern with ice in his voice replied, "For your information Frank, the ball that Victor belts for four is exactly the same one with which you can barely make contact."*

The following anecdote, although a grand cricketing yarn, is of dubious authenticity. During the 1914 Tour of New Zealand as Victor went out to demolish the Canterbury bowling at Christchurch, a tiny boy ran up with a bat and pleaded with him to use it. Trumper patted the youngster on the head and said, "All right, Slogger, you hold mine until I've finished batting." The first ball was sent high over the bowler's head for six and when nearing the hundred the shoulder of the bat parted company with the blade and still the score mounted until finally he reached 293 with only half a bat in his hands. Unfortunately the story is apocryphal as Trumper's first scoring stroke in this innings was a single and he did not hit the first of his three sixes until well into his second century. Not one of the reporters covering the match that day made any mention of a small boy or a broken bat.

Percy Fender described an incident which centred around Sir Donald Bradman's early demise on a beastly pitch at Lord's in a 1934 Test Match. During this tour Bradman made 304 and 244 in two successive Tests but on the sticky wicket in the second innings of the second international Fender considered that Bradman's departure was due to the belief that the match was a lost cause.† Afterwards while keeping company in the member's bar with Warwick Armstrong, Fender inquired of the big man how Trumper and Bradman compared on such a wicket. "If you really want to know Percy, I'll tell you. When we went in on a sticky dog, if Victor didn't like its looks, he restrained his natural impulse to thrash the bowling until the wicket improved; then he hit the cover off the ball. Need I say any more?"

At Leyton against Essex in 1909 Warren Bardsley reached and

---

* H. V. Hordern, *Googlies*. Angus & Robertson, Sydney, 1932.
† Richard Streeton, *P. G. H. Fender, A Biography*. Faber & Faber, London, 1979.

then passed two hundred and looked set for his third century when Victor joined him and politely said that it was time that he got out so that others might occupy the crease for valuable practice for the forthcoming Test encounters. Bardsley declined to do this so his partner called him through for an impossible run as the bails were dutifully removed by the wicket-keeper. Later Bardsley remonstrated with Trumper for deliberately running him out for 219, but Victor remained firm, "You had a good innings Warren, and there are others in this team who don't always get the chance to bat as you do."

Sydney neswpapers in June 1954 reported that just before the 39th anniversary of Trumper's death an anonymous gentleman in his sixties approached the Sydney Cricket Ground manager Keith Sharp for permission to touch up the gold lettering on the memorial granite plaque on the back of the Sheridan Stand. One paper reported, "Yesterday the lettering was bright and shiny for the 39th anniversary of the death of a cricketer who lived only 38 years."

Shortly before she died in 1963 Annie Trumper, a tall, handsome and deeply religious woman who attended Mass nearly every day, sat watching a Test Match in the Members' enclosure at Sydney. Annie Trumper, turned to her companion and said with some disdain, "I wish modern day cricketers would move their feet more often down to the pitch of the ball!" She had lived eleven remarkable and happy years with the Crown Prince of Cricket and had witnessed the heights of glory to which batsmanship could ascend.

As Hugh Trumble so aptly stated in 1925, "Trumper stands alone as the best batsman of all time."*

---

* The *Sunday News* 30 August 1925.

Appendix

THE SYDNEY DWELLINGS OF VICTOR TRUMPER

1877–1883	—unknown—
1883–1886	432 Riley Street, Surry Hills
1886–1888	30 Little Arthur Street, Surry Hills
1888–1889	487 Crown Street, Surry Hills
1889–1890	10 Nichols Street, Surry Hills
1890–1896	119 Cooper Street, Surry Hills
1896–1899	31 Selwyn Street, Paddington
1899–1902	31 Liverpool Street, Paddington
1902–1909	112 Paddington Street, Paddington
1909–1915	"Auckland", Help Street, Chatswood

VICTOR TRUMPER'S SPORTS STORES IN SYDNEY

1904–1906	Trumper and Carter, Cricketing and Sports Depot, 108 Market Street Sydney
1906–1909	Trumper and Carter, Cricketing and Sports Depot, 124 Market Street, Sydney
1909–1913	Victor Trumper and Company, Sports Depot and Mercer, 317 George Street, Sydney
1913–1915	Victor Trumper and L. W. Dodge, Ltd (Reg. Office), 317 George Street, Sydney

References: New South Wales Electoral Rolls, *Sands' Directories*, 1877–1915

Bowlers Who Most Frequently Dismissed Victor Trumper

	Dismissals	Catches
W. Rhodes (England and Yorkshire)	18	6
S. F. Barnes (England, Lancashire and Warwickshire)	14	1
G. H. Hirst (England and Yorkshire)	11	3
L. C. Braund (England and Somerset)	10	9
G. L. Jessop (England, Cambridge University and Gloucestershire)	7	2
J. V. Saunders (Australia and Victoria)	7	1
W. J. Whitty (Australia, N.S.W. and South Australia)	7	—
W. Brearley (England and Lancashire)	6	—
H. H. Young (England and Essex)	6	—
C. Blythe (England and Kent)	6	—
A. E. Trott (Australia, Victoria, England and Middlesex)	5	3
C. B. Llewellyn (South Africa and Hampshire)	5	—
A. Fielder (England and Kent)	5	—
J. T. Hearne (England and Middlesex)	5	—
G. A. Faulkner (South Africa)	4	—

A. A. Lilley (England and Warwickshire) was by far the most successful wicketkeeper against Victor Trumper. He caught Trumper seven times and stumped him on two occasions.

238

VICTOR TRUMPER'S CENTURY INNINGS IN FIRST CLASS CRICKET (42)

292* N.S.W. v. Tasmania, Sydney, December 1898
253 N.S.W. v. New Zealand, Sydney, February 1899
135* Australia v. England, Lord's, June 1899
104 Australia v. Gloucestershire, Bristol, July 1899
300* Australia v. Sussex, Brighton (Hove), July 1899
208 N.S.W. v. Queensland, Sydney, November 1899
165 N.S.W. v. South Australia, Adelaide, December 1899
230 N.S.W. v. Victoria, Sydney, February 1901
101 Australia v. Surrey, The Oval, May 1902
121 Australia v. Oxford University, Oxford, May 1902
105 Australia v. M.C.C. & Ground, Lord's, May 1902
128 Australia v. Cambridge University, Cambridge, June 1902
113 Australia v. An England Eleven, Bradford, June 1902
104 Australia v. England, Manchester, July 1902
109 Australia v. Essex, Leyton, July 1902
119 Australia v. Essex, Leyton, July 1902
125 Australia v. Gloucestershire, Cheltenham, August 1902
127 Australia v. Eleven Players of England, Harrogate, September 1902
120 Australia v. South of England, Hastings, September 1902
178 N.S.W. v. South Australia, Sydney, January 1903
130 N.S.W. v. Victoria, Sydney January 1903
185* Australia v. England, Sydney, December 1903
113 Australia v. England, Adelaide, January 1904
172 Australia v. New Zealand, Wellington, March 1905
108 Australia v. Gloucestershire, Bristol, June 1905
110 Australia v. Worcestershire, Worcester, August 1905
101 N.S.W. v. Victoria, Sydney, January 1906
135 N.S.W. v. South Australia, Sydney, December 1907
119 N.S.W. v. Victoria, Melbourne, December 1907
166 Australia v. England, Sydney, February 1908
133 Australia v. Cambridge University, Cambridge, June 1909
113 Australia v. Derbyshire, Derby, July 1909
150 Australia v. An England Eleven, Blackpool, August 1909
105 N.S.W. v. Rest of Australia (C. T. B. Turner's Benefit Match), Sydney, January 1910
142 N.S.W. v. Victoria, Melbourne, December 1910
159 Australia v. South Africa, Melbourne, January 1911
214* Australia v. South Africa, Adelaide, January 1911
113 Australia v. England, Sydney, December 1911
201* N.S.W. v. South Australia, Sydney, January 1913
138 N.S.W. v. Victoria, Sydney, January 1913
126* N.S.W. v. Rest of Australia (V. T. Trumper's Benefit Match), February 1913
292 Australian Eleven v. Canterbury, Christchurch, February 1914
*Not Out

VICTOR TRUMPER'S FIRST CLASS ANALYSIS

	Matches	Innings	Not Out	Runs	Highest Score	Average	100	50	Catches	Runs	Wickets	Average	Best Bowling
1894–95	2	4	1	22	11	7.33	-	1	-	-	-	-	-
1897–98	5	10	-	192	68	19.20	-	-	5	135	6	22.50	4/32
1898–99	9	15	1	873	292*	62.36	2	2	2	90	-	-	-
1899 England	33	48	3	1556	300*	34.58	3	9	15	29	1	29.00	1/10
1899–1900	7	10	-	721	208	72.10	2	2	1	225	12	18.75	3/26
1900–01	4	7	-	458	230	65.43	1	2	2	232	6	38.66	3/71
1901–02	10	18	-	486	73	27.00	-	3	12	319	7	45.57	2/19
1902 England	36	53	-	2570	128	48.49	11	11	24	415	20	20.75	5/19 (2 × 5)
1902 South Africa	4	8	1	307	70	43.86	-	2	4	175	6	29.16	3/60
1902–03	5	9	-	446	178	49.56	2	1	6	89	3	29.66	2/33
1903–04	11	21	3	990	185*	55.00	2	7	14	152	1	152.00	1/38
1904–05	2	4	-	198	81	49.50	-	2	2	6	-	-	-
1905 New Zealand	4	5	1	436	172	109.00	1	3	3	-	-	-	-
1905 England	30	47	1	1667	110	36.24	2	12	28	4	-	-	-
1905–06	3	6	-	250	101	41.66	1	1	-	-	-	-	-
1906–07	2	3	-	23	11	7.66	-	-	-	-	-	-	-
1907–08	10	19	-	797	166	41.95	3	2	10	9	1	9.00	1/9
1908–09	1	1	-	0	-	-	-	-	-	-	-	-	-
1909 England	34	45	2	1435	150	33.37	3	7	19	151	1	151.00	1/24
1909–10	1	1	-	105	105	105.00	1	-	1	-	-	-	-
1910–11	11	20	2	1246	214*	69.22	3	8	5	-	-	-	-
1911–12	12	20	3	583	113	34.29	1	4	10	-	-	-	-
1912–13	8	13	3	843	201*	84.30	3	5	2	-	-	-	-
1913–14	4	5	-	107	32	21.40	-	-	3	-	-	-	-
1914 New Zealand	7	9	-	628	293	69.78	1	3	4	-	-	-	-
TOTAL	255	401	21	16939	300*	44.57	42	87	172	2031	64	31.73	5/19 (2 × 5)

* Not Out

N.B. When recording the second decimal place for an average the standard mathematical convention has been used; e.g. 1899 England, Trumper's average of 34.578 becomes 34.58.

240

VICTOR TRUMPER'S PERFORMANCES IN SYDNEY GRADE CRICKET

	Matches	Innings	Not Out	Runs	Highest Score	Average	100	50	Catches	Runs	Wickets	Average	Best Bowling
For South Sydney													
1894–95	9	10	1	191	77*	21.22	–	1	3	1	–	–	–
1895–96	8	12	1	107	22*	9.73	–	–	3	157	6	26.17	3/17
Total South Sydney	17	22	2	298	77*	14.90	–	1	6	158	6	26.33	3/17
For Paddington													
1896–97	10	9	2	149	48	21.29	–	–	6**	380	16	23.75	3/9
1897–98	8	8	3	1020	191*	204.00	6	2	2	204	7	29.14	4/57
1898–99	6	8	1	562	260*	112.40	3	1	3	177	12	14.75	5/18
1899–1900	6	6	–	354	119	59.00	2	–	2	261	13	20.08	4/30
1900–01	8	10	1	557	213*	61.89	1	2	6	310	28	11.07	9/90
1901–02	5	6	–	479	158	79.83	3	1	3	218	11	19.82	6/37
1902–03	4	5	–	374	335	74.80	1	–	4	183	7	26.14	4/55
1903–04	4	4	1	315	134	78.75	2	1	1	156	7	22.29	3/8
1904–05	6	6	1	488	215	97.60	2	1	4	155	9	17.22	4/31
1905–06	7	8	1	363	101	51.86	1	3	7	66	3	22.00	3/36
1906–07	11	11	–	945	212	85.91	3	4	7	59	1	59.00	1/28
1907–08	6	7	1	365	136	60.83	1	2	2	–	–	–	–
1908–09	6	7	–	604	260	86.29	3	–	–	–	–	–	–
Total Paddington	87	93	10	6575	335	79.22	28	17	47**	2169	114	19.03	9/90
For Gordon													
1909–10	7	12	1	518	105	47.09	2	3	10	–	–	–	–
1910–11	8	9	–	482	105	53.56	1	4	7	–	–	–	–
1911–12	6	8	–	259	71	32.38	–	2	7	–	–	–	–
1912–13	7	8	1	448	127	56.00	2	1	3	–	–	–	–
1913–14	7	7	1	503	157*	83.83	2	2	2	–	–	–	–
1914–15	4	4	–	159	123	39.75	1	–	2	–	–	–	–
Total Gordon	39	48	2	2369	157*	51.50	8	12	31	–	–	–	–
TOTAL	143	163	14	9242	335	62.03	36	30	84**	2327	120	19.39	9/90

* Not Out
** Trumper made one stumping; versus Leichhardt 12–2–1897

241

VICTOR TRUMPER'S FIRST CLASS ANALYSIS BY TEAM

	Matches	Innings	Not Out	Runs	Highest Score	Average	100	50	Catches	Runs	Wickets	Average	Best Bowling
TEST CRICKET													
Australia v. England	40	74	5	2263	185*	32.80	6	9	25	142	2	71.00	2/35
Australia v. South Africa	8	15	3	900	214*	75.00	2	4	6	175	6	29.17	3/60
Total Test	48	89	8	3163	214*	39.05	8	13	31	317	8	39.63	3/60
Australian XI in England	113	159	3	6365	300*	40.80	17	36	78	498	20	24.90	5/19 (2 × 5)
Australian XI in New Zealand	11	14	1	1064	293	81.85	2	6	7	–	–	–	–
Australian XI v. The Rest of Australia	4	5	–	152	62	30.40	–	1	2	30	3	10.00	1/0
Australian XI v. M.C.C.	1	1	–	30	30	30.00	–	–	–	–	–	–	–
Australian XI v. N.S.W.	1	2	–	75	60	37.50	–	1	–	–	–	–	–
Australian XI in South Africa	1	2	–	68	49	34.00	–	–	1	–	–	–	–
Total Australian XI	131	183	4	7754	300*	43.32	19	44	88	528	23	22.96	5/19 (2 × 5)
N.S.W. v. South Australia	24	42	4	1701	201*	44.76	4	7	14	515	21	24.52	4/32
N.S.W. v. Victoria	22	38	1	1926	230	52.05	6	10	18	289	6	48.17	3/94
N.S.W. v. M.C.C.	11	21	–	533	74	25.38	–	3	13	314	4	78.50	1/21
N.S.W. v. Queensland	6	7	1	421	208	70.16	1	3	3	24	2	12.00	2/12
N.S.W. v. The Rest	3	5	1	304	126*	76.00	2	1	1	–	–	–	–
N.S.W. v. New Zealand	2	2	–	285	253	142.50	1	–	2	–	–	–	–

N.S.W. v. Tasmania	2	2	2	379	292*	–	1	1	–	12	–	–	–
N.S.W. v. South Africa	2	4	–	168	78	42.00	–	2	–	–	–	–	–
N.S.W. v. Western Australia	1	2	–	106	55	53.00	–	2	1	–	–	–	–
Total N.S.W.	73	123	9	5823	292*	51.08	15	29	51	1154	33	34.97	4/32
The Rest v. Australian XI (1898–99)	3	6	–	199	75	33.17	–	1	1	32	–	–	–
TOTAL	255	401	21	16939	300*	44.58	42	87	172	2031	64	31.73	5/19 (2 × 5)

* Not Out

VICTOR TRUMPER'S FIRST CLASS ANALYSIS BY VENUE

	Matches	Innings	Not Out	Runs	Highest Score	Average	100	50	Catches	Runs	Wickets	Average	Best Bowling
IN AUSTRALIA													
Sydney	65	110	6	5344	292*	51.38	15	21	49	887	29	30.59	4/32
Melbourne	22	41	–	1697	159	41.39	3	12	15	84	–	–	–
Adelaide	16	30	5	1094	214*	43.76	3	5	10	274	7	39.14	2/1
Brisbane	3	4	1	118	77	39.33	–	1	1	12	–	–	–
Hobart	1	1	1	87	87*	–	–	1	–	–	–	–	–
Total in Australia	107	186	13	8340	292*	48.21	21	40	75	1257	36	34.92	4/32
IN ENGLAND													
Bath	2	3	–	88	86	29.33	–	1	–	–	–	–	–
Birmingham	7	11	1	189	45	18.90	–	–	3	84	2	42.00	2/35
Blackpool	1	2	–	199	150	99.50	1	–	–	66	–	–	–
Bournemouth	2	4	–	98	52	24.50	–	1	–	–	–	–	–
Bradford	4	5	–	165	113	33.00	1	–	3	–	–	–	–
Brighton (Hove)	4	5	1	394	300*	98.50	1	–	2	–	–	–	–
Bristol	4	5	–	337	108	67.40	2	1	2	19	5	3.80	5/19
Cambridge	3	3	–	264	133	88.00	2	–	2	–	–	–	–
Canterbury	4	6	–	226	69	37.67	–	3	4	–	–	–	–
Cheltenham	4	6	–	232	125	38.67	1	–	1	–	–	–	–
Crystal Palace	3	5	–	107	64	21.40	–	–	1	5	–	–	–
Derby	4	5	–	209	113	41.80	1	–	4	–	–	–	–
Eastbourne	2	4	–	107	64	26.75	–	1	2	–	–	–	–
Edinburgh (Scotland)	2	4	–	81	55	20.25	–	1	1	–	–	–	–
Harrogate	1	1	–	127	127	127.00	1	–	–	–	–	–	–
Hastings	2	4	–	163	120	40.75	1	–	3	–	–	–	–
Hull	1	–	–	–	–	–	–	–	1	–	–	–	–
Leeds	4	8	1	126	38	18.00	–	–	2	33	–	–	–
Leicester	4	7	1	179	70	29.83	–	1	2	76	5	15.20	5/33
Leyton	6	9	–	414	119	46.00	2	2	1	–	–	–	–
Liverpool	4	6	–	171	89	28.50	–	2	6	–	–	–	–

Ground				Runs	HS	Avge				Runs	Wkts	Avge	Best
Lord's	15	17	1	753	135*	47.06	2	4	6	63	3	21.00	2/23
Manchester	8	13	—	487	104	37.46	1	3	—	6	—	—	—
Northampton	2	2	—	124	68	62.00	—	2	2	4	—	—	—
Nottingham	6	9	1	311	94	38.88	—	3	6	80	3	26.67	3/59
Oval	13	22	—	707	101	32.14	1	4	12	40	1	40.00	1/23
Oxford	4	5	—	270	121	54.00	1	1	4	31	—	—	—
Portsmouth	1	1	—	55	55	55.00	—	—	—	—	—	—	—
Scarborough	3	5	—	152	62	30.40	—	2	3	—	—	—	—
Sheffield	4	5	—	161	85	32.20	—	2	7	39	—	—	—
Southampton	3	4	—	123	92	30.75	—	1	2	—	—	—	—
Taunton	2	3	—	61	51	20.33	—	1	3	29	2	14.50	1/10
Truro	1	1	—	19	19	19.00	—	—	—	—	—	—	—
Uttoxeter	1	1	—	12	12	12.00	—	—	—	24	1	24.00	1/24
Worcester	2	2	—	117	110	58.50	1	—	1	—	—	—	—
Total in England	133	193	6	7228	300*	38.65	19	39	86	599	22	27.23	5/19
IN NEW ZEALAND													
Auckland	1	1	—	81	81	81.00	1	1	—	—	—	—	—
Christchurch	4	5	1	504	293	126.00	1	2	3	—	—	—	—
Dunedin	2	2	—	159	87	79.50	—	2	—	—	—	—	—
Hastings	1	2	—	65	42	32.50	—	—	—	—	—	—	—
Wellington	3	4	—	255	172	63.75	1	1	4	—	—	—	—
Total in New Zealand	11	14	1	1064	293	81.85	2	6	7	—	—	—	—
IN SOUTH AFRICA													
Cape Town	2	4	1	176	70	58.67	—	1	2	26	1	26.00	1/26
Johannesburg	2	4	—	131	63	32.75	—	1	2	149	5	29.80	3/60
Total in South Africa	4	8	1	307	70	43.86	—	2	4	175	6	29.17	3/60
TOTAL	255	401	21	16939	300*	44.58	42	87	172	2031	64	31.73	5/19 (2 × 5)

* Not Out

Bibliography

ALTHAM, H. S. *A History of Cricket, Vol. 1.* George Allen & Unwin, London, 1926.

ANON ("by the author of *Cricket on the Brain*"). *Cricket at the Breakfast Table.* Jarrold & Sons, London, 1909.

ARLOTT, JOHN (ed.). *Cricket: The Great Ones.* Pelham Books, London, 1967.

ASHLEY-COOPER, F. S. *Cricket Highways and Byways.* George Allen & Unwin, London, 1927.

ASHLEY-COOPER, F. S. *Curiosities of First-class Cricket.* Edmund Seale, London, 1901.

BELDAM, G. W. and FRY, C. B. *Great Batsmen: their Methods at a Glance.* Macmillan, London, 1905.

BELDAM, G. W. and FRY, C. B. *Great Bowlers and Fielders: their Methods at a Glance.* Macmillan, London, 1906.

BROWN, LIONEL H. *Victor Trumper and the 1902 Australians.* Secker & Warburg, London, 1981.

CARY, CLIF. *Cricket Tests and Records.* T & H Pty Ltd, Sydney, 1946.

CARDUS, NEVILLE. *The Summer Game.* Rupert Hart-Davis, London, 1948.

CARDUS, NEVILLE. *Autobiography.* Collins, London, 1947.

DARLING, D. K. *Test Tussles On and Off the Field.* J. Walch & Sons, Hobart, 1970.

EDEN, GUY. *Bush Ballads and Other Verses.* Sisley, London, 1907.

FINGLETON, J. H. *The Immortal Victor Trumper.* Collins, London, 1978.

FERGUSON, W. H. *Mr Cricket.* Nicholas Kaye, London, 1957.

FRY, C. B. *Life Worth Living.* Eyre & Spottiswoode, London, 1939.

FREWIN, LESLIE (ed.). *The Boundary Book.* MacDonald, London, 1962.

GIBSON, ALAN. *The Cricket Captains of England, A Survey.* Cassell, London, 1979.

HORDERN, H. V. *Googlies: coals from a Test-cricketer's fireplace.* Angus & Robertson, Sydney, 1932.

HUTCHEON, E. H. *A History of Queensland Cricket.* Queensland Cricket Association, Brisbane, 1946.

IREDALE, FRANK. *Thirty-three Years of Cricket.* Beatty, Richardson, Sydney, 1920.

JESSOP, G. L. *A Cricketer's Log.* Hodder & Stoughton, London, 1922.

KNIGHT, A. E. *The Complete Cricketer.* Methuen, London, 1906.

LAVER, FRANK. *An Australian Cricketer on Tour.* Chapman & Hall, London, 1905.

LILLEY, A. A. *Twenty-four Years of Cricket.* Mills & Boon, London, 1912.

LORD HAWKE et al. *The Memorial Biography of W. G. Grace.* Constable, London, 1919.

MACARTNEY, CHARLES GEORGE. *My Cricketing Days.* Heinemann, London, 1930.

MAILEY, ARTHUR. *10 For 66 and All That.* Phoenix House, London, 1958.

246

MESSENGER, DALLY R. *The Master.* Angus & Robertson, Sydney, 1982.

MONFRIES, J. ELLIOTT. *Not Test Cricket.* Gillingham, Adelaide, 1950.

MOYES, A. G. *Australian Batsmen from Charles Bannerman to Neil Harvey.* Angus & Robertson, Sydney, 1954.

MOYES, A. G. *Australian Cricket, A History.* Angus & Robertson, Sydney, 1959.

MOYES, A. G. *The Changing Face of Cricket.* Angus & Robertson, Sydney, 1963.

NOBLE, M. A. *The Game's the Thing.* Cassell, London, 1926.

PADWICK, E. W. *A Bibliography of Cricket.* London Library Association, 1977.

POLLARD, JACK. *Australian Cricket, The Game and the Players.* Hodder & Stoughton, Sydney, 1982.

REESE, DANIEL. *Was It All Cricket?* George Allen & Unwin, London, 1948.

SMITH, E. J. and MURPHY, P. *Tiger Smith of Warwickshire and England.* Readers Union, Newton Abbot, 1981.

STANDING, PERCY CROSS. *Anglo-Australian Cricket 1862–1926.* Faber & Gwyer, London 1926.

STANDING, PERCY CROSS. *Cricket of Today and Yesterday.* T. C. & E. C. Jack, London, 1902.

STREETON, RICHARD. *P. G. H. Fender, A Biography.* Faber & Faber, London, 1979.

SWANTON, E. W. (ed.). *The World of Cricket.* Michael Joseph, London, 1966.

THOMPSON, A. A. *Hirst and Rhodes.* Epworth Press, London, 1959.

TREVOR, PHILIP. *With the M.C.C. in Australia 1907–08.* Alston Rivers, London, 1908.

TREVOR, PHILIP. *Cricket and Cricketers.* Chapman & Hall, London, 1921.

WARNER, P. F. *Cricket Across The Seas.* Longmans, London, 1903.

WARNER, P. F. *How We Recovered The Ashes.* Chapman & Hall, London, 1904.

WARNER, P. F. *The Book of Cricket.* Sports Handbooks, London, 1911.

WARNER, P. F. *England v. Australia (1911–1912).* Mills & Boon, London, 1912.

WARNER, P. F. *My Cricketing Life.* Hodder & Stoughton, London, 1921.

WARNER, P. F. *Lord's 1787–1945.* George G. Harrap, London, 1946.

WHITINGTON, R. S. *The Courage Book of Australian Test Cricket. 1877–1974.* Wren Publishing, Melbourne, 1974.

WILSON, F. B. *Sporting Pie.* Chapman & Hall, London, 1922.

Wisden's Cricketers' Almanacks, 1894–1916. Sporting Handbooks, London.

Index

250

251